Unforgettable Places

Unforgettable Places

Unique Sites and Experiences Around the World

Steve Davey, Marc Schlossman,
Steve Watkins and Clare Jones

Firefly Books

CONTENTS

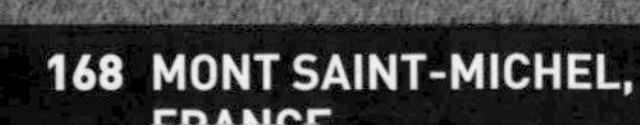

HISTORIC
ROUTE
66

Introduction

We only get one life so we owe it to ourselves to see as much of this beautiful world as possible. For many of us, lying on a beach for two weeks each year is just not enough any more. We want to see ancient monuments, extraordinary scenery, endangered wildlife, foreign cultures, architecture and art – places that give us the chance to grow and expand our horizons. *Unforgettable World* will help you search out some of these essential destinations and experiences.

Steve Davey, Steve Watkins, Marc Schlossman and Clare Jones drew on their years of experience as international travel writers and photographers in selecting their favourite places, journeys and activities for the acclaimed *Unforgettable* books. And the very best are featured in this inspirational compilation. Some, such as the famous Taj Mahal in India and Gaudí's astonishing architecture in Barcelona, are relatively well-known, but many others, such as the remote island of Rapa Nui in the south-east Pacific and Bolivia's Uyuni Salt Flats, are very much off the beaten track. Some, such as the Florida Keys and Italy's beautiful Amalfi Coast, can be reached in relative comfort, whilst others present more of a challenge – tracking mountain gorillasin the foothills of a Rwandan volcano, for example, or trekking for nine days at altitude to see the stunning Himalayan scenery around Makalu in Nepal. Whatever your interests, tastes and abilities, there is something here for everyone.

Although you'll find plenty of tips for travellers, this is not a travel guide, and it's certainly not definitive, but it will introduce you to a host of spectacular locations, all of which can be visited within the space of a two-week break. (The map on pages 600–1 shows the locations of all the places featured.) Illustrated throughout with specially commissioned photographs, this is a book that will inspire you to think beyond the walls of your room and take that trip of a lifetime.

River-running
Zambezi River, Zambia

Tackling powerful grade four and five rapids are the highlight of any descent

Whether it involves getting drenched by one of the seven natural wonders of the world or rafting the planet's most awesome rapids, a journey on the mighty Zambezi River is a guaranteed thrill.

Rising from a small spring in north-western Zambia, the Zambezi, Africa's fourth-largest river, travels a massive 2700 km and traverses six countries on its way to the Indian Ocean. En route this majestic body of water weaves an unmistakable path, and has carved out the spectacular Victoria Falls where, on the border between Zambia and Zimbabwe, the 2-km-wide river plunges more than 100 metres into the steep-sided and ever-deepening Batoka Gorge, a white-water-rafting paradise.

Water explodes over the bow

The tranquillity of the upstream river, home to giraffes, elephants, hippos, crocodiles and innumerable forms of birdlife, is dramatically shattered as the Zambezi approaches the plunging drop of the falls. At peak flood a staggering 550,000 cubic metres of water thunder over the edge every minute, creating serious white-water rapids below.

For the best views of the falls from the Zambian side follow the network of paths to the none too encouragingly named Knife Edge Bridge, where a hair-raising traverse through swirling clouds of spray takes you on to a downstream island in the river with views of the gaping abyss below. As the falls plunge downwards and ricochet off the rocks in the gorge, spray can spiral upwards as high as 500 metres. This remarkable plume of water can be seen up to 70 km away, earning the Victoria Falls their local name: Mosi-oa-tunya (the smoke that thunders).

Safety kayakers follow every raft

The falls are incredible enough in themselves, but the real adventure lies downstream. If pitting your wits against roller-coaster waves, big drops and swirling eddies grabs you, you will find that white-water rafting on the Zambezi is in a class of its own. Depending on the time of year, you may even find yourself bobbing about at the base of the falls in your inflatable raft, with just a paddle for support, before you launch into a descent.

The 25 raftable rapids come one after the other and form the most daunting commercially-run white water anywhere in the world. They are classified as grade five by the British Canoe Union – the official definition is 'extremely difficult, with long and violent rapids, steep gradients, big drops and pressure areas'. If this doesn't get your adrenalin flowing, the names of some of the rapids just might. With titles like 'The Terminator', 'Oblivion' and 'Stairway to Heaven' they give

Flying over Victoria Falls in a microlight provides a sensational view

Rafting on the Zambezi River takes place in the Batoka Gorge a pretty clear indication that this is a river not to be messed with. A raft can be overturned in a split second and its paddling party scattered liberally along the sides of the gorge.

No previous experience of rafting is required to join any of the trips, which can be day-long or, if you want to explore the lower, more tranquil reaches of the river towards Lake Kariba, several days. Don't be alarmed, though – you won't be thrown in at the deep end. Qualified raft guides provide thorough training and instruction before you depart.

Gentle paddling sections do exist

If you need to calm frayed nerves, and have enough energy left after all this adventure, it is well worth hopping on board an upstream cruiser for a sunset wildlife safari. Meandering through the calm and sedate waters of the upper Zambezi, it is hard to imagine how wild the river gets after the Victoria Falls. But keep your eyes peeled – you may just have some close-up encounters with hippos and crocodiles. It seems that even here, on tranquil waters and sipping wine, the prospect of a swim is less than desirable.

Experienced guides steer the raft

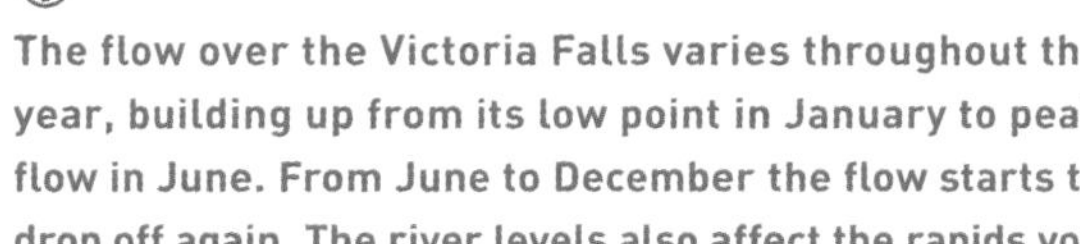

The flow over the Victoria Falls varies throughout the year, building up from its low point in January to peak flow in June. From June to December the flow starts to drop off again. The river levels also affect the rapids you will be able to run. During the low-water season you can raft rapids 1 to 18, approximately 24 km. In the high-water season only rapids 11 to 23 can be run, approximately 18 km. Most visitors base themselves in the town of Livingstone on the Zambia–Zimbabwe border. If you really want to indulge yourself the quintessentially colonial-styled Royal Livingstone hotel, owned by Sun International, nestles on the banks of the Zambezi, with views down to the thundering falls. All activities can be booked and organized through the hotel's dedicated centre on site.

Driving Californian surf

Big Sur, USA

No country conjures up images of driving through spectacular scenery like the USA does. Its dramatic landscapes and open roads create several world-class drives, such as Route 66 and the Big Sur. The former is fine if you are on an eternal holiday, but for a quicker driving fix wind down the windows, load up the rock CDs and opt for the Californian classic: Big Sur. It follows US Highway 1 along the rugged Pacific coastline and is as thrilling a drive as you can possibly pack into a few days.

The highway threads its way down the country's entire west coast from Oregon to California, but it is the 145 magnificent kilometres from Carmel-by-the-Sea to San Simeon that make up Big Sur.

Crashing surf pounds the beach near San Simeon

Rear view of Santa Lucia Mountains

Whatever you do, don't miss the popular sunset crawl when cars cruise the bends as the sky bursts into orange and red, and the ocean becomes mercury blue.

From Monterey, home to a fantastic aquarium, take the scenic Seventeen-Mile (27-km) Drive around the peninsula to quaint Carmel-by-the-Sea. The real Big Sur will still be lying in wait for you, though. Almost immediately after leaving Carmel, Point Lobos, the first of many state parks, will greet you, its jagged promontory acting as a barrier against crashing Pacific waves. Point Lobos is good but the drive gets better.

Soon Highway 1, with its eclectic mix of sports-car drivers, Harley riders and motorhomes, begins to climb above the shoreline with striking views almost beyond the horizon. Despite all this natural

Coastline near Julia Pfeiffer Burns State Park

Driving over Bixby Bridge at dusk

beauty Big Sur's best known icon is the dramatic Bixby Bridge. Spanning high above a plunging canyon, it is backdropped by the Santa Lucia Mountains. The cliffs here are so lofty and imposing that the area's notorious early morning sea fog often struggles until after midday to rise up and over them. Patience usually pays off, so hang around for the views.

After passing Point Sur lighthouse you move inland through the layered, gentle hills of the Andrew Molera State Park – a good spot for hiking and riding. The Pfeiffer Big Sur State Park, named after the family who were the area's first European settlers, warrants a couple of days of exploration. Among towering, prehistoric, coast redwood trees, a network of excellent hiking trails includes the gentle Nature Trail and more demanding mountain escapades to Buzzard's Roost and Pfeiffer Falls. If you are fortunate you may see black-tailed deer or bobcats. If you are extremely unfortunate you may encounter a mountain lion!

Big Sur is not all nature and wildlife, though, and there is a thriving community of artists here. Its favourite son was Henry Miller,

Big Sur sunset over the Pacific Ocean

McWay waterfall in Julia Pfeiffer Burns State Park

Looking north up Big Sur coastlines

US Highway 1 clings to the Big Sur coastline

author of the controversial erotic novel *Tropic of Cancer*. Renowned for his straight talking, Miller spent his final years in Big Sur. He was a painter as well as a writer, and you can see his intriguing work at the funky Coast Gallery and the offbeat Henry Miller Memorial Library.

Arguably, Big Sur's finest coastline lies in the south around Julia Pfeiffer Burns State Park. Here, natural rock arches and islets dot the surf and headlands stretch off to infinity. In the park itself a short trail leads to a picture-perfect cove graced by the 24-metre-high McWay waterfall.

Strolling along the beach at Carmel-by-the-Sea

The final stretch to the sea-lion colonies and endless sandy beaches around San Simeon is a gentle comedown from the drama of the cliffs to the north. If the wilderness bug didn't bite you, San Simeon's outrageous and outlandish Hearst Castle awaits. A gaudy fusion of every architectural style of recent centuries, it was the home of the newspaper publisher William Randolph Hearst. As Henry Miller might say, 'Everyone to his own'.

If you can, avoid weekends in the high season when traffic congestion detracts from the driving experience. Hotel accommodation along Big Sur is limited but what there is, such as the Ventana Inn & Spa and Big Sur Lodge, is high quality. Petrol stations are rare. There is one in Big Sur village but the prices it charges are extortionate, so fill up in Carmel-by-the-Sea or San Simeon. For great food and views, you can't beat the Nepenthe restaurant, just north of the Coast Gallery.

Climbing a volcano

Pacaya, Guatemala

Pacaya erupts spectacularly into a moonlit dusk sky

Climbing Pacaya in the afternoon is best to see it erupt

Seeing a volcano erupt is an awesome experience – and in southern Guatemala you can really feel the heat by climbing to the summit of Pacaya (Volcán de Pacaya) for a spectacular close-up view. And no, you don't have to be crazy! There are guided tours every day up this highly active volcano, giving adventurous travellers a chance to see Mother Nature at her most powerful.

Pacaya lies 30 km south of Guatemala City and is an easy drive from Antigua, a beautiful colonial city and now a World Heritage Site. Once the capital of the Spanish kingdom of Guatemala, which included southern Mexico and much of modern-day Central America, it is magnificently surrounded by three dormant volcanoes: Agua, Fuego and Acatenango – all good trek options. Fittingly, given its location, it

Molten lava steams on the flanks of Pacaya

Antigua is a beautiful colonial city

was the power of nature – severe earthquakes have struck Antigua over the centuries – that resulted in the seat of government being shifted to Guatemala City in 1776.

Unlike the newer capital, Antigua has retained its grace and charm, with scores of churches and monasteries mixed in with the colourful, colonial houses along its cobbled streets. It also hosts one of the most elaborate Holy Week festivals around, when entire streets are turned into artworks with multicoloured sawdust-and-flower carpets. The solemn processions and massive floats carried by people are unforgettable in themselves.

No matter when you come to Antigua, you won't be able to miss the Pacaya-tour companies and their leaflet distributors in the Plaza Mayor. But climbing the volcano is no mean feat – it is 2560 metres high, and reaching the summit takes two to three hours of seemingly

Volcanoes surround Antigua and caused it to lose its capital status

Mayan highland tribes come to market in Antigua

one-step-forward and two-steps-back, edging up frustratingly loose, black lava, scree fields. There are two routes up Pacaya and organized groups stick to the easier option, leaving from San Francisco de Sales. Many tour departures are timed so that you arrive at the cone of the volcano in plenty of time for sunset and the full impact of the contrast between the – hopefully – erupting red lava and the darkening sky.

As the hike begins, you hear the slightly ominous, dull thunder-like sounds of eruptions high above. And, just in case you need any more warning that this is not a tour to take lightly, steaming, hot remnants from recent eruptions begin to line the path as you near the active summit: the McKenney Cone. Underfoot, things start to get heated, too, and thick-soled walking boots come into their own. Just as it seems as though you are going to walk over the rim of the cone, the trail turns to the left and up to the relative safety of the old, dormant summit.

On a good day the view from here is awesome. The active vent bubbles and boils, spewing red lava over its sides, and intermittently sends streaming Strombolian volleys of the hot stuff up to 100 metres into the air. The stench of sulphur is all-consuming even if you take care to be upwind of the cone. Beyond Pacaya's breathtaking pyrotechnic show, the conical, silhouetted peaks of Antigua's three other volcanoes provide a stunning backdrop. As dusk heads deeper into the night, the burning red and orange lava creeps down the side of the volcano. For you, too, it is time to descend.

ⓘ

Volcanic activity on Pacaya can be checked at the Inguat tourist office, near the cathedral, in Antigua. Its staff will also recommend authorized volcano-tour companies, such as Eco-tour Chejo's. Ascending Pacaya without a guide is not advised. Some climbers brave going right up to the rim of the active cone, but beware – doing so is a complete lottery as no sequence of gentle eruptions ensures that the next one isn't going to be huge. This is no sanitized tourist experience and it is important to stay very aware of what is going on as you ascend. The Hotel Posada de Don Rodrigo in central Antigua is a unique, colonial place to stay.

Mayan woman and her daughter preparing flowers for sale

Finding paradise

Dhoni Mighili, the Maldives

A speck in the Indian Ocean, Dhoni Mhigili is paradise found

If you want to escape to paradise, surround yourself with nothing but ocean views and indulge in spa treatments, secluded Dhoni Mighili, set in the crystal-clear waters of the Maldives, is the island you have been dreaming of.

A tiny speck in the middle of the Indian Ocean – it takes only 800 footsteps to round its sandy circumference – Dhoni Mighili ('boat island') is a dreamy world of luxurious indulgences. With only six bungalows, it never caters for more than 12 guests at a time, so you will have most of its white sands and shimmering turquoise sea to yourself. To get to it from the airport at Male takes either a

30-minute seaplane ride over a necklace-like string of atolls or a four-hour cruise on your own private *dhoni*, a traditional Maldivian sailing boat.

These lovingly crafted, 20-metre wooden boats with double sails have been specially built to allow guests to live on board if they want a change from their bungalows, as well as using them to journey, explore and indulge. With such enticing names as *Sublime*, *Serenity*, *Dream*, *Passion*, *Seduction* and *Bliss* they will take you to visit nearby islands or go snorkelling; or you can simply enjoy a sail, a glass of wine and the chilled-out decadence of lounging on deck on one of the huge, cushioned daybeds.

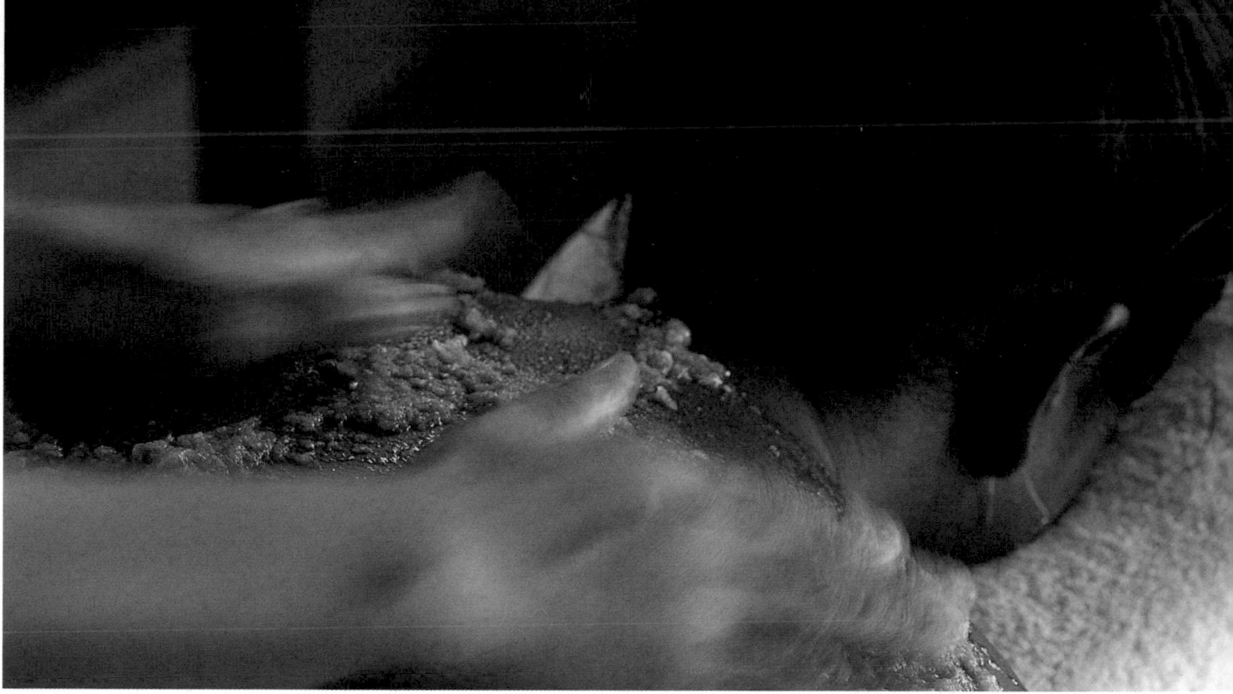

Spa treatments include 'holistic heavenly bliss'

And the relaxing need not stop when you are on land. You can take a dip in your own private plunge pool, lie back in the shaded garden of your bungalow or simply curl up on an *undholi*, the luxurious, wood-carved swing bed traditionally used by Maldivian families

Spa foot bowl

Throughout your stay you will also have your own dedicated *thakuru* (butler) on hand 24 hours a day, as well as a captain and two crew members, all immaculately dressed in the traditional colourful *mundu* (sarong). The service is 'wherever and whenever'. So if you fancy sailing off into the sunset, or having a land-based candlelit dinner under the stars at midnight, you quite simply can.

For the more adventurous, there's windsurfing, catamaran sailing and kayaking, as well as a dive school if you want to enjoy the Maldives' world-class underwater action. But if you just want to unwind and spoil yourself, the Sen Spa can provide some serious pampering. With indoor and outdoor treatment rooms, both overlooking the sea, it's not difficult to drift off to sleep to the sound of water gently rising and falling.

The spa menu includes the deliciously named 'holistic heavenly bliss', an all-over body treatment that is as good as it sounds, scrubbing, cleansing and polishing your skin so that it feels like new. And after a long flight to the Maldives you may wish to take advantage of the 'jet lag reviver' – or even the hot-stone treatment, which uses

hot, black basalt to restore flagging energy. The tropical fruit wrap, made with fresh fruits including coconut, papaya and pineapple, almost looks good enough to eat.

Wining and dining is definitely a key part of the Dhoni Mighili experience, and with water all around it's no surprise that seafood is a big hit on the menus. Tropical fruits are also in abundance and make any meal truly exotic. Before you arrive you will have been asked about any special requests you have, including food you like and don't like. This means the resident chef can rustle up your favourite dishes at just a moment's notice. When it comes to where to eat you can choose between the restaurant, dining on board your *dhoni* or picking a secluded spot on the beach – some people even ask for their table to be in the water.

Relaxing and unwinding is the easy part of staying on Dhoni Mighili – the hardest part will be leaving the paradise you have found.

Sunset over traditional *dhoni* boats

There is a wide choice of operators and resorts in the Maldives to suit a variety of budgets. Specialist operators Seasons in Style provide tailored itineraries to Dhoni Mighili. And if you want another unforgettable experience, the company behind Dhoni Mighili has opened the first-ever underwater spa on Huvafen Fushi in the North Male Atoll, a 30-minute journey by speedboat from the international airport at Male, the Maldivian capital. Here you can enjoy treatments and therapies while watching the amazing underwater world go by.

Trekking the Milford Track

Fiordland, New Zealand

If you are going to pull on a pair of hiking boots and strap a rucksack to your back just once, New Zealand's Milford Track, hailed as the 'world's greatest walk', has to be the trek to take. Traversing the heart of South Island's dramatic wild fiord country, it winds through native bush and rainforest, glaciated valley systems and up into the high mountains at the Mackinnon Pass. It then skirts majestically downwards past rivers and waterfalls, including the awesome Sutherland Falls, to Milford Sound crowned in scenic splendour by the jagged Mitre Peak.

Milford Sound

Dramatic mountains line the trail from Glade House

Mitre Peak dominates Milford Sound

Ever since Quintin Mackinnon and Ernest Mitchell first pioneered the route in 1888, walkers ranging from hardened trekkers to novices literally wearing their first hiking shoes have been taking up the challenge of this four-day, 53-km trail. And there is an easy and a hard way to do it. Guided walks offer the relative luxury of lodge accommodation, three-course meals, hot showers and a glass of wine at the end of the day. Independent walkers use a system of huts along the track, but are required to carry and cook their own food.

If you join a guided walk your experience begins with a trek briefing in Queenstown after which you travel by coach to Te Anau. Here you board a launch for the head of Te Anau Lake. The boat ride is a memorable approach to the track with mountain vistas rearing loftily in the distance, their edges blanketed in deep forest. When you arrive at your destination it is only a 20-minute stroll along the fern-lined trail to the first lodge: Glade House.

The Wetland Walk is a short detour

Rainforest cloaks the trail near Glade House

On the second day of the trek, a suspension bridge strung across the Clinton River brings the first bit of precarious excitement. The trail then winds through thick, beech forest past Mackinnon's hut to a sidetrack called the Wetland Walk, which takes you through a unique reserve area of protected ferns and mosses. After this you can savour the luxury of some level walking as you follow the old, broad, packhorse trail before climbing into the western branch of the

A waterfall tumbles down a narrow canyon

The trek high point, Mackinnon Pass, is overlooked by Mount Balloon

Wispy waterfall near Pompolona Lodge

Clinton valley – its 1220-metre walls can make you feel incredibly small.

After an overnight stay at Pompolona Lodge you will have to be up at the crack of dawn to give yourself plenty of time for the daunting ascent to the 1073-metre Mackinnon Pass. You cross another wobbling suspension bridge and then the climb begins in earnest, with a series of forested switchbacks. Gradually getting higher you finally emerge to an awesome view of the Nicholas Cirque, a natural amphitheatre at the head of the Clinton valley. One final push, and you will make it up to the pass and the memorial cairn built in 1912 to commemorate Mackinnon and Mitchell's efforts. A sea of jagged mountain tops and deep valley systems stretches far into the distance.

The track follows along the saddle, skirting the edges of imposing Mount Balloon, before descending almost another 6 km to Quinton Lodge. It can be hard going on the rocky and uneven ground, so concentrate instead on the towering cliffs, glacial streams and a pretty boardwalk through a canyon of tumbling waterfalls. If your legs are still up to it, take the 90-minute return walk from the lodge to the Sutherland Falls – which, at 540 metres, stands as the fifth-highest waterfall in the world.

After all the efforts of the previous three days the final stretch will probably seem like a breeze. The track descends steadily, and by the time you reach the 43-km peg you will be back in the rainforest and on fairly even ground. The refreshing sight of Lake Ada means you are close to Sandfly Point, where you can finally hang up your boots. From here, a boat transports you into the majestic, glacially carved Milford Sound. There's no better way to celebrate completing the trail than boarding the *Milford Mariner* sailing boat for a tranquil overnight voyage into the sound to see the sun set over the Tasman Sea. A short walk up on deck will be the only exercise required.

A few airlines, including Air New Zealand, fly several times daily to Queenstown, directly and via Auckland. The Dairy Guest House, a converted dairy in Queenstown provides perfect pre- and post-trek accommodation. Guided walks can be arranged through Ultimate Hikes, while the perfect end to the trek is to sail with Real Journeys through Milford Sound on the *Milford Mariner*. For an exhilarating return journey to Queenstown, take a scenic flight for some breathtaking mountain views.

Sunrise catches a peak en route from Glade House

Festival of the Sahara
Douz, Tunisia

When fiercely proud Bedouin nomads and their camel caravans converge on the Tunisian oasis town of Douz for the spectacular Festival of the Sahara, sand and sparks are bound to fly. The event is still relatively unknown outside Tunisia, but with camel racing, poetry competitions, tribal plays and traditional music, this flamboyant gathering is the best desert festival for your diary.

Mehari camels race to the finish line

Young Bedouin horse rider

Douz itself seems to float between the shimmering, endless dunes of the Great Eastern Erg and the mirage-making, ocean-sized salt flat of Chott El Jerid, in central Tunisia. Driving across the latter's 50-km-wide, blinding white expanse invokes thoughts of Antarctica, and is a sure-fire way to exhaust your supply of superlatives before you even reach the oasis.

The town is the social and trading hub for five Bedouin groups, with the 15,000-strong Mrazrig tribe holding sway. During spring, many tribesmen still move their sheep and goats south towards Ksar Ghilane to graze on the Nefazaoua plains. In winter they return to Douz to work on the date harvest, and it was this seasonal regrouping that first inspired the festival (nobody really knows when it started although it has been official for over 35 years). It was a chance for tribes to test each other's wits in games and horsemanship, a time for musical and poetical celebration, and an opportunity for youngsters to marry – a tradition that continues today.

Tribal musicians come from all over Tunisia

Life for the Bedouin has always been a delicate balancing act between desert survival and oasis exuberance, a relationship mirrored in the location of H'Niche Stadium, a one-stand, open-sided affair that is site of the main action. Built on the very edge of town, it is held in place on one side by overhanging palm trees and dissolves seamlessly into wind-whipped dunes on the other.

With crowds filling the whole stadium, the festival bursts into life with the thud of drums and the piercing tones of the flute-like *zoukara*. The players, swathed in billowing white skirts and bright red waistcoats, their fezzes topped with lengthy black tassels, whirl like

Tribal elders parade at the festival opening

Drums and *zoukaras* set the festival rhythm

spinning tops, almost drilling themselves into the ground. Line after line of Bedouin tribesmen fire ear-cracking shotgun volleys into the sand as horse riders behind them fight to control their fiery mounts.

The most prestigious event is the camel race. With around £2000 at stake, victory must be won at any cost. In a loping version of the Olympic 800 metres, the pale-cream mehari camels – speedy sprinters normally employed to search out new pastures ahead of caravans – race shoulder to shoulder. After a series of qualifying

Dancers twirl during the festival opening parade

heats, the final is on the fourth and last day, and includes two exhausting laps of the circuit. Such is the prize, it is not unknown for fights to break out between the jockeys.

In between the sporting action, an elaborate, traditional play unfolds with the Saharan dunes as a stage. It tells the story of a brave Bedouin warrior, Mandour, who falls in love with a girl from a rival tribe. Trouble and strife follow before... well, let's not spoil the ending. Another event well worth catching is the unique 'hair dance'. Dozens of girls, clothed in vivid dresses and with their faces veiled, kneel on the ground and swing their long hair around in great swishing arcs to the sound of hypnotic music, until they collapse.

As well as the final of the camel race, the fourth day also sees Sloughi greyhound racing, and a sand-hockey competition with the teams using shepherd's crooks for hockey sticks. However, the most spectacular display is by acrobatic horsemen who, at full gallop, bounce around and on and off their mounts, like vaulting gymnasts. A rousing procession formally closes the festival and within hours the site is cleared. Black woollen tents are dismantled, earthenware cooking pots packed and camel trains prepared.

As the Bedouin meander through an ocean of sandy waves towards the targetless horizon, it seems that their journey home will take for ever. There is no doubt that their collective body-clock will bring them back next year, but their speedy departure suggests that their hearts belong more to the Sahara than the oasis.

ⓘ

The festival is held at the end of November or the beginning of December; the actual date is different every year. Douz is packed during the festivities, so book your accommodation early. Other events, including a 'Miss Sahara' competition, take place in the town in the evenings. The first day and the last day of the festival are usually the most spectacular and boisterous.

Bedouin horsemanship is a star attraction

Souk shopping
Marrakech, Morocco

The vivid colours of its bustling souk, the red of its medina walls, the mingling aromas of a thousand spices and the sounds of story-tellers, fire-eaters and snake charmers make Marrakech the world's most exotic location for bargain-hunting.

For centuries the city has been a renowned trading centre. Berbers and Arabs, nomads and tribespeople from the surrounding Atlas Mountains converged in its chaotic central square, Jemaa El Fna,

Feasting begins at dusk in Jemaa El Fna

while merchants from Timbuktu, Egypt and Europe came to deal in cotton, gold, silver, slaves and spices. Today it feels as though little has changed and shopping remains a reason in itself to visit Marrakech's medina, or old quarter.

A maze of alleyways stretches northwards out of Jemaa El Fna, into the heart of the souk. Tightly packed rows of closet-sized stalls line them on both sides and keen salesmen vie for your attention. While they, like Marrakech's hawkers, once had a reputation for high-pressure sales

tactics, things have changed. Now, thanks to the introduction of plain-clothes tourist police, bartering for arts and crafts is a relatively relaxed affair.

It's almost guaranteed that at some point you will get lost in the souk's twist of shadowy, narrow streets, where the sky is crowded out by overhanging carpets and metalwork or leather displays. With so many tightly packed stalls selling an array of products from traditional babouche (bright yellow slippers) to ornamental ironwork lanterns,

Silk cushions at Dar Les Cigognes

Babouche slippers in the souk

it's easy to let browsing take over and lose your bearings. You will usually find that the next turn brings you back to a familiar spot.

An area not to be missed is Rahba Kedima (the 'old place') off Rue Semaine in the north-east part of the souk, where herbalists tout potions, lotions and spices to cure all manner of ailments or diseases. Here you can pick up black scorpions, bottled leeches and even dried chameleons for medicinal purposes. You may prefer to settle for a simple but effective neck and shoulder massage.

When the hustle and heat of the souk starts to take its toll on your will to barter, retreat to Jemaa El Fna. Its many shady pavement cafés offer refreshing mint tea – or you can try one of the fresh juices from the orange-laden carts that line its perimeter.

It is at sunset that the action really gets under way in the square as musicians, brightly costumed water-sellers, dancers, scribes writing letters, dentists pulling teeth and henna tattooists gather en masse. And shortly after the sun goes down the open-air restaurants take centre stage. Neat, orderly rows of benches, strings of twinkling

Pot-pourri in the souk

Marrakech's souk is bustling with life

lights, tables covered with white cloths and plates piled high with salads, couscous and skewered lamb are promptly assembled, and hazy smoke and enticing aromas fill the air.

The thud of drums and the sound of whining instruments enticing snakes from wicker baskets, street sellers shouting their wares, the hiss of flames and the clatter as snails are cooked in their shells on the food stalls combine in an intoxicating concoction. Although Jemaa El Fna translates as 'assembly of the dead', it brims with life every evening.

Traditional red walls in the medina

Crenellated roof at Dar Les Cigognes

For a more chilled-out view of proceedings, watch the scene unfold from the vantage point of the Café Glacier, which has a panoramic view of both the square and the Koutoubia mosque, the other dominant feature in the centre of the medina.

If you want to escape the bustle entirely, you can find solace in one of Marrakech's *riads* – traditional homes centred around a courtyard – many of which have been converted into stylish boutique hotels in recent years. They are typically hidden behind sturdy, thick, wooden doors, and there is no way of knowing that these conceal retreats with interiors that make you feel you are in an art gallery. Rooms are arranged around the courtyard, so all the windows face inwards overlooking this cool inner sanctum. Stepping into a *riad* is to step into a haven removed from the chaos, noise and hustle of the city, where you can unwind, relax and rest before your next shopping spree.

Souk mosque door

Ornate ceiling and lantern, Dar Les Cigognes

Several airlines, including Royal Air Maroc, fly daily to Marrakech. Across from the Royal Palace and the Badi Palace, Dar Les Cigognes is one of Marrakech's luxurious *riads*. A merchant's house in the 17th century, it has been carefully restored and the rooms individually decorated. They include the lavish Sahara room with a desert landscape mural, and the Harem room with its red and gold furnishings. Dar Les Cigognes gets its name from the storks that nest on its ramparts (*dar* is Arab for 'house' and *cigognes* is French for 'storks'). Local guides are available to help visitors find their way around the complex alleyways of the souk.

Post box and leather foot stool in the souk

'Lost World' river journey

Angel Falls, Venezuela

'Paradise on Earth' claimed Christopher Columbus when he encountered Venezuela's coastline in 1498. If he had only ventured further inland, what words would he have used to describe Venezuela's richest natural treasure: Angel Falls (Salto Angel), the world's highest waterfall? Words might have failed him even sooner – getting to Angel Falls along the Carrao River, which weaves between a 'Lost World' archipelago of table-topped mountains afloat on a jungle sea, is perhaps one of South America's best wilderness river journeys.

A hiking trail hewn from the rock runs behind powerful Sapo Falls

Set within the Canaima National Park (Parque Nacional Canaima), in the Gran Sabana region buried deep in Venezuela's south-east corner, these bizarre rock islands, or *tepuís*, provided the inspiration for Sir Arthur Conan Doyle's 1912 novel, *The Lost World*. Convinced that their inaccessibility meant there was hope of finding dinosaurs and pterodactyls still alive atop them, he wrote this classic tale that eventually inspired Steven Spielberg's *Jurassic Park*.

To reach the Gran Sabana from Venezuela's capital, Caracas, it is necessary to fly first to unspectacular Ciudad Bolívar. Then the adventure begins, with an exhilarating flight southwards either in a small four-seater plane or an old, silver, twin-prop DC-9 that comes straight out of

the golden age of flying. As you near Canaima, a tiny village populated by Pemón Indians and the base for river trips to Angel Falls, *tepuís* begin to pop their summits through sporadic clouds.

Before departing upriver for the falls, be sure to take the short boat trip and hike to Sapo Falls (Salto Sapo), one of seven waterfalls above Canaima Lake (Laguna Canaima), which you will have seen from the plane. At over 100 metres wide and 20 metres high, the tannin-brown fall is spectacular in itself, but the real treat lies behind

Pemón Indian guides on Carrao River

it: a literally breathtaking path hewn from the rock behind the torrent. The path was cut by a hermit, Tomás Bernal, and traversing it requires a swimsuit – and a dose of courage when you experience the air-sucking power of a massive waterfall.

Although it is feasible to get to Angel Falls and back in a day the pace will be feverish, so if time allows it is better to take a two- or three-day option. Overnighting in a hammock at one of the rustic camps near Auyan Tepuí will add immeasurably to your sense of exploration.

The boats to the falls are driven by experienced Pemón Indian guides, and as the narrow, outboard-motor-powered craft battle against the strong currents of the Carrao, the snaking, jungle-cloaked river plays tricks on your sense of direction. 'New' *tepuís* seem to appear and disappear until it eventually becomes clear that most of them are just one: Auyan Tepuí. Rising above the treeline like an immense, medieval fortress, and turreted with tall, standing, pillar stones, it is a forbidding sight. The name means 'Hell Mountain' and

Auyan Tepuí rises above the clouds

Boat on the Carrao River

it is revered and feared by the Pemón Indians, who believe that *marawitón* (bad spirits) live up there with the god Tramán-chitá.

If Conan Doyle had gone looking for dinosaurs he would have been hard pressed to find them on Auyan Tepuí's summit. At a staggering 700 sq. km it is four times as big as Washington DC. Angel Falls launches itself spectacularly from the 807-metre-high plateau in a fine misting, dancing spray.

Missouri-born adventurer, pilot and gold prospector Jimmy Angel brought the first reports of this natural wonder to the outside

Sapo Falls tumbles into Canaima Lake

Hammocks at camp

world in 1935. Two years later he deliberately crash-landed his plane, *Río Caroni*, on the summit of Auyan Tepuí and took 11 days to find a way down the treacherous cliffs – a stunt that gave the waterfall its name.

Although Angel Falls can be seen from the river, a short hike towards its base takes you to a far better vantage point. Crane your neck, peer skywards and watch in wonder as the water tumbles down the red rock-face to form the world's highest waterfall.

ⓘ

Boat trips to Angel Falls usually operate only from May to November – the wet season, when river levels are higher – but prolonged rainfall may see this period extended. In Canaima and Ciudad Bolívar several airlines, such as Rutaca and LTA, offer flights over the waterfall. National Airline Servivensa offers package tours to Canaima from Caracas, with accommodation in its comfortable Campamento Canaima lodge. Better value can be found with tour operators in Ciudad Bolívar and Canaima.

Angel Falls

Walking the Wall

Jinshanling to Simatai, China

Outrageous in scale and visible from space, the Great Wall of China barely needs an introduction. Walking along it inspires visions of steadfast Chinese soldiers and charging Mongol hordes, imperious defence and futile attack. Almost everyone has this on their 'to do' list when they visit China, but you can avoid the milling crowds of walkers by heading for the part that starts at Jinshanling.

Stretching for more than 6700 km across the harsh, jagged mountains and the deserts and grasslands of northern China, from the Shanhai Pass in the east to the Jiayu Pass in the west, the Great

The Great Wall winds its way through the harsh mountains near Jinshanling

Watchtowers line the wall

Wall was built over a period of about two thousand years. The Badaling section is by far the most popular one to visit, but it has been highly restored and this, together with the number of tourists, means it is a struggle to get a feeling for its true nature. For anyone who is reasonably fit, a better option is the 12-km-long trek from Jinshanling to Simatai, where the wall and its surroundings retain an appealing air of ruggedness, raggedness and natural disrepair.

Jinshanling is about 120 km north of Beijing, in the Hebei region, and is serviced by a number of tour operators in the capital, who will drop you off there and pick you up again in Simatai later in the

Building the wall across mountainous northern China cost many lives

View of wall near Simatai

afternoon. Although the wall is visible on entering the Jinshanling gate, it is not until you climb the first flight of steps to look along its snaking, crenellated length that you stop in awe. With contouring mountain ridges as far as the eye can see, every high peak crowned with a hefty watchtower, this gargantuan piece of engineering defies gravity as it rears up then plunges down slopes steep enough for extreme skiing.

Initially a series of separate walls built by warring dynasties during the late Spring and Autumn Period (770 BC to 476 BC), the Great Wall itself dates from after 214 BC, during the Qin dynasty, when most of the existing walls were linked and their overall length extended under the emperor Qin Shi Huangdi. The futility of attacking its 7-metre- to 8-metre-high ramparts, coupled with the exhaustion brought on by traversing the mountains that surround it, must have broken the hearts of many an enemy. Even the notorious Mongol hordes of Genghis Khan (Chinngis Khaan) struggled to breach it before capturing Beijing in 1215. When the Yuan dynasty founded by

Genghis' grandson Kublai, who completed his grandfather's conquest of China, fell in 1368 the Ming emperors went on a massive building spree to strengthen the wall, in particular to try to keep the Manchus at bay during the 16th and early 17th centuries.

At first, when you leave Jinshanling, the wall is in good condition, which helps to warm your legs up for the relentless series of steps that take you from one watchtower to another. At the height of China's power, over a million soldiers guarded the Great Wall against attackers. Looking out from a watchtower at the endless, bleak folds of rough mountainside, it is not difficult to imagine the suffering of enemy soldiers, especially in winter, as they marched or rode from the north for months to mount an attack. With each watchtower placed to give sweeping views, and a series of horseback messengers

Walking to Simatai avoids the crowds of other sections

ready to alert defenders on other sections of the wall, the Chinese had an overwhelming advantage.

As you edge closer to Simatai and start to get a feel – even if it is only the ache in your legs – for the magnitude of this giant, brick dragon, the state of the wall begins to deteriorate. In a couple of areas where it is too unstable for walking, footpaths lead off around the mountainside, giving you the enemy's view of the wall's daunting, towering brickwork.

Above Simatai a modern swing bridge now crosses the river and the more adventurous can take a final ride down to the village on a flying-fox zip wire. It seems a pity, though, to spoil an encounter with one of the world's truly great monuments by making such a sharp exit.

ⓘ

Many Beijing tour operators offer trips to popular sections of the Great Wall, including Jinshanling. Make sure they allow you enough time, about four or five hours, for an unhurried walk to Simatai. The constant up and down makes for slow progress. Persistent local 'guides' will latch on to you from the start of the wall, offering postcards and books. Ignore them – the route is straightforward and the books are heavily overpriced – and they will eventually look elsewhere for business.

Ruined wall near Simatai

A bridge crossing at Simatai

Walking the wall from Jinshanling to Simatai is surprisingly strenuous

Trekking Torres del Paine

Patagonia, Chile

The striking spires, or Torres, that give their name to the park

Crossing a rickety bridge on the Circuit trek

Grazing the sky with their ragged, saw-toothed summits, the red granite peaks of the Torres del Paine national park are the popular icons of Patagonia, one of the wildest places on the planet. Remote, unpredictable and committing, the park has a network of trekking trails that are hard to rival. They encompass a clutch of iceberg-strewn, azure and jade lakes, white-water rivers and waterfalls, and the largest glaciers in the southern hemisphere outside Antarctica. It is unsurprising, then, that Torres del Paine is often dubbed the world's most spectacular national park.

Covering some 240,000 hectares, this UNESCO Biosphere Reserve is usually approached by bus or ferry via the small town of Puerto Natales. Some 500 km south of Puerto Montt, the gateway to Chilean Patagonia, Natales is set on the shores of the dramatic Last Hope Sound (Seno Ultima Esperanza). From otherworldly cloud formations

and menacing storms to unbelievable sunsets, this vast body of windswept waters can be a show in itself.

If you have time, the best way to reach Puerto Natales is by taking the ferry from Puerto Montt. It threads its way along the route of Charles Darwin's *Beagle*, through the hundreds of islands that line the Chilean south-west coastline, where icebergs and whales are common

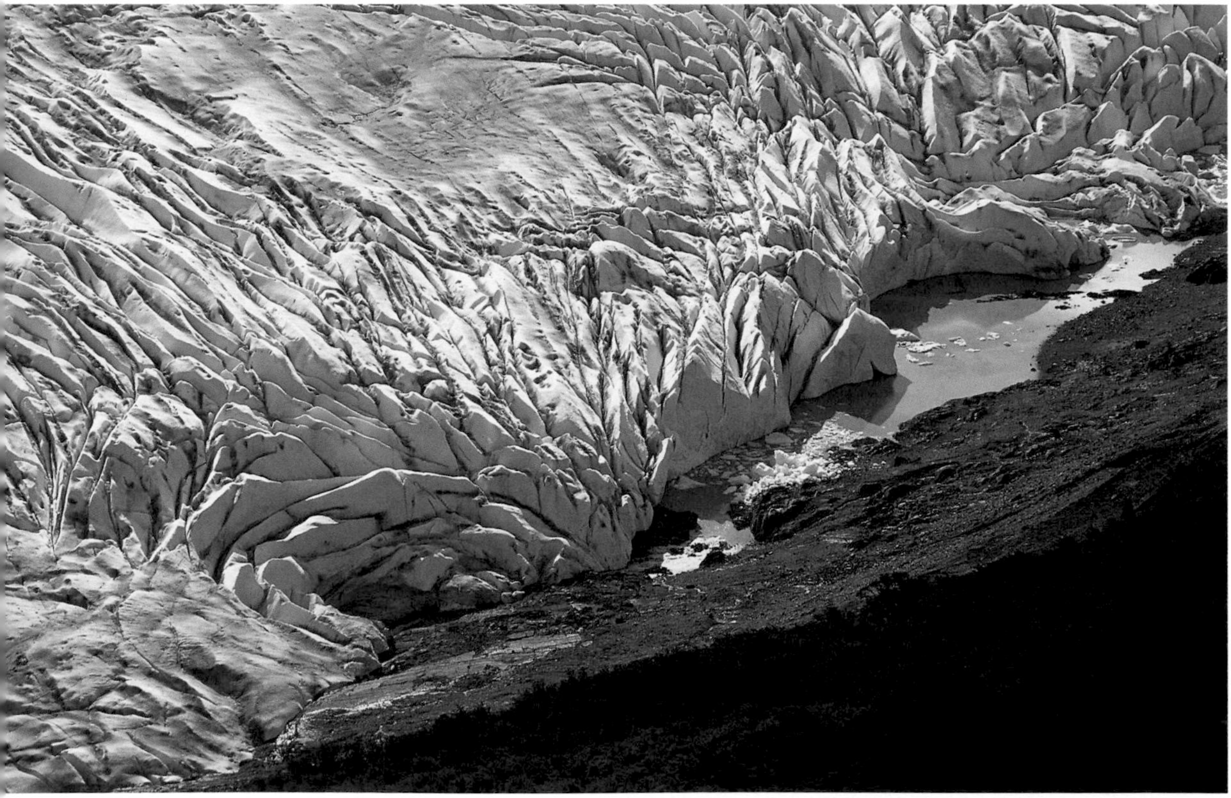

Fissured surface of Glacier Grey

sights. The four-day journey is a fantastic introduction to Patagonia, and, compared to almost any other cruise, an absolute bargain.

From Natales a four-hour bus ride along 112 km of dirt roads to the park entrance gives you plenty of time to contemplate the meaning of 'remote' as you drive through uninhabited countryside. Once inside Torres del Paine, the more serious trekkers take off on the Paine Circuit, a six- to eight-day epic – but navigationally straightforward – route that is well worth getting fit for. While the other trails, such as the not-to-be-missed trek to the soaring pinnacles (Torres) that give their name to the park, are magnificent the circuit is undoubtedly the one to attempt, given the time and ability. You can tag the one- to two-day Torres trail on to the start or end of it. If it is

Glacier Grey forms part of the great southern Patagonia ice field

solitude you are after, avoid embarking on the circuit for a day or two after the ferry pulls into Puerto Natales, bringing with it a cargo of eager hikers.

Weather permitting (snow sometimes closes the highest pass), the 100-km circuit takes you around, through and over the Paine massif. It is best tackled anticlockwise – in this direction the scenery

Trekkers can cross Lago Grey by boat for views of the Paine massif

Looking down over Glacier Grey

improves constantly and the trail builds to the tougher sections. En route, you encounter lush meadows, cross small rivers and skirt beautiful wilderness lakes like Lago Dickson, surrounded by ice-topped mountains. Other lakes, such as Laguna Siete Perros (Seven Dogs), brim with icebergs and provide a stark contrast to the dense forests that line the lower to mid levels of the massif.

There are several challenging climbs to high passes, some of which have steep descents that offer little respite for weary legs, but the scenery is always spellbinding. Any aches and pains are forgotten when you look down at the immense, fissured valley of ice that is Glacier Grey. This remnant of the great southern Patagonian icefield, which once encased the entire region, is about 1500 years old and regularly calves chunks of ice into Lago Grey, the home run on the circuit.

For those in search of a touch of luxury, Hosteria Grey on the shores of Lago Grey is an outstanding if somewhat ungainly lodge, where the wind is kept at bay by double glazing and normal hotel service is resumed. Though we wouldn't recommend that you spend your entire time there, it is an ideal end-of-trek treat. Experience the alluring wilderness that is Torres del Paine just once, and it will always call you back.

Trekking the Paine Circuit involves either sleeping in huts, which must be booked ahead, or camping. You will also need to reserve accommodation at the Hosteria Grey well in advance. The best, but also the busiest, time to go to Torres del Paine is from December to March. Blue Green Adventures run a full range of adventure trips, including trekking, biking and horse trekking. Venture south of Patagonia and it's 'next stop Antarctica', so expect – and equip yourself for – some wild weather during the trek. It may not arrive, but if it does being caught out will be a recipe for misery. The winds, in particular, can be ferocious.

Exploring around Lago Dickson

Rocky scenery from the Balcões near Ribeiro Frio

Pico Ruivo
Madeira, Portugal

Terraces in the interior of Madeira

Long synonymous with sweet wine and winter breaks for the elderly, Madeira is also a paradise for hikers and nature lovers. The tip of an underwater mountain range, it shoots abruptly out of the Atlantic Ocean some 950 km from the Portuguese coast.

The island is only 57 km long and 22 km wide but its highest point, the craggy and atmospheric Pico Ruivo, rises 1861 metres above sea level. This sudden height amid the wet waters of the Atlantic creates microclimates. Although the temperature hovers in the 20s all year round, Madeira's mountainous centre is often enveloped in rolling impenetrable cloud that, seemingly magically, gives way to hot sunshine before the mist sweeps in again. And the weather can be different on each quarter of the island: if it is raining in one area drive over a pass, or through a road tunnel, and there is a good chance you will be bathed in sunshine.

Rugged coastline on the north of the island

Peaks at Pico do Arieiro

Coastline at the foot of Reid's Palace

The starting point for treks to Pico Ruivo is the atmospheric peak of Pico do Arieiro, reached via a switchback road with many hairpin bends. From here you look across seemingly endless knife-like jagged peaks and out to the sea nearly 2 km below. Between the rock-blades deep valleys slice into the island – their floors see daylight only at midday when the sun is high enough to pierce their hidden depths. The walk is only 4 miles, but includes a number of vertiginous climbs and descents of over 450 metres.

Not all the hikes are as strenuous as the trek to Pico Ruivo. Many trails follow Madeira's *levadas* (watercourses), which date back to 1452. Cut into the contours of hills, they were developed to move water around the island and sometimes run for dozens of kilometres. They have a gradient of only a few degrees, so the water always flows – but not too fast. Alongside the *levadas* are walking tracks, some a few metres wide, others just narrow ledges cut into a hillside. There are also long tunnels hacked through rock, initially by slaves brought to work on sugar-cane plantations.

Steeply terraced village of Curral das Freiras

Jagged mountains at Pico do Arieiro

Plants on the summit of Pico do Arieiro

As well as being the island's main thoroughfares as recently as the mid-20th century, the *levadas* allowed seemingly inaccessible places to be irrigated for agriculture. The result can be seen in a key feature of the Madeira landscape: the *poios* (terraces) on many of the mountainsides. Nowhere on the island is there a better example of this terracing than in the remote Curral das Freiras (Nun's Valley). Viewed from the top of the surrounding hills, seemingly sheer walls drop to the gloomy valley floor below. There are *poios* most of the way down and the effort required to bring these relatively small areas under cultivation must have been phenomenal. The sun reaches the village at base of the valley for only a few hours a day, and it is a shame that *levadas* can't bring in sunlight as well as water.

Funchal is Madeira's main town and it is here that you will find Reid's Palace, one of the world's classic hotels. Perched on cliffs overlooking the sea, it has quiet gardens, tennis courts and three heated saltwater pools. Once patronized by Winston Churchill, George Bernard Shaw and a host of kings and queens, this is old-world luxury. Even if you can't afford to stay here you should sample afternoon tea on the terrace overlooking the sea.

Funchal is famous for the wicker toboggans that run down from Monte in the hills above it. Not quite a white-knuckle ride, they clatter noisily through streets polished over the years by their runners, propelled by two *carreiros* wearing straw boaters. A cable-car ride to the top of the hill will give you commanding views of the town and its surroundings.

Cabo Girão, the second highest sea cliffs in the world

ⓘ

British Airways fly direct from Gatwick to Funchal. During the summer season a charter flight is the best option. Hiring a car is vital if you want to explore. Distances aren't great so it is possible to base yourself in one place. The doyen of Madeira hotels is the historic Reid's Palace. Owned by Orient Express, it occupies the best viewpoint in Funchal.

Looking out to Ilhéu de Farol from Pico do Arieiro

Neist Point, Duirnish

Isle of Skye
Scotland

Clouds building over the peaks of the Red Cuillin

The Isle of Skye is the largest of the islands in the Inner Hebrides and is dominated by the mighty Cuillin Hills, which can be seen from all but its most remote parts. Many of their peaks are accessible without technical skills and they are justifiably popular with mountaineers and climbers.

The Cuillin are split into two groups. The Red Cuillin are composed of granite that takes on a characteristic reddish tinge at sunrise and sunset, and are round in profile. The Black Cuillin are made from basalt and gabbro, a rough, dark rock that gives them their name, and are far more striking. While they are relatively low – none of them reaches over 1000 metres – they loom impressively over the island. Craggy peaks and sheer cliffs form deep gullies and ravines, unsoftened by vegetation and often wreathed in cloud. The highest point on Skye is the summit of Sgurr Alasdair in the Black Cuillin.

The Cuillin are not the island's only spectacular feature. Much of the coastline is striking, with great cliffs plunging down to the sea or rolling farmland sweeping down to pebble beaches. On the most

western point of Skye is the Neist Point Lighthouse; painted yellow and white, an incongruous colour scheme in this remote location, it stands on a vertical cliff, the top of which is coated with meadows and wildflowers. Seabirds soar in the surrounding air currents.

The Storr, a rocky hill on the Trotternish Peninsula, is noted for the pinnacles at the foot of its steep cliff face, in an area called the Sanctuary. These are volcanic plugs, strangely shaped by the violence of their creation and erosion. The best known is the Old Man of Storr.

The wildlife on Skye is as spectacular as the scenery. The rare white-tailed sea eagle is sometimes seen here, and golden eagles are relatively common in the Cuillin Hills. In summer you may come

Western coastline of Trotternish seen from Sconser

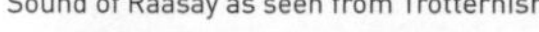

Sound of Raasay as seen from Trotternish

Farmhouse at Drinan, Strathaird

Cemetery on the shore of Portree Loch, Portree

Red clover and lichens on the coast at Ord, Sleat

Pier on Armadale Bay at Isleornsay, Sleat

across dolphins, minke whales and even basking sharks in the island's lochs and inlets, and otters can be found all year round. On land there is a good chance of seeing majestic red deer.

Skye is steeped in history. There are cairns and standing-stone circles from Neolithic times – even dinosaur footprints at Staffin Bay – and it was known to the Romans and recorded by Ptolemy, the 2nd-century Greek geographer. The name itself is said to come from Old Norse, hinting at contact with the Vikings.

More recently, Dunvegan Castle has been the seat of the Clan MacLeod since 1237. It has been augmented by a keep and tower over the centuries, although most of the battlements were added in the 19th century. For all its fortifications – until the 18th century the only entrance was via a sea gate – the castle has seen little action, although it was besieged by the Macdonalds, the sworn enemies of the MacLeods, in the 15th century.

Although Skye is on the same latitude as Moscow, the Gulf Stream makes it much milder. However, the weather is changeable and you can be engulfed in a sudden downpour at any time, only to have the sun break through grey clouds a short while later. If it does rain you could visit the Talisker distillery at Carbost. Named after Talisker Bay, or possibly the Talisker River, it is the only single-malt distillery on the island. It dates back to 1840, and Robert Louis Stevenson mentioned it in his poem *The Scotsman's Return from Abroad.*

Gaelic and the culture it represents are highly valued on Skye – almost half the population speak the language and the island is sometimes called by its Gaelic name: Eilean á Cheò (Isle of Mist). There is also a strong heritage of folk music, and the annual Isle of Skye Music Festival in June attracts many well-known folk singers.

ⓘ

The island is easily reached by car or bus from Inverness and Glasgow over the Skye Bridge. There are train services to Mallaig and the Kyle of Lochalsh on the mainland side, and ferries to Skye and many of the nearby islands from Mallaig. Inverness and Glasgow have good rail and air links with the rest of the UK.

Farm at Tormore on the Sound of Sleat, Sleat

Kilmore, Sleat

The Golden Temple
Amritsar, India

Detail on the roof of the Sri Harimandir Sahib

Golden temple reflected in the Amrit Sarovar

The Sri Harimandir Sahib, or Golden Temple, arguably the most beautiful building in India, is set on an island in the middle of the Amrit Sarovar (Pool of Nectar), the lake that gives the town of Amritsar its name.

Construction of the temple, the holiest building of the Sikh religion, started in 1589, after someone who was disabled had reputedly been cured by bathing in what was then a small lake. The lake was expanded to form the Pool of Nectar. The land for this enlargement was granted by the Mogul emperor Akbar. The original temple was destroyed by invading Afgans in 1757 and the site had to be retaken by the Sikhs. It

was rebuilt in 1764, and in 1830 its roof was covered with 100 kilograms of gold – the reason why the building is known as the Golden Temple. Up close, the detail of the gilding is exquisite.

As the spiritual centre of the Sikh faith the temple is about far more than beauty. Sikhism is noted for its egalitarianism and anyone is welcome here, irrespective of religion, race or caste. The overriding impression is one of peace and spirituality, despite the crowds of visitors. Every Sikh tries to make the pilgrimage to the Golden Temple at least once, and the atmosphere is surprisingly cosmopolitan. Doctors from the US mingle with fierce old men from rural villages.

As at other Sikh temples (*gurudwara*) there is no organized worship. Some pilgrims stroll around the Pool of Nectar. Others sit and stare at the Golden Temple in quiet contemplation. Many bathe, lowering themselves into the water with the help of great chains anchored to the sides of the lake.

The inside of the temple is even more beautiful than its exterior, with breathtaking detail and a pietra dura inlay of precious stones in marble that is even finer than that in the Taj Mahal. The place is imbued with an air of deep devotion. In the main sanctum a priest surrounded by hundreds of quietly sitting pilgrims reads from the *Granth Sahib*, the holy book of the Sikh religion. A complete reading takes 48 hours. The atmosphere is incredibly moving, yet humblingly simple. The feelings of reverence and awe are palpable. Another reading of the *Granth Sahib* takes place upstairs, and yet another in a chapel on the roof. Early in the morning the book is ceremonially processed from the Akal Takht, where it is kept, and returned late at night.

Looking down the causeway

The Golden Temple complex

Temple guard contemplates the Sri Harimandir Sahib

Inside the Sri Harimandir Sahib

Handing out plates at the Guru Ram Das Langar

The Pool of Nectar is a special place for sitting and contemplating, but make sure you don't point your feet at the temple or dip them in the water. Doing either is considered to be an insult, and you certainly don't want to insult Sikhs. They are proud people with warrior traditions – as is shown by the wall plaques that commemorate army detachments. A priest or guard may fix you with a fierce gaze, looking like thunder – then smile, like a rainbow breaking across clouds.

No one could be more welcoming than a Sikh. Hospitality is central to Sikhism and you may well be offered free cups of tea. You will certainly be offered free meals. The Guru Ram Das Langar is an enormous kitchen and dining hall where vegetarian food is provided for pilgrims. Everyone sits in long lines on the floor of the hall holding metal trays on to which their portions are put. Extra chapattis are offered – just hold your hands together and one will be dropped into them. At the back of the dining hall is the kitchen, where chapattis are made in a remarkable production line and volunteers wash up the trays.

The peace and spotlessness of the temple complex contrast markedly with the bustling, dusty and run-down old town that surrounds it. Narrow bumpy streets are thronged with garrulous cycle-rickshaw drivers and crowds of pilgrims. It would be a shame to rush through this area, though, as there are a number of fascinating shops with everything a devout Sikh could ever need: religious pennants, turbans, bracelets and even martial swords.

Jet Airways fly directly to Amritsar from London. Most of the better hotels are some way out of town. Local arrangements can be made through Atithi Travels in Delhi. Although visitors are welcome inside this holiest place in the Sikh faith, all photography is banned. We obtained special permission from the temple authorities to take the pictures shown here.

Man reading at an upper window of Sri Harimandir Sahib

Golden Temple floodlit at night

Yasawa Islands
Fiji

Overlooking the Yasawa chain from a seaplane above Nanuyalailai Island

The Yasawa Islands have a brooding malevolence that is a complete contrast to the relaxed and easy-going nature of their inhabitants. Black rocks pepper soft golden beaches, and craggy green hillsides covered in ominously dark grassland are rent with valleys and ridges that show the violence of their volcanic creation.

The people of Fiji have not always been friendly. Historically, they have fought with each other and any outsiders, and built up a reputation for warlike behaviour. Although the islands were briefly

Rugged interior of Nacula Island

visited by the explorers Abel Tasman, in the 17th century, and Captain Cook in the 18th, they were largely avoided by Europeans until the discovery of valuable sandalwood in 1804.

Trade led to settlers and missionaries coming to the islands from Europe, but this exacerbated the conflict between the Fijian chiefdoms, and the country was eventually ceded to Britain in 1874. The British introduced Indian labourers, whose descendants now make up almost half the population, and ruled Fiji until it gained its independence in 1970.

The Yasawa are a string of some 20 volcanic islands that stretch in an 80-km line in the west of the country. The water between Nanuyalailai, Nanuya, Matacawalevu and Tavewa is particularly clear and in the sunlight it glows an iridescent blue – so blue that the 1980 Brooke Shields film, *The Blue Lagoon*, was shot here. The lagoon is now universally known by the name of the movie, and is fantastic for diving and snorkelling – the water so clear that visibility is near perfect.

Beach on the island of Tavewa

Nacula Island

What I particularly like about the Yasawa Islands is that the accommodation includes a number of stylish mid-range and even backpacker places, as well as a couple of super-expensive ones. This means you don't have to be rich to swim in the fabled Blue Lagoon, or even stay on the beach.

The looming height of many of the islands means there are some perfect vantage points if you are prepared to climb. Getting to the top of Tavewa is a bit of a slog, but the views over the Blue Lagoon are amazing. Nacula provides even more spectacular scenery. Stand on a high ridge and you will be rewarded by a 360-degree panorama, with the lagoon and the islands stretching away in the distance on one side, and the harshly weathered valleys and inlets of Nacula on the other. The combination of colours – dark green hills running down into dark blue waters fringed by golden sand – is outstanding.

Blue lagoon off Tavewa Island

There are villages on most of the islands, and many of them are linked to guest houses and resorts. This gives the Yasawas a strong feeling of culture and means the local people benefit from tourism. Almost all the houses are made from modern materials, but you will still see some traditional thatched huts. Instead of being centred around their chief's house, most villages are now focused on churches, but a chief is still treated with great respect and runs the

Boat passing Matacawalevu Island at sunset from Nanuyalailai Island

community. It is possible to visit the villages, but you should take a guide – and kava for the chief.

Kava (*yaqona* in Fijian) is a traditional and bitter-tasting drink made from a root. It is mildly intoxicating and used in a number of ceremonies. Village elders drink it before making decisions and it is

Volcanic rock of Nanuyalailai Island with Nacula behind

Palm fronds outside a traditional hut, Nanuyalailai Island

often offered to guests. Sampling *yaqona* is as much a part of a visit to the Yasawa Islands as lying on the beach or swimming in the Blue Lagoon – although it is drunk more for its effect, and for cultural reasons, than for its taste!

ⓘ

Fiji's main island, Suva, is easily reached from Australia or New Zealand. Air Vanuatu also has regular flights from Port Vila, allowing you to combine a visit to Fiji with one to Vanuatu. From Suva a fast ferry, the *Yasawa Flyer*, stops off daily at all the main Yasawa island groups. There is also a small four-seater seaplane, run by Turtle Airways. The family-owned and run Nanuya Island Resort is right on the Blue Lagoon and is a perfect blend of style and affordability. There is a PADI dive centre and the food in the open-sided restaurant is excellent.

Newfoundland
Canada

Just off the east coast of Canada, Newfoundland is known as the 'crossroads of the world' to its inhabitants – and it lives up to its nickname. As the island is closer to Europe than any other part of the American continent it was – and is – strategically important for travel, navigation and communications.

Lobster Cove Head Lighthouse

The Vikings established the first non-indigenous settlement in North America here, and Amelia Earhart took off from Harbour Grace when she became the first woman to fly the Atlantic in 1932. The first trans-Atlantic cable was laid to the small village of Heart's Content in 1866; and Marconi received the first trans-Atlantic wireless message at the aptly named Signal Hill in St John's, the island's capital, in 1901.

Today, if you are flying between Europe and North America the chances are that the striking scenery you see out of the plane window when you're close to Canada is Newfoundland: the curvature of the earth's surface means the shortest flight path between London and New York often takes you over it. The *Titanic* was following a similar route when she struck an iceberg less than 640 km from the island –

Bonne Bay, town of Woody Point and Tablelands, Gros Morne National Park (background)

Cape St Mary's Ecological Reserve

its Cape Race Lighthouse was the first to receive the SOS signal from the stricken ship.

Because of global warming there are fewer icebergs than there were in the days of the *Titanic*, but they can still be seen in June and early July. The convergence of the northbound, warm Gulf Stream and southbound, colder Labrador Current off Newfoundland drags in icebergs that have calved from the Greenland ice shelf. The two currents also bring in vast amounts of plankton as well as fish and the whales that feed on them – humpback, fin and minke whales are often seen in the island's offshore waters.

On land, Newfoundland is home to the highest concentration of moose in North America, and there are caribou on the Avalon Peninsula. The island's birdlife is spectacular, especially in the Cape St Mary's Ecological Reserve, which has some of the most accessible seabird colonies in the world. In the breeding season, from April to June, vast numbers of northern gannets, kittiwakes and common murre form noisy garrulous colonies. Rarer species that nest here include black guillemots, razorbills and double-crested cormorants. It is possible to get to within a few metres of the birds.

Woody Point Lighthouse

The most dramatic region of the island is arguably Gros Morne National Park. Its landscape is the result of a combination of glaciation and tectonic plate movements, and the Western Brook Pond is set in a classic example of a valley that was carved out by a glacier. A boardwalk leads through a series of bogs (where you will find orchids, carnivorous plants and even moose) to the so-called pond – it is actually 3 km long. A boat tour will take you to where it narrows through a steep gorge with sheer cliffs and peaks that rise to 650 metres. The Tablelands area was formed by tectonic movements that forced peridotite up from the ocean floor. This part of

Tablelands, Gros Morne National Park

Fair and False Bay, Burnside

The Battery, St John's

St John's

the park is barren, as peridotite, rare at the earth's surface, inhibits the growth of vegetation, yet nearby slopes are forested.

There are a number of remote settlements on the Newfoundland coast. Known to the local people as 'outports', some are small clusters of weathered dwellings but others are complete villages, and visiting them is like stepping back 100 years in time. These are not just tourist traps; they are well-preserved working fishing communities, even though the cod industry has been hard hit by dwindling stocks. Trinity on the Bonavista Peninsula is a particularly atmospheric outport.

The oldest city in North America, St John's is lively and colourful, with a vibrant feel that contrasts well with the island's unspoilt natural scenery and long cold winters. It has numerous bars and nightclubs – George Street, with 28 on each side, has the highest concentration in the northern part of the American continent – and the houses that line many of the city's other streets are painted in different vivid colours.

Hatchet Harbour

Only Air Canada flies to Newfoundland so flights are relatively expensive. You need to hire a car well in advance, especially if you visit the island during the peak summer months. Be aware that it is not possible to get unlimited mileage on your car hire. Distances are vast and extra mileage charges can mount up.

Sagar
India

India is intense. Eternal. Nowhere else in the world is there the same balance between ancient and modern. On the one side are industrialists and computer programmers; on the other a spirituality that permeates and orders the very nature of society. And nowhere is this more apparent than on the island of Sagar during the Ganga Sagar *mela* (festival) at Makara Sankranti.

This is one of the great gatherings that are a key feature of Hinduism, India's main religion, during which pilgrims bathe in sacred waters to wash away their mortal sins and so free themselves from the endless cycle of reincarnation. Sagar is in West Bengal, near Kolkata

Boarding a ferry to Sagar island for the *mela*

Ferries sailing to Sagar island for the *mela*

(Calcutta), at the point where the sacred River Ganga (Ganges) reaches the Bay of Bengal. And in mid-January each year over half a million pilgrims travel there to celebrate Makara Sankranti at the start of the sun's journey to the northern hemisphere.

The ethereal nature of the island is accentuated by a night-time fog that often lasts long into the morning. Swirling and all-enveloping, it is coloured orange by sodium lights, and green, blue and red by coloured ones that demarcate the main roads so that the many – often illiterate – pilgrims can orientate themselves.

Pilgrims making offerings

Although people bathe a couple of days before Makara Sankranti, the most auspicious time is on 14 January, just after midnight. Streams of pilgrims make their way to a beach where the Ganga is said to meet the sea. The real confluence is slightly further away, but currents

Pilgrims bathing in the sea

Pilgrims at the Ganga Sagar *mela*

make entering the water dangerous and during the *mela* the authorities forbid bathing there and ground the local boats to enforce the ban.

It is impossible not to be affected by the sheer number of people, many of whom have travelled great distances, and all of whom share a single belief and intent. The spirituality is palpable and the feeling of euphoria infectious. Hinduism is a joyful religion and there is little solemnity at the bathing area. People smile and splash each other. They dare each other to duck under the waves for a full immersion and surface, spluttering and laughing. Smiling, happy, cleansed.

Walking through this throng you will not feel excluded or unwelcome. The pilgrims draw you in far more than celebrants of any other religion would. And the pressure to bathe is irresistible – people find it inconceivable that you would come all the way to Sagar and not do so.

After they have immersed themselves in the cold water the shivering pilgrims make their way up to the Kapil Muni Temple, where they crowd around the priests, attempting to give them offerings in return for *prasad* (sugary sweets that have been blessed).

Pilgrim praying in the sea

As they move away from the temple they walk along a road lined with the cell-like ashrams of naga sadhus. These ascetic holy men, who are often considered to be living saints, eschew material possessions including clothes – all that covers them is ash from fires. In prudish India the fact that they choose to walk round naked is taken as being completely normal. They also sport long dreadlocks and smoke *charras* (hashish) when they meditate.

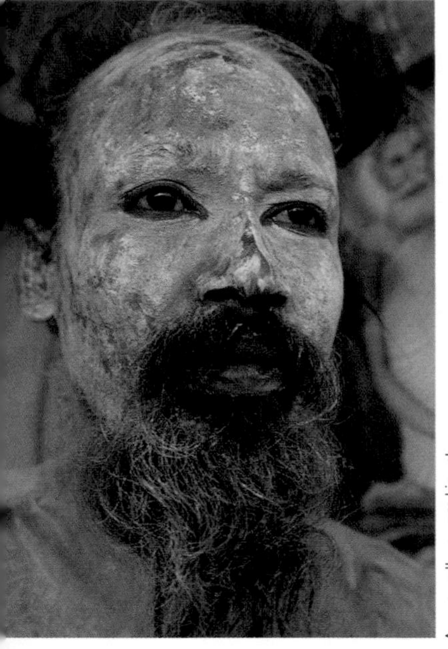
A naga sadhu covered in ash

Naga sadhus are renowned for their extreme approach to spirituality: yoga, fasting, days of meditation. Some even perform standing penances and remain on their feet for years at a time. Although they are primarily at the *mela* for religious reasons, Ganga Sagar is also a peak time for business. They bless the pilgrims in return for a few rupees – making the money that will see them through until there is another festival to attend. Sagar receives pilgrims throughout the year, and has a semi-permanent contingent of holy men, but during the *mela* their numbers are swollen in that uniquely Indian, indistinguishable blend of the spiritual and the commercial.

Kapil Muni Temple

Crowds of pilgrims on the temporary main street of the *mela*

Pilgrims pushing to make offerings at the Kapil Muni Temple

Pilgrims struggling to receive *prasad*

Indian festivals are like this. Amid all the spirituality there are sprawling bazaars and even fairground attractions. Many pilgrims invest what to them is a phenomenal amount of money to get to Sagar, and they combine their visit with shopping for goods and clothes that are not available at home. As the *mela* winds down they board buses that carry them to the embarkation point and the ferry boats that will take them to the mainland. Some of the more devout pilgrims (and the poorer ones) walk 30 km or so across the island.

At times the site of the festival resembles a great refugee camp. People plod great distances to reach it and many sleep rough in the cold January nights of West Bengal. They are sent on long diversions to avoid potentially fatal crushes and endure many hardships in addition to their immersion in the bitterly cold waters of the Bay of Bengal. But Ganga Sagar is a happy and fulfilling time. A time that will reward the faithful and the curious alike with memories of one of the world's last great pilgrimages.

Ferry arriving at Sagar island at sunset

The *mela* on Sagar takes place on 14 January every year. Jet Airways flies to India from many international airports, including Heathrow, and connects with their extensive domestic network, which has daily flights to Kolkata. From here the easiest way to get to Sagar is by private car. Accommodation at the *mela* is very basic and should be booked well in advance. Atithi Voyages in Delhi can make all the arrangements.

Hong Kong Island
China

Looking down on the Victoria Harbour from the Peak

Hong Kong Island, dominated by the severe bulk of the Peak and with its craggy and thickly forested slopes littered with skyscrapers, is testament to man conquering nature. Developers here are masters at – and challenged by – taming the environment. The old colonial water-front is now well back from the murky waters of Victoria Harbour, and land is constantly being reclaimed from the sea with new signature buildings rising to give Hong Kong a dynamic and fluid face.

The busy streets of Hong Kong Island

Britain forced China to cede the then undeveloped island in 1841, at the height of the first Opium War. In 1898 they leased it from China for 99 years, together with the Kowloon Peninsula and the New Territories on the mainland, and developed the colony of Hong Kong into one of the world's great financial centres. When the lease expired in 1997 it was handed back to the Chinese government. It was formed into a Special Administrative Region and its trade, growth and prosperity have continued unchanged.

Today Hong Kong Island is an alluring mixture of the new and the old. There seems to be no end to its architectural marvels – including the angular Bank of China Tower, which so offended adherents of feng shui. But enough of the old city has been preserved for this part to retain its original atmosphere. Stores in Wing Lok Street still sell

Skyscrapers on Hong Kong Island

Detail of the International Finance Centre on Hong Kong Island

Reflection of Jardine House

Star Ferry on Victoria Harbour

traditional remedies and birds' nests for soup, and in the Man Mo Temple massive incense coils hang from the ceiling, dispensing a fragrance that will live in your clothes for days. On the streets leading down from the Peak, small street markets sell everything from vegetables to fish, padlocks to batteries – and, of course, traditional fast food to workers hurrying to the banks and offices on the waterfront.

Asia Pacific Tower with the Bank of China building behind, seen from Hong Kong Park

Traditional Chinese medicine pharmacy

Signboards on Hong Kong Island

Star Ferry passing Hong Kong Island

The centrepiece of the old city is Statue Square, which dates back to the colonial era. The Legislative Council Building is the only one that survives from that period, but its granite bulk gives an idea of what the square – now dominated by the extravagant design of Norman Foster's HSBC Building – would have looked like.

One of the most unmissable sights in Hong Kong is the view from the Peak as the sun sets and the lights of the city come on. And at any time the scenery is breathtaking, although it can be obscured by a foggy haze created by pollution from the mainland. From here, the New Territories and Kowloon look closer than ever.

You can take the Peak tram to the summit or, to experience a world-class commute, go on the Mid-Levels Escalator – the longest moving staircase in the world. In the morning it runs down from the Peak, and in the afternoon it reverses. In a place where temperatures and humidity soar, the people of Hong Kong find it a useful way to get around. For another of the island's commutes – one that has to be the best in the world – board the double-decked Star Ferry, which will take even less time, and make the journey to the New Territories. The views are spectacular and the trip costs a couple of Hong Kong dollars.

Horse racing is a great passion in Hong Kong, and if you are in town on a Wednesday night there is a good chance that there will be a race meeting at the Happy Valley Racecourse. An institution in the city, it is always packed. You can buy a tourist ticket, which includes a meal in one of the private boxes on the top of the stands, or stand at the rail with the serious race-goers and see the action up close.

Happy Valley Racecourse

ⓘ

There are many international flights to Hong Kong. Visa rules are different from those for the rest of China, so check whether you need to get a visa before you leave. The classic place to stay on Hong Kong Island is the newly renovated Mandarin Oriental on Statue Square. Just a short walk from the Star Ferry, it has tremendous views across Victoria Harbour.

Giant incense coils at the Man Mo Temple

Fishing marina, Key West

The Florida Keys are a unique chain of 1700 islands that stretch 177 km into the Atlantic Ocean from mainland Florida and are linked by the Overseas Highway. One of the world's great drives, this takes you over a series of 40 bridges that skim the blues of the Atlantic on one side and the aquamarines of the Gulf of Mexico and Florida Bay on the other.

In its strict sense, a key is an ancient coral reef raised above sea level. The Florida Keys are split into three groups – Upper, Middle and Lower – whose characters change the further you get from the mainland.

In the Upper Keys the first main island is Key Largo, made famous by Humphrey Bogart and Lauren Bacall in the gangster film of the same name. Continuing the Bogart theme, you can visit the boat that was used in the 1951 movie *The African Queen*. The next notable

The Florida Keys

USA

Sunset, Key Largo

stopping point in this part of the Florida Keys is a group of islands called Islamorada (Purple Isle). It is thought that Spanish explorers named them after floating purple sea snails. Islamorada bills itself as the Sportfishing Capital of the World.

Long Key is one of the Middle Keys, and in its state park you can walk through the sort of untouched tropical forest that covered much of the keys as little as a hundred years ago.

About halfway down the Florida Keys chain, and spanning a number of separate islands, is the small town of Marathon. Its name is said to come from the seemingly 'marathon' workload of the men

Long Key State Park, Long Key

Islamorada

Papa Joe's Restaurant, Islamorada

who built the Florida East Coast Railway that once ran the entire length of the keys. Here you will find the Crane Point Hammock Reserve, which has more Pre-Columbian archaeological remains than anywhere else in the keys.

Like Long Key, Bahia Honda in the Lower Keys is the site of a state park. Its beach is a 4-km sweep of white sand and is reputed to be one of the most beautiful in the United States.

A myopic local, Key West

The Seven Mile Bridge spans the Middle and Lower Keys, and is among the longest bridges in the world. It has featured in countless films and crossing it is probably the highlight of the whole drive. In the middle it rises 20 metres above the water to allow boats to pass under it.

The last island in the chain, Key West, is closer to Cuba than it is to the United States mainland. This gives it a unique atmosphere, and makes it a haven for anyone seeking an alternative way of life. Its reputation for 'living for today' has attracted writers and artists for generations. Of these, the one who is most synonymous with Key West is Ernest Hemingway, who lived and worked here for some of his most prolific years. His house on Whitehead Street is now a museum, and the descendants of his six-toed cats still wander the grounds. When he wasn't writing (or drinking and fighting) Hemingway used to fish for blue marlin and sailfish in the Florida Straits between the island and Cuba.

A typical Key West house

Hemingway's study

Sloppy Joe's Bar, Duval Street, Key West

Key West is very much at the edge in the meteorological as well as the geographical sense. With nowhere for people to go but 200 km back up the Overseas Highway, each hurricane season brings with it the potential for disaster, which is dismissed with studied nonchalance by the local population, who call themselves 'Conchs'.

The Everglades, a vast wetland of subtropical marshes on the coast of the mainland, provides an interesting contrast to the Florida Keys. Reachable from the top of the Overseas Highway, its southern part is incorporated as the Everglades National Park. It is most famous for its alligator population, but the area is also home to a vast array of birdlife.

ⓘ

The Florida Keys are easily reached by driving from Miami, which has some of the best international flight connections of any city in the United States. The hurricane season is from June to early November, and is a good time to avoid the keys, even though they won't necessarily be hit by hurricanes!

Madagascar is known the world over for its unique wildlife. It split from the east coast of Africa millions of years ago and its flora and fauna developed in isolation, producing many endemic species – 80 per cent of which are found only on the island.

Red *tsingy* near Diego Suarez

The signature animal of Madagascar has to be the lemur, a member of the primate family. It comes in all shapes and sizes, from the large sifaka, which leaps along the ground between trees on its hind legs, to the tiny aye-aye, which is nocturnal and lives in the hollows of trees. Because it uses its abnormally long middle finger to kill its prey, local people believe it is a bringer of death, and many are killed on sight.

The capital of Madagascar, Antananarivo is in many ways more like a provincial French town than an African city. Centred on a long rocky ridge, it is topped by two cathedrals, government buildings and even the remains of a royal palace that was set on fire in 1995. Spreading down from the ridge is a jumble of ancient streets and houses.

Madagascar

Baobab at sunset, near Morondova

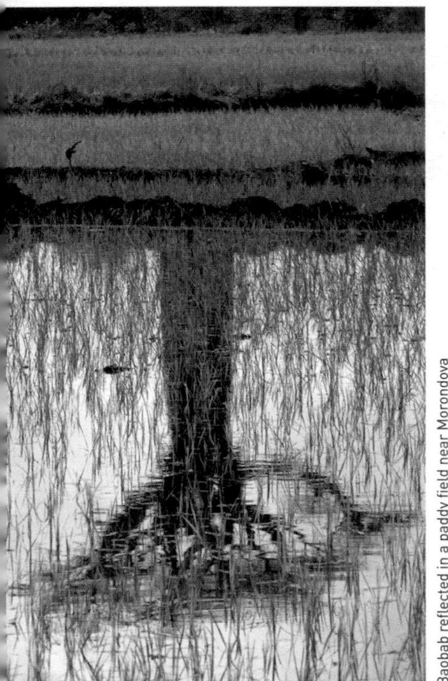
Baobab reflected in a paddy field near Morondova

Zebu cart passing the Avenue of Baobabs, Morondova

Deeply rooted beliefs are part of the culture of the Malagasy of Madagascar, who are predominantly a mix of Asian and African peoples. For instance, chameleons are said to be the spirits of dead ancestors, and many local people go out of their way to avoid hurting one – even when they are driving. There is a wide variety of species on the island including a minuscule chameleon less than a centimetre long. Because their eyes rotate, allowing them to see in all directions, it is believed that chameleons are able to see into the future and the past.

The landscape of Madagascar is striking. The island is noted for its *tsingy*, the Malagasy name for a bizarre, spiky karst limestone rock formation caused by erosion. Many of the spikes are razor sharp and there are great crevices, some of which allow trees and bushes to grow.

The *tsingy* include one in the Ankarana Reserve in the north, near the Diego Suarez, and the Tsingy de Bemaraha in the south. They often form vast fields that stretch as far as the horizon and create impenetrable barriers. Any vegetation that manages to find a foothold struggles to thrive in this hostile environment.

There are six endemic species of baobab in Madagascar, and the Morondova region is where to find them – as your plane comes in to land you will see what seem to be thousands of the trees littering the countryside. A visit to the Kirindy Reserve in search of lemurs will take you through the Avenue of Baobabs – a dirt road that leads through a small village and is lined with these great trees. The ones here are particularly tall and thin, and tower over the local people.

Tsingy at Ankarana Reserve

Antananarivo

Male common chameleon (*Chamaeleo oustaleti*)

Crowned lemur (*Eulemur coronatus*)

Verreaux's sifaka lemur (*Propithecus verreauxi*)

Large day gecko (*Phelsuma madagascariensis*)

If the lemur is the signature wild animal of Madagascar, the signature domesticated one must be the humpbacked zebu, an animal that is much prized for its milk and meat, and even for transport. As the baobab avenue glows a golden red at sunset, carts drawn by zebu clatter slowly through the giant trees, which cast their long shadows over villagers returning home at the end of a day spent working in the fields.

ⓘ

Air Madagascar flies to the capital, Antananarivo, from Paris, Milan and Johannesburg among other places. It also has an extensive network of internal flights to Madagascar's main cities. Le Voyageur, a Swiss-run, Madagascan-based company, can make local arrangements and organize tours around the island.

Avenue of Baobabs, Morondova

Countryside near Diego Suarez

Stockholm
Sweden

Stockholm is built on 14 islands that lie between Lake Mälaren and the Baltic Sea and are part of Sweden's most extensive archipelago. And the heart of the city, the 13th-century Gamla Stan or medieval old town, spreads over three of them.

This part of Stockholm is a meandering warren of picturesque streets and alleys lined with towering red, orange and yellow façades. If you wander around you are virtually guaranteed to get pleasantly lost. Its biggest attraction is the huge Royal Palace (Kungliga Slottet), the official residence of the Swedish royal family. It has been rebuilt a

Riddarholmen (left) and Gamla Stan seen from Södermalm

Royal Palace

number of times, most recently following a fire in the 17th century. The current building dates from 1754, although work on it continued for another 80 years. The Swedes have learnt to make the most of their short summer, before the darkness of the northern winter closes in, and this is the perfect time to visit Stockholm. People take advantage of the long hours of daylight to enjoy late-night visits to the city's parks and outdoor spaces. Work hours are relaxed, there are free festivals and concerts, and alfresco bars and cafés are packed.

June, July and August are also the best months for exploring the archipelago that sprawls to the east of the city. The islands – more

than 24,000 cover an area of 150 km by 80 km – are reckoned to be 2 billion years old and are low and rounded, shaped by the smoothing effect of glaciers during the last ice age. The ice affected them in another way too: its massive weight pushed them down into the sea, and now that they have been released they are rising by about 4 mm a year.

Sailing is immensely popular in Sweden and the waters around the archipelago are treated like a lake – even though they are actually part of the Baltic Sea. Because it is fed by many rivers, and only

Östermalm seen from Skeppsholmen

Riddarholmskyrkan

meets other oceans at two points, the Baltic has a relatively low salt content and often freezes in the winter.

The network of channels in the archipelago forms an intriguing maze that is perfect for island hopping by sail, motor boat or ferry. The shorelines of the islands, with their bays and inlets, are typically covered with coniferous and deciduous trees, peppered with worn rocks and boulders and studded with stocky wood cabins and boat sheds.

There are some 50,000 holiday homes in the archipelago and the islands near Stockholm can be crowded at weekends. To get a taste

Strömgatan and Riksbron

Ferry from Nämdö Böte at sunset

of the true isolated beauty of the more outlying ones it is worth heading for Nämdö – 40 km and a whole world away from the city centre. It has 35 permanent residents, a single dirt road, a restaurant, a grocery store and a school with seven pupils. Amid its picturesque, moss-covered forests and wildflower-speckled meadows there are a number of hiking trails where you will be sure to see roe and fallow deer – even elk, which often swim here from other islands. At the northern end of Nämdö there is a high vantage point, complete with a

Östanvik, Nämdö

Sunset seen from Nämdö Böte

tower that affords a 360-degree view over the surrounding archipelago – perfect as the setting sun turns both sky and water a vivid gold.

ⓘ

Scandinavian Airlines (SAS) flies to Stockholm from many countries. The world's largest fleet of steamships operates between the city and the islands of the archipelago. Ferries are run by Waxholmsbolaget. Schedules vary with the season. For Nämdö, take a bus from Stockholm to Stavsnäs, then the one-hour ferry ride.

Giant Buddha, Dambulla

Sri Lanka

Sri Lanka has to be one of the world's most varied islands. Individually, its history, culture, wildlife or stunning beaches would justify a visit in their own right; together they make travelling through the island a unique experience.

Temple of the Tooth, Kandy

The very best of Sri Lanka can be seen in a simple loop from the international airport at Colombo. Within just a few hours you reach Sigiriya and its famous palace on top of an enormous rock – a hardened plug of magma from an ancient eroded volcano – that towers some 200 metres above the surrounding plain.

The Singhalese king Kasyapa built the palace at the end of the 5th century AD on what was formerly the site of a Buddhist monastery. The climb to see its ruins is steep and not for the faint-hearted, especially if you take a detour about halfway up the cast-iron spiral staircase to see the exquisite frescoes of scantily clad women under an overhang. Once you arrive at the top the views – as far as the hills around Kandy – are spectacular.

Sigiriya is a good base from which to explore Anuradapura and Polonnaruwa, the island's deserted former capitals. Both have a number of Buddhist relics, including stupas and giant images of the

Lion Staircase at Sigiriya

Buddha, and Polonnaruwa is home to the iconic reclining Buddha seen in so many Sri Lankan tourist publications. It is also home to a number of particularly cheeky langur monkeys.

Sri Lanka has a relatively large population of wild elephants, many of which seemingly wander around the countryside; migration corridors link a number of national parks. Minneriya, a short distance from Sigiriya, is set around an ancient man-made reservoir, a permanent source of water, and in the dry season it can attract hundreds of elephants, making it one of the best parks for seeing these animals.

Kandy is a few hours' drive south of Sigiriya, and on your way there it is well worth visiting the fascinating series of caves at Dambulla. These house ornate frescoes and ancient images of the Buddha, some of which date back as far as the 1st century BC.

Reclining Buddha, Dambulla

Drummer at the Temple of the Tooth, Kandy

Tea plantation and waterfall, Nuwara Eliya

The city of Kandy is noted for the the Temple of the Tooth (Sri Dalada Maligawa), which houses the most sacred relic in Sri Lanka: a tooth of the Lord Buddha. The golden casket that encases it is presented to the faithful three times a day, in a crowded and somewhat noisy ritual. To the accompaniment of frenetic drumming and horn playing, a long line of pilgrims and tourists files past the open chapel in which the tooth is kept. Kandy is also known for its sprawling botanical gardens, which date back to the era when Britain ruled the island – then known as Ceylon.

Elephants at Minneriya National Park

Sri Lanka is famous for its tea, still marketed as Ceylon Tea. The plants were brought here from India by the British when their attempts to grow coffee failed, and the centre of tea production is Nuwara Eliya, about three hours' drive south of Kandy and some 2000 metres above sea level. The slopes of all the hills around and leading up to the town are covered in tea plants, and are often worked into intricate patterns by the tea pickers as they move around. The new leaves of this remarkable plant are harvested by hand when they are a month old by legions of women who work six days a week, often on vertiginous hillsides.

Botanical Gardens, Kandy

Stormy coastline, Galle

If you have always hankered after seeing leopards, Yala National Park on Sri Lanka's south coast (about five hours' drive from Nuwara Eliya) must be one of the best places in the world to go. Not only is the population here high, but as the top predators these big cats aren't as elusive as they are in Africa. Yala is also home to a good many elephants and a number of bears.

As you drive back to Colombo you will pass the historic coastal town of Galle. The area was among those worst hit by the Boxing Day tsunami in 2004. Thousands were killed, although many people in the old town, protected by the walls of the 1663 Dutch fort, survived. The coastline around Galle boasts some of the most beautiful beaches on the island, many of which are deserted, with little or no development.

Painted stork and deer at Yala National Park

ⓘ

Emirates flies to Colombo from a number of UK airports, with a connecting flight in Dubai. Public transport is somewhat unpredictable in Sri Lanka, but hiring a car and driver is good value. Jetwing Holidays can arrange this for you, and you will stay at a number of their properties, including the stylish Vil Uyana in Sigiriya, the historic St Andrews in Nuwara Eliya and the luxurious lighthouse in Galle. Their Kandy property is at the stunning Hunas Falls, 32 km from the city. If you want to be closer Jetwing suggest the Citadel. Their property in Yala was destroyed by the 2004 tsunami so they recommend the Yala Village.

Big Island
Hawaii, USA

Big Island is arguably the most spectacular of the Hawaiian islands. It is home to the highest mountain on earth – measured from the seabed Mauna Kea reaches 9700 metres – and also to Mauna Loa, which is 30 metres lower than Kea but together with its underwater mass it is taken to be the largest object on the planet. The island's distance from Honolulu's international airport means it is also refreshingly free from the excesses of tourism seen on the more popular islands.

Keokea Beach Park, Big Island

Akaka Falls, Big Island

Sometimes known as Hawaii, Big Island is the youngest of the islands in the Hawaiian group – so young that some areas are still volcanically active. It is made up of five overlapping shield volcanoes, including Kohala, now extinct, and Mauna Loa and Mauna Kea. Kilauea, on the flank of Mauna Loa, has been erupting continuously since 1983.

A unique combination of north-east trade winds and elevation means the summit of Mauna Kea provides some of the world's

clearest conditions for astronomy. There are 13 observatories here with telescopes that are among the most sophisticated ever made. It is possible to drive to them, but a four-wheel-drive vehicle is essential as the road is all but impassable without one, and car rental companies specifically exclude it if you hire any other kind of car. You should also be aware that Mauna Kea's tremendous altitude – the volcano rises to 4205 metres above sea level – could impair your driving skills and even lead to acute mountain sickness (AMS).

North Shore, Oahu

Waipi'o Valley, Big Island

Big Island has 11 of the earth's 14 climate zones, and as you drive around it you will see many of the resulting terrains, from beaches and lush vegetation to lava deserts and even alpine tundra.

Hilo, the main city on the wetter eastern side of the island, is a good place to start your tour. As you drive north the road loops through tropical rainforest towards the Akaka Falls, where a plume of water falls 128 metres into a round pool. At the northern end of this coast is the Waipi'o Valley overlook, where steep cliffs channel a flat valley floor out to the open sea. This valley was the birthplace of the legendary chief Kamehameha the Great, who unified the Hawaiian islands in 1810. From the overlook you can also see the cliffs of the other valleys that scour Kohala, all inaccessible by land.

Sunset, South Kohala coast, Big Island

Inland from Kohala is the cattle-rearing centre of Waimea, home to Parker Ranch, one of the largest ranches in the world. Incongruously, cows graze on open pasture in the foreground against views up to the summit of Mauna Kea and its observatories.

Sunset Beach, Oahu

The terrain on the drier Kona coast to the west is the result of recent lava flows and there is little vegetation. Tourism is centred on this part of the island, around the town of Kailua and luxury resorts to the north. To the south, the slopes of Mauna Loa are a

Waimea, Big Island

Kahua Ranch, Big Island

Kilauea Iki Crater, Big Island

prime coffee-growing area that produces Kona, one of the world's best-known coffees. Further south you will come to Kealakekua Bay, where an obelisk marks the spot where Captain Cook was killed in 1779 during a fight with local people.

The Hawaii Volcanoes National Park in the south of the island, geologically the youngest part of the all the Hawaiian islands, is home to two of the most active volcanoes in the world. At its heart lies the 1200-metre Kilauea, on the side of Mauna Loa, which looms almost 3000 metres above the rim of the smaller volcano's caldera. The heights of these mountains are almost inconceivable.

A drive around the Kilauea caldera takes you through one of the most desolate landscapes on earth – one that looks more like a moonscape, except for signs that indicate the date of each lava flow. The road circles the sheer cliffs that plunge to the continuously steaming floor of the crater.

The island of Oahu, with its capital Honolulu, is not as striking as Big Island, but all the interisland flights pass through it and it is worth taking the time to stop off and head for the North Shore – the surfing Mecca of the world. Winter storms in the northern Pacific create swells that are amplified by the shoreline and regularly result in waves that reach a height of 6 or 9 metres – and some that soar to 15 metres.

Legendary surf spots here include Sunset Point, the Bonzai Pipeline and Waimea Bay. Sunset is a good time to watch as the surf dudes line up waiting for the big wave, then take their lives in their hands and ride the violent wall of water.

ⓘ

Honolulu International Airport on the island of Oahu is a major airline hub in the Pacific and a number of flights to the USA, Asia and the Pacific Rim land there. Aloha Airlines and Hawaiian Airlines fly from Honolulu to Big Island.

Slopes of Mauna Kea, Big Island

A telescope in the Submillimeter Array, summit of Mauna Kea, Big Island

Sicily
Italy

The harbour at Cefalù, Palermo province

The largest island in the Mediterranean, Sicily is a smorgasbord of European history. Because of its strategic position it was colonized by the Greeks and Romans, and ruled by Byzantines, Arabs, Normans and, lastly, the Spanish before it became part of Italy in 1860. This led to a mix of bloodlines that has given rise to a culture that is unique to the island: the local people consider themselves Sicilians first and Italians second.

One of the best ways to appreciate all that Sicily has to offer is to hire a car and drive through its many centuries of history. Near the capital Palermo is Monreale, a hill town at the end of the picturesque Conca d'Oro Valley. It has spectacular panoramic views down to Palermo,

Hill town of Castiglione di Sicilia, Catania province

Hills near Segesta, Segesta province

and the sea beyond. The interior of the 12th-century Norman cathedral is covered with mosaics, and when you view them from a distance it is almost impossible to believe they are made just from tiny coloured squares. Their complexity and subtlety are breathtaking, with every major event in the New and Old Testaments depicted in almost overwhelming detail. The cloisters of the adjacent Benedictine abbey have an Arabic flavour blended with Byzantine and Norman styles, indicative of the varied influences on the island.

On the south-east corner of the island, Siracusa is steeped in more than 2500 years of history. The city was founded by Corinthians in 734 BC and later became one of the most important cultural centres of its time –

rivalling Athens in the Greek world. Its medieval heart is on the tiny offshore island of Ortygia.

A number of hill towns to the south-west of Siracusa were rebuilt after a devastating earthquake in 1693, at the height of the baroque period, and the architecture of Noto is some of the finest on the island. Walking through the massive Porto Reale arch and along the Corso Vittorio Emanuele it is impossible not to be humbled by the grandeur of the buildings with their ornate details. Elaborate towers and balconies

Cathedral window, Monreale, Palermo province

Figure of Christ in the central apse of the cathedral, Monreale, Palermo province

augment façades decorated with gargoyles, cherubs and lions.

The Valley of the Temples in Agrigento, west of Noto, is the largest and best-preserved site of Greek ruins outside Greece. The most striking structure is the Temple of Concord – its walls are largely intact and give a strong impression of the scale and the complexity of the original building. The yellow stone glows golden at the beginning and end of the day.

Further west are the ruins of the Greek city of Selinus. Dating back to the 7th century BC, they cover a much wider area than the

The town of Ragusa Ibla, seen from Ragusa

Valley of the Temples and it is possible to visualize the extent of the ancient city. They are on the coast, and a walk amid their Doric columns gives tremendous views out to sea. About 35 km away, isolated in rolling green hills, is the site of the Greek town of Segesta. All that remain of it, perched on a high outcrop, are an amphitheatre and a temple that was started in the 5th century BC but never completed. At times in their histories Selinus and Segesta fought border wars with each other.

Castle above the town of Cáccamo, Palermo province

Garden and quadrangle of the cloisters, Benedictine monastery, Monreale, Palermo province

Detail of a carved pillar in the monastery cloisters, Monreale

Sicily is famous for Mount Etna, at 3323 metres the highest active volcano in Europe. The best way to approach it is through the mountainous interior, past a string of hill towns that are all you would expect them to be on this island: atmospheric jumbles of houses topped by churches and ancient castles. Groves of olive trees stretch across dry valleys. The road weaves around hairpin bends and across viaducts and bridges.

The first views of Etna are stunning: as you look down from the hillside towns broad sweeping valleys lead to forests on the volcano's

South-western edge of the hill town of Gangi, Palermo province

Mount Etna over Maletto town, Catania province

lower slopes and lava flows on its upper ones, topped by snow at its summit. Some of the best vantage points are in the town of Centuripe, south-west of Etna.

It is possible to reach the higher slopes of Etna by road, cable car or even the Circumetnea Railway, which originates at Catania on the east coast, but the most striking views are from afar with the volcano dominating the surrounding countryside.

ⓘ

There are a number of international flights to Palermo. Accommodation can be tricky in the peak summer months, but if you avoid these it shouldn't be necessary to book in advance. The weather is usually warm for much of the year. Hiring a car is the best way to explore the island.

Doric temple at Segesta, Trapani province

Socotra
Yemen

Crabs on the beach at Erher

Socotra lies in the Arabian Sea, off the Horn of Africa, and is the main island in a small archipelago of the same name. Unlike most other remote islands, which are the result of volcanic activity, its origin is continental – it split from Africa some 6 million years ago. This spawned a great biological diversity, and Socotra is a botanical paradise. Around 800 plant species can be found here – over a third of which are endemic.

The quintessential plant is *Dracaena cinnabari*, the dragon's blood tree. A succulent, it looks like an upturned umbrella and great forests of this strange species can be seen on the rocky slopes of the island's mountainous interior. It is said that Romans travelled to Socotra to

'Bottle tree' at Erher

acquire the tree's blood-red sap, which they used as a disinfectant when they treated wounded gladiators.

The strangely shaped bottle tree – its trunk resembles the distended leg of an elephant – is also found all over the island. It seems to grow everywhere and clusters can often be seen clinging to steep cliffs like watching sentinels. It is also known as the desert rose, as after the monsoon rains it produces shocking-pink flowers.

There are also forests of frankincense trees. Their burnt sap releases a strong fragrance, and was used in ancient Egypt to treat the bodies of the dead. Inscriptions describe how terraces of the trees were cultivated here to meet the demands of this lucrative trade.

The harsh, often dry conditions on the island don't support many animals, but vultures, especially white Egyptian vultures with their bright yellow beaks, seem to be everywhere. They congregate wherever people are eating, to scavenge leftovers, or squat on the low stone houses waiting for their next meal.

The rugged mountains in the centre of Socotra are often enveloped in a misty shroud, which gives the highlands a completely different feel to that of the arid plain encircling them. They are green even during the dry summer months, so this is the time to visit the island if you want to see the greatest contrasts of desert and lush vegetation.

Egyptian vulture

The coast is virtually unspoilt, with long stretches of white sand. At Erher on the east of the island great dunes have formed against high craggy cliffs. The beach extends for kilometres, broken only by fantastically eroded rocks. The shore fringes a brilliant aquamarine

Coastline at Qalansia

Lizard walking over dead coral

Mountainous interior of the island

Frankincense trees in the interior

lagoon and I saw a large pod of dolphins mooching quietly along, just a metre or so away. Nearby, and set into one of the cliffs, is the immense Huq Cave; more than 3 km long, it is lined with ornate stalactites and stalagmites. Unlike many caves, it is open and airy and it is possible to walk almost its entire length without stooping.

Dragon's blood trees

Tourism is very much in its infancy here. The airport was built only in 1999 and apart from a couple of guest houses in Hadibo, the main town, it is a case of camping – or enjoying the hospitality of the local people. And they are certainly hospitable. Many of Socotra's 40,000 or so inhabitants live in isolated villages in the deep fertile valleys of its central mountains, and as you travel around the island you will no doubt often be invited to share their meals. Although most

Rugged valley in the interior of Socotra

Old town of Sana'a, the capital of Yemen

people speak Socotri, the local Semetic language, Arabic is also widely spoken.

Socotra is part of the Republic of Yemen, and if you fly to the island you will have to spend a night in Sana'a, the Yemeni capital. Don't miss the chance to visit its old town, home to what are reputed to be the world's first skyscrapers. These 800-year-old brick buildings soar up to nine storeys and some even incorporate hotels. All the men walk around with traditional curved Jambiya daggers – and often mobile phones – attached to their belts.

ⓘ

Yemenia, Yemen's national airline, flies to Sana'a and on to Socotra from a number of countries. Independent travel is all but impossible on the island, and the Yemen-based Universal Touring Company can organize an itinerary for you. November to February are the best months to visit. The strong winds of the south-west monsoon make travel on the island impossible from June to the beginning of September. Supplies of food and bottled water are low in September as supply boats can't run to Socotra from the mainland. Ramadan is also a difficult time to travel.

Mud-brick building in old Sana'a

Sark

Channel Islands, United Kingdom

Sark is the smallest of the main group of Channel Islands between England and France, and arguably the most distinctive. Its age-old political system – it is governed by the *seigneur* and a parliament called the Chief Pleas – means it has the last feudal constitution in the western world.

Although Sark was granted in perpetuity to Helier de Carteret, the first *seigneur*, by Elizabeth I in 1565, it is part of the British Isles and owned by the British Crown. It is quaintly English but with a number

La Coupé leading to Little Sark

Lighthouse

of unique quirks, the first of which becomes apparent when you arrive on the ferry from Guernsey or Jersey. Save for tractors that transport supplies from the tiny harbour and take tourist bags to visitors' accommodation there is no motorized transport. You simply tell the baggage handler where you are staying and your luggage arrives in a couple of hours. There are a number of horse-drawn carriages that take tourists on sightseeing tours, but these are officially discouraged from working on Sundays. Alternatively, for more run-of-the mill transport you can hire a bicycle.

Cliff-top heather

Tractor parking by the pub

Although there is little crime on Sark, the island has a couple of part-time police officers who are elected from the community, and a tiny two-cell prison that dates back to 1856. Anyone who has been arrested for a minor crime such as vagrancy or drunkenness can be imprisoned for up to two days, simply at the behest of the officers. More serious cases are referred to Guernsey. The prison has a distinctly Victorian feel, and is still used occasionally.

Sark consists of two separate islands, Big Sark and Little Sark, linked by a vertiginous causeway known as La Coupé, built in 1945 by German prisoners of war. Although it has railings cyclists must dismount and wheel their bicycles over it, while passengers in carriages have to get out and walk. On one side a cliff drops sharply to Convanche Bay 300 metres below; on the other, the slope down to Grand Grêve, one of the most popular sandy beaches on the island, is less forbidding.

Much of Sark consists of rolling farmland that leads to steep cliffs; the edges of many of these are exposed and covered with bracken and heather. There are few roads, and those that do exist often run between high banks topped with hedgerows. In some places they are lined with trees whose branches meet to create shady canopies.

The small main settlement, known as the Village, is just up from the harbour. Its high street, the Avenue, has a few shops and cafés, and a post office with the only postbox on the island – painted blue and not red. Many of the houses in the neighbouring streets are at least a couple of centuries old and built from local stone.

The Seigneurie, the official residence of the *seigneur*, was built in 1675 on the site of a 6th-century monastery to the north of the Village, but there have been additions over the years – notably a large tower added in the Victorian era. Its beautiful formal gardens are open to the public and are one of the most popular attractions on Sark.

Hay bales

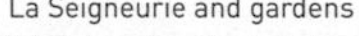

La Seigneurie and gardens

There are a number of walks around the island. Alternatively, you can take one of the boat trips around Sark run by George Guille. His ancestors were among the original Sarkese who came here in 1565, and after the trip he will happily regale you with tales about the island in the Bel Air Inn, one of its traditional English pubs.

La Sablonnerie on Little Sark

Stone house in the Village

Sark can be reached by regular ferries from Guernsey and Jersey. Aurigny Air Services links these islands with a number of airports in the United Kingdom, including London Gatwick. It also flies to Dinard in France, which allows you to combine a visit to Sark with one to Mont Saint-Michel **(see page 168)****.**

Carriage crossing La Coupé

Marigot Bay

St Lucia
Windward Islands

Britain and France fought over St Lucia 14 times in the 150 years leading to 1814 and, politics apart, it is easy to see why: the landscape is stunning. More mountainous than the other Caribbean islands, St Lucia's highest point is 950-metre Mount Gimie, but its most notable feature is the twin Gros and Petit Pitons, which peak at 798 metres.

The Pitons and Soufrière

Most tourism is centred on Rodney Bay in the north-west, but it is worth hiring a car to explore the rest of St Lucia. The road around the island follows the coast for much of the way, but also takes you inland where it winds up into the lower slopes of the rugged and mountainous interior, much of which is covered with impenetrable, lush rainforest.

There is a very traditional side to St Lucia. Gros Islet, just to the north of Rodney Bay, is an unspoilt Caribbean village and Friday nights here, when the weekly 'jump-up' street party happens, are unmissable. Stalls sell jerk chicken, there are loud sound systems, and tourists and locals alike dance and drink cold Piton beer and large slugs of the local rum.

Soufrière

Marigot Bay

Fishing boat in the harbour at Soufrière

North of Gros Islet is the Pigeon Island National Historic Park. This peninsula was the home of the pirate Francois 'Wooden Leg' Le Clerc in the mid-16th century. It was also the site of the British stronghold from which Admiral Rodney launched a 36-year struggle against the French; in 1814, this brought France's possession of St Lucia to an end. It is still possible to stand on the ruins of the fortifications and enjoy commanding views as far as the island of Martinique.

Soufrière is the oldest town on St Lucia and was its capital when it was ruled by France. The main square has a typical French colonial feel, with many surviving buildings. Luxury hotels in the nearby hills and on the coast have stunning views of the Pitons. Synonymous with the island, these are eroded lava domes and, together with the ridge between them, they support eight rare plant species and five endemic bird species. An impressive way to appreciate the twin peaks is to take a scenic helicopter ride; this skirts around them and skims low over the verdant rainforest that coats their lower slopes.

There are a number of reserves where you can visit pristine rainforests. The 7690-ha Central Rainforest Reserve lies at the foot of

Anse La Raye

The Pitons

Balenbouche Estate

Mount Gimie and encompasses rainforest, cloud forest and woodland – all of which can be seen as you climb the mountain's slopes. The Enbas Saut trail leads to two waterfalls on the Troumassee River.

Further south, on St Lucia's south-west coast, is the tranquil Balenbouche Estate with its historic plantation house. The rusted remains of an 18th-century sugar mill have been overgrown by the trunks and trailing roots of massive ficus trees, which seem to grow out of its very walls. Ficus are also known as strangler figs and they really do look as if they are strangling this crumbling ruin.

Although tourism is important to St Lucia, the island's main foreign currency earner is bananas, which are grown in plantations in its interior. They play a major role in the cuisine of the island, so you may find yourself dining out on banana salad, or boiled green bananas and saltfish, while watching the sun set behind the mighty Pitons.

ⓘ

The dry season, from January to April, is the best time to visit St Lucia. There are direct flights from Europe and the USA to Hewanorra International Airport, about a 90-minute drive from Rodney Bay. Inter-Caribbean flights use the George F. L. Charles Airport in Castries.

Unicorn in Rodney Bay

Pigeon Island National Park

Cannon at Pigeon Island National Park

Balenbouche Estate

Mont Saint-Michel
France

The imposing and atmospheric bulk of Mont Saint-Michel makes a memorable impression when you first see it, as part of the Normandy countryside. It dominates, yet integrates with, the surrounding farm land, filling in the gap in an avenue of tall poplar trees, hiding behind rolled bales of straw in a harvested field or looming out of the pink pre-sunrise mist. Even in silhouette it is instantly recognizable.

Mont Saint-Michel is a tidal island in the mouth of the Couesnon River. It is home to a number of old dwellings and is topped with a steepled church and a Benedictine abbey – the archangel Michael reputedly appeared to St Hubert, Bishop of Avranches, in 708 and instructed him to build a monastery here.

Mont Saint-Michel looms over a flock of sheep, seen from Bas-Courtils

Village on the slopes of Mont Saint-Michel

The series of walls and towers on Mont Saint-Michel's perimeter protected it against the English during the Hundred Years War between England and France in the 14th and 15th centuries. They repeatedly attacked the island, but failed to take it because of a combination of these fortifications and its isolation from the mainland. Its defensive nature was turned around during the French Revolution when it was used to imprison high-profile political prisoners. Despite protests by prominent figures, including Victor Hugo, Mont Saint-Michel remained a prison until 1863.

Hugo was a great fan of the island. It was he who coined the phrase 'à la vitesse d'un cheval au gallop' to describe how the tides here race in at the speed of a galloping horse. At more than 14 metres,

they are among the highest in the world. The water rushes in at over 32 km an hour and there is a real risk of being drowned if you venture too far out on the sand that surrounds Mont Saint-Michel at low tide. Be aware, too, that there are also patches of quicksand.

Light floods through one of the fortified gates on the Rue Grande

Village of Mont Saint-Michel

Mont Saint-Michel was originally more of an island than it is today. Historically it was connected to the mainland by a narrow, natural land bridge that was completely under water at high tide. However, the construction of polders to reclaim land for farming, and the permanent causeway that was built towards the end of the 19th century, have led to the bay silting up. There are plans to replace the causeway with a bridge, to reverse this process and make Mont Saint-Michel a true island again.

A giant car park at the island end of the causeway is used as an impromptu campsite for motor homes in summer. The sea of cars, and the crowds on the island and in the small town on the mainland with its hotels and restaurants, can be off-putting. So make sure you visit Mont Saint-Michel at the right time: in the early morning – the narrow alleyways of the village at the foot of the abbey are deserted

Towering apse of the church at Mont Saint-Michel

Looking down the cloisters at the Benedictine abbey

Village of Mont Saint-Michel seen from the causeway

just after sunrise – or in the evening when the crowds have dissipated.

The abbey opens at 9 a.m., long before most visitors arrive, which will allow you to walk around in relative peace – even in the summer months. Look out from the battlements at about 11 o'clock and the people swarming up the causeway will resemble an invading army. This is a good time to head out into the countryside to view Mont Saint-Michel from afar, and appreciate how it fits into its environment.

ⓘ

Mont Saint-Michel is a short drive from Dinard Airport. Aurigny Air flies to Dinard from London via Guernsey, which makes it possible to combine your visit with one to Sark (see page 156). There are a number of hotels on the mainland end of the causeway, but staying on Mont Saint-Michel itself will allow you to appreciate the island's unique atmosphere.

St Aubert's Chapel at the rear of Mont Saint-Michel

Mont Saint-Michel seen from the bay at low tide

Rapa Nui
Chile

Moai at Ahu Tahai just outside of Hanga Roa

Rapa Nui is one of the most remote inhabited islands in the world. The flight to reach it deep in the south-east Pacific takes you over a seemingly endless expanse of sea, and when you arrive you will feel you have reached the very end of the earth.

The island (also known as Easter Island) is famous for its iconic *moai*, enigmatic stone figures that, over a period of about six hundred years, from the 10th century, were erected on stone platforms, or *ahu*, on various sites along the coast. Many of these locations are now rubble – all that remains of *moai* that were tumbled by malevolent hands as Rapa Nui tore itself apart in internecine conflict, or that have broken up

with the long passage of time. The origins and purpose of these great monuments is unknown, as is the mechanics of how they were transported.

The original inhabitants of Rapa Nui were Polynesians who, it is believed, sailed the Pacific on the trade winds that blew towards the island for half the year, then reversed, allowing these early explorers to find their way home. According to archaeologists, the first settlers came to Rapa Nui to escape the wars, and even cannibalism, that swept the islands of the south Pacific about 1500 years ago. A number of clans were established and the golden age of the creation of the *moai* was ushered in.

A culture thrived in the isolation of Rapa Nui and the population increased to an unsupportable level, peaking in the late 16th century. By

Rano Kao

Rugged coastline on Rapa Nui

this time, however, the islanders had cut down most of the trees, and it is thought that there wasn't enough wood for them to build the boats they needed to leave Rapa Nui. It is also believed that there was famine leading to violence and warfare. The population dropped from a peak of ten thousand to a few thousand over the following 200 years.

There must have been some degree of cooperation in the island's history because the stone for all the *moai* was mined and carved in the same place, before the statues were transported to their platforms, often kilometres away. This place was the spectacular volcanic crater of Rano Raraku, one of two on the island. Here many of the statues can be seen *in situ*. Scores dot its inside and outside, lying at eclectic angles like broken teeth, carved yet awaiting transportation. Others are part-carved in the rock – still waiting for workers to come and finish them, as they have for many hundreds of years. The red stone for the topknots on most of the *moai* was mined from a separate quarry.

Rano Kao, on the north of the island, is the larger of the two craters. Almost a perfect circle, its walls drop vertically for over 100 metres to a lake, speckled with floating reeds, that is rumoured to be twice as deep as the unflooded part of the volcano. On the crater's edge a series of low stone huts provided shelter during the *tangata*

Moai at Anakena

manu, the annual birdman festival. Each clan on the island trained an athlete who competed in a race to climb down the volcano's steep cliffs to the sea, swim to the nearby island of Motu Nui and return with an egg from the *manutara* (sooty tern) in his hand. Ornate petroglyphs record this tradition, which some people believe was a way of distributing scarce resources after the age of the *moai*.

The *moai* are seemingly all over Rapa Nui, and even in the most remote locations. The easiest to reach are on the outskirts of the small but thriving town of Hanga Roa with its colourful harbour, but probably the most spectacular are those of Ahu Tongariki, lying at the end of a shallow valley that leads down from the Rano Raraku crater. Fully restored, 15 of these great statues stand on a platform; with their crushed noses and cauliflower ears they look for all the world like a lined-up rugby team. And like all but one of the *moai* installations, they are on the coast but staring inland – perhaps prophesying danger from within rather than from the sea.

Moai at Rano Raraku quarry

Double rainbow over Rano Raraku

The landscape of Rapa Nui would be spectacular even without

the *moai*. Apart from the Rano Raraku and Rano Kao craters, a number of volcanic cones are dotted around the island's rolling grasslands, where hundreds of semi-wild horses wander and graze. On the coast, waves that have built up over many kilometres of open sea dash mercilessly against rugged black shores.

On Rapa Nui you can sit in baking sunshine and see a storm in another part of the island. And from a high vantage point you can observe weather fronts sweeping in from the sea. Truly, as you watch

Wild horse by fallen *moai*, Ahu Tongariki

Petroglyphs at Orongo on Rano Kao volcano

the slate-grey clouds dragging the sun in their wake, often with rainbows ahead of them, you will feel that you are on the very edge of the world.

Standing *moai* at Ahu Tongariki

LAN Chile is the only airline that flies to Rapa Nui. In peak periods there are daily flights from Santiago and twice weekly from Tahiti. Fares are excessive but cheaper internet deals are available. The small Chilean-run Explora group's package is recommended as it includes all food and drinks, and guided tours around the island with committed and friendly local guides. Rather than relying on motor coaches, the Explora ethos is to conduct a series of walks around Rapa Nui that take in the landscapes and show the *moai* in the best possible context.

Angkor Wat
Cambodia

Although the trees that surround Angkor have been tamed, it is still possible to imagine how this ancient city was 'lost' to the outside world for centuries until the French explorer Henri Mahout discovered it smothered in the jungle in 1860.

Angkor was the capital of the Khmer civilization, which spanned some 500 years, until it was sacked by Thai invaders in 1431. It reached its zenith in the 12th century, first with the building of the temple that came to be known as Angkor Wat and later with the construction of Angkor Thom, a royal city-within-a-city.

The temple was built by King Suryavarman II as a representation of Mount Meru, the mythical holy centre of Hinduism. Surrounded by a large moat bridged by a stone causeway, it is a west-facing rectangular stone structure comprising three levels. The uppermost

Angkor Wat reflected in the waters of the north pool at sunrise

Monks climbing down steps from the third level of Angkor Wat

level, formerly open only to priests and the king, is topped with four corner towers and a central sanctuary 65 metres from the ground. Originally devoted to the Hindu god Shiva, the temple later became a Wat, or Buddhist monastery, and is now accepted as a spiritual monument by the predominantly Buddhist Cambodians. Images of the Buddha can be found among its vaulted galleries.

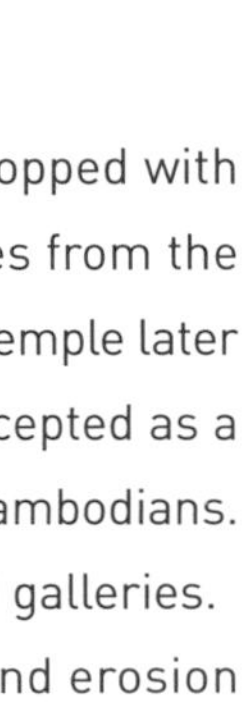

Even after more than 800 years of plundering and erosion the carvings of Angkor Wat remain exquisite and the wealth of detail is bewildering. Galleries of bas-reliefs – the longest in the world – depict scenes from the Hindu religious epic, the *Mahabharata*, battle scenes from Khmer history and warnings about the tortures of hell.

The temple is best seen in the golden light of early morning when the rays of the sun pick out the *apsaras* (celestial nymphs)

Novice monks on the terrace of the first level of Angkor Wat

Bas-relief of a marching army

carved into its walls, seeming to breathe life into them. Amid the quiet beauty, it is hard to imagine that this place was one of the final refuges of the notorious Khmer Rouge communist movement – until you notice scars from the impact of bullets on the stone of the building.

Direct flights from Bangkok in Thailand have made the temples of Angkor more accessible, and they are now visited by more tourists than ever. Most tend to gather at the north pool to photograph the reflections of the rising sun, but those seeking peace and tranquillity should head straight to the principal sanctuary of Angkor Wat. This is reached by one of four flights of steep and worn stairs, signifying just how difficult and arduous is the path to heaven. It was once the

Looking out from the third level to the second level and surrounding trees

exclusive preserve of Hindu priests, but now you too can have it to yourself – providing you get there early enough.

The top level of Angkor Wat seems to have been designed for the sunrise. Golden fingers slide through the unique, stone-pillared windows and illuminate details that quickly recede in the brilliant light of the day, and some of the most beautiful *apsaras* – which can be found in the central sanctuary – are uncovered by the rising sun, only to be hidden in shadow again just 20 minutes later.

It can sometimes be half an hour before the first few explorers from the sunrise party reach here. Most don't bother; they go back to their hotels for breakfast, and return here later in the day, when the sun is intense and energy-sapping, and the atmosphere far from spiritual.

Other parts of the Angkor complex not to be missed are the Bayon and Ta Prohm. Built later than Angkor Wat, the Bayon is a small temple covered with giant, impassive stone faces reminiscent

Apsaras carved into the principal sanctuary of Angkor Wat

Sun shining through the pillared windows of the cloisters on the third level of Angkor Wat

of Lord Buddha, and perhaps marking the transition from Hinduism to Buddhism in the Khmer civilization. Ta Prohm is a largely ruined temple complex, with roots of banyan and kapok trees growing out of the stonework – and sometimes so much a part of it that neither would survive any attempt at separation.

ⓘ

Siem Reap, the nearest town to Angkor (10 km away), can be reached by plane from Bangkok, Thailand (Bangkok Airways has several flights a day in both directions) or from the Cambodian capital, Phnom Penh. Alternatively, you can get there by boat across Tonle Sap. This lake trip takes most of the day but is an interesting journey. A wide range of accommodation is available in Siem Reap, from inexpensive guest houses to the exclusive Amansara Resort. Tickets for the ruins can be bought for one, three or seven days. Three days is a good amount of time. The site is very spread out, but the better hotels can organize a guide with a car, or you can hire a bicycle, motorbike or motorbike-taxi from many places in town.

Grand Canyon
Arizona, USA

As you stand in the cold darkness of an Arizona night, waiting for dawn, you will have no comprehension of the enormity of the landscape in front of you. In the dull early light your first view of the Grand Canyon will be a flat, almost painterly composition. Then gradually the sky turns to blue and red, and golden sunlight starts to pick out details – first the edge of the far ridge, then the tallest pinnacles inside the canyon itself.

Sunset at Yapavi Point

Grandview Point

As the sun rises higher, more is revealed. Rock formations sculpted by years of erosion are illuminated, and long, convoluted shadows are cast on to giant screens formed by cliffs.

Only when you notice details, such as a row of trees, or a flock of geese flying overhead, do you come to realize the true scale of the canyon. That far ridge might be 15 km away, and the mighty Colorado River – a mere stream viewed from above – is 1500 metres below.

Consisting of an inner and outer gorge, the canyon is some 450 km long in total, so it is impossible to try taking it all in at once. Far better to spend some time at one or two of the lookout points that punctuate the roads along the rim of the canyon and see the changing light from them. From Hopi Point, a short distance from the Grand Canyon Village, you can look both ways along the canyon, getting

View from Hopi Point

spectacular views of the scenery and watching it change colour throughout the day. You can also see the Colorado River looking deceptively small and tranquil far below.

There are a number of trails down into the canyon. Some of the longer ones will involve camping en route but you can hike down and back up in a day on others, such as Bright Angel Trail – provided you start early enough. However, even for this shorter trail, the park authorities recommend that you break your journey at Indian Garden campsite and spread your hike over two days. Remember, it will take twice as long to walk back up the trail as it took to walk down, and it's a hard uphill slog. Those not used to exercise can hire a mule to carry them, but the ride is fairly uncomfortable. Trail-walking provides some idea of the scale of the canyon. Distances become more real as you descend, and details of the scenery unfold around you. Soon the walls of the canyon tower above you, and you realize that the landmarks that looked so close from the rim take hours to reach.

View from Yaki Point

View from Yapavi Point

The canyon receives over a million visitors a year, although most stay only a few hours and tend to congregate on the more accessible south rim. To avoid the worst of the crowds, visit in spring or autumn. Although it will be cold at night and in the mornings, the air is clearer and you can observe the canyon in very different conditions. The weather can change suddenly, giving clear blue skies one day and a white-out blizzard the next. However, the great depth of the canyon leads to huge temperature variations between the top and the bottom, so in the course of one day you might walk through heavy snow at the top and hot sunshine at the bottom.

Sunrise at Yaki Point

The Colorado River from Desert View Point

ⓘ

The nearest major airport to the Grand Canyon is at Flagstaff, a couple of hours' drive away from the south rim. If you are coming from Las Vegas you can fly directly to Grand Canyon airport at Tusayan. There is a free bus service around the park, but hiring a car is recommended as it will give you more freedom to explore. Grand Canyon Village offers a range of accommodation, but as it is all run by the same company there is little competition in pricing. The best place there is El Tovar Lodge, which is right on the rim. It gets very booked up, though, so make a reservation well in advance. The National Parks Department's website (www.nps.gov/grca/grandcanyon) covers all aspects of the Grand Canyon.

The head of Bright Angel Trail

Iguassu Falls
Brazil and Argentina

If you were to design the perfect waterfall then Iguassu would have to be it. Straddling the border between Brazil and Argentina, where it is known as Saltos do Iguaçu and Cataratas do Iguazú respectively, it comprises a range of cataracts.

One such is the Devil's Throat (Garganta del Diablo), which has a classic horseshoe shape and drops into a deep chasm. A walkway runs from the Argentinian side to the edge of the cataract, allowing you to stare directly at the wall of water as it drops into the void below.

Spray over Iguassu Falls at sunrise

Salto Tres Mosqueteros on the Argentinian side

The Argentinian side in the setting sun

The Santa Maria Cataract, which falls over the Brazilian side of the border, is interrupted halfway down by a plateau. Here the water is dotted with moss-encrusted rocks and spanned by a walkway that provides views up and down the falls and is festooned with rainbows.

Both walkways provide an experience for all the senses: the endless rushing sound that grows to a roar as you approach, the sheets of cooling spray as you get closer, and the buffeting winds, caused by the great volume of water pushing the air out of the way.

The whole waterfall stretches for a couple of kilometres and includes many other cataracts, some approachable only by boat, others visible only from an island that sits in the middle of the river above the falls. Iguassu is surrounded on both sides by verdant rainforest, which has been made into two national parks.

Uniquely for the sights in this book, an early start is not required as the sunlight barely hits the lower parts of the falls until an hour or two after dawn.

The Devil's Throat (Garganta del Diablo)

The Argentinian side of the falls

While most of Iguassu is in Argentina, some of the best views are on the Brazilian side, especially at sunset. It is a simple process to cross over for the day as travel agents on both sides offer inexpensive trips.

The Brazilian side of the border is probably the least developed, and those seeking seclusion should consider staying at the Hotel das Cataratas eco-hotel. Built in a Portuguese colonial style, with some rooms overlooking part of the waterfall, and a clock tower from which you can watch the sunset, the hotel is actually inside the national park. Although there are signs warning against jaguars and snakes you can stroll down to the falls at night, when the dull roar seems even louder, and you might just be able to make out the spray in the moonlight.

If you can combine your visit with a full moon there are special night visits open to everybody, and the moonlight is bright enough to make out many details of the falls.

The Devil's Throat (Garganta del Diablo) and the top of Salto Santa Maria

ⓘ

There are flights to Foz do Iguaçu, the town on the Brazilian side of the falls, from both Rio de Janeiro and Saõ Paulo. Though many people do day trips from these cities it is better to stay for at least a couple of days to allow time to visit the Argentinian side. This is very easy – most local hotels arrange trips – and you won't even need a visa. You can also raft on the river, explore the surrounding forest and even take a helicopter ride. The Hotel das Cataras hotel on the less-developed Brazilian side will give you privileged access to the falls – especially on Monday mornings when the park is officially closed to non-guests.

Rio de Janeiro

Brazil

View from Corcovado Mountain to Sugar Loaf Mountain at dusk

The mountain of Corcovado, topped by a 32-metre statue of Christ the Redeemer facing out over Guanabara Bay, has to be the great enduring image of Rio de Janeiro. From up here, on a clear day, you can see almost the whole city, from the downtown business district to the internationally famous beaches of Ipanema and Copacabana. It also has one of the best views of Sugar Loaf Mountain, another of the city's great landmarks.

Rio is arguably the most stunning harbour city in the world, pipping both Sydney and Hong Kong in my estimation. While the last two are amazing in their own way, Rio has the advantage of being built on a series of hills, some of which are still covered by virgin forest, and looks out over the most beautiful natural scenery of the granite islands in Guanabara Bay. Corcovado, set within a park that opens at 8 a.m., can be reached either by taxi or by a creaking old tram that

Looking down from Corcovado Mountain

Christ the Redeemer

winds its way up to the summit. You should really make the effort to reach the top early in the morning when misty clouds, backlit by the rising sun, sometimes fill the bay, with just the tops of the islands peeking above them. It's also well worth visiting at sunset, when the sun sinks into the hills behind Rio and the city lights up.

Ipanema Beach

Similarly, the view of both Rio and Corcovado from Sugar Loaf Mountain is worth seeing at both ends of the day, when the city assumes quite different appearances.

If you want to see the actual sunrise you will have to take a taxi to San Cristobel Point, which lies outside the park. Although not as high as Corcovado, it still enjoys a commanding view over the bay.

From the top of Sugar Loaf Mountain it is possible to take a very short helicopter ride that flies you up and around the statue of Christ the Redeemer for less than £30.

Rio, however, is about so much more than sights or even natural beauty. No other city in the world epitomizes the 'Life's a Beach'

Copacabana Beach

philosophy more than Rio. And where better to see this than at Copacabana and Ipanema? Both immortalized in song, these beaches mirror the character of the cariocas, as the citizens of Rio call themselves. As the clubbers who congregate there to wind down after an all-night party give way to the first of the morning's joggers, the next 24 hours will see everything from holidaymakers to beach boys, from volleyball players to bodybuilders – all set to a background of bossa nova music and perhaps accompanied by a cocktail.

Rio has endured a bad reputation for street crime over the years, but has gone a long way to clean up this problem. As with most major cities, drugs and poverty make certain parts of the city riskier than others, but if you stick to the main areas (which include all the principal tourist sites) and don't carry valuables conspicuously, you will probably find Rio far less threatening than many European

Santa Teresa tram

capitals. In fact, the biggest annoyance I suffered – though totally well meaning – was that the locals constantly warned me to be careful with my possessions.

Many airlines fly to Rio from all over the world. Most of the hotels are out along the beaches of Copacabana and Ipanema. The most famous hotel is the Copacabana Palace, run by the Orient Express Group. Even if you do not stay there you should visit the terrace bar for a sundowner. When on the beach, leave all your valuables in your hotel or with the guards posted on the beach by most of the top hotels. The downtown area is quite a way from the beaches, but taxis are cheap and plentiful. The stunning views from Sugar Loaf Mountain and Corcovado are not to be missed.

View from Corcovado Mountain

Taj Mahal
Agra, India

The most evocative views of the Taj Mahal are across the Yamuna River, and getting to the Taj is part of the magic. Although it is quicker to take a boat across, taking a cycle-rickshaw through the village of Katchpura is more atmospheric. In the cool of a pre-dawn morning, you will pass villagers sleeping on low charpoy beds outside their small dwellings, often passing so close that they could reach out and touch you.

On arriving at the river you might have to share the view with a fisherman or a small herd of water buffalo, but these merely add to the feeling of timelessness.

From across the river the Taj Mahal is best seen at sunrise, when the light turns from cold misty blue to any variation of pink,

The Taj Mahal viewed from across the Yamuna River

The east corner of the Taj Mahal???Overleaf: The Taj Mahal from across the Yamuna River at sunrise

pale gold or orange. The Taj mirrors these colours, eventually reaching a soft creamy white, changing, in turn, to a blinding white in the glare of the midday sun. Those who visit at that time of day often come away disappointed. It is worth visiting at different times over several days to appreciate both the might and grace of the structure as it changes with the light. You'll have to pay to enter the Taj Mahal and grounds, but it currently costs nothing to view it from across the river.

The Taj sits on a marble platform with a marble minaret at each corner, and these minarets actually lean out slightly so that they won't fall on the main structure in the event of an earthquake. Each face of the Taj has a giant arch and is decorated with exquisite

calligraphy from the Koran and ornate carvings of flowers inlaid with pietra-dura mosaics of semi-precious stones.

The Taj Mahal is set in a relaxed but formal garden complex, with pools of water leading to it from the main gate – a special view that has inspired a generation of photographers. The distance from the gate to the Taj is deceptive and the building seems to grow in both size and stature as you approach.

The Taj Mahal was built in 1632 by Emperor Shah Jahan as a mausoleum for his favourite wife, Mumtaz. Legend has it that he intended to build a duplicate Taj in black marble on the opposite side of the river as his own tomb. In recent years the ruins of foundations and gardens have been discovered there, which seems to support this theory, but the truth will probably never be known. Shah Jahan was overthrown by his son and spent his last days locked up in Agra Fort, just down the river from the Taj.

Western mosque flanking the Taj Mahal

Agra Fort with the Taj Mahal behind

Agra can be reached by plane or fast train from New Delhi, although the latter has a reputation for pickpockets. All the rooms in the new luxury Amarvilas hotel in Agra look out on the Taj Mahal so uniquely, you don't have to pay a premium for good views if you stay there. The bustling streets of Taj Ganj, just outside the main gate, were once the home of the craftsmen who constructed the Taj. It is now a backpacker's ghetto with very cheap accommodation. Some of the best views can be had from the roof-top restaurant of the budget Shanti Lodge. Other attractions include the fort in Agra, which has good views down the Yamuna River to the Taj, and also the deserted city of Fatehpur Sikri a few hours away.

Detail of a door in the pedestal of the Taj Mahal

Detail of the Dome

Petra
Jordan

The city of Petra was carved from red sandstone in the 3rd century BC by nomadic Arabs known as Nabataeans. The only entrance is through a *siq* – a long, narrow gorge. This channel, eroded by thousands of years of floods, forms a twisting and convoluted pathway through solid rock that looms up to 100 metres on either side.

At some points along its 1.2-km length the *siq* is wide enough for the sunlight to flood in and lift the dark and oppressive atmosphere, but at others it is no wider than a couple of metres, and the walls appear to close above your head. An early morning visit can be an eerie experience, with just the wind whistling through the gorge and the strangely tinny echo of your own footsteps.

The royal tombs seen from the High Place of Sacrifice

Looking down the *siq* to Al Khazneh (the treasury)

At one time the *siq* would have been crowded with camel trains laden with wealth, and even the invading Romans, who finally conquered the city in AD 106, would have had to fight their way down its entire length.

Rounding the final and narrowest corner of the *siq* you are confronted by the towering façade of Al Khazneh (the treasury), which is the enduring image of the city. Although the carvings on the treasury have been damaged by Bedouin, who once lived among the deserted ruins and used the statues for target practice, there is still much to be seen. This includes the large urn on the top of the structure, that the Bedouin shot at in the belief that it contained the lost treasure of King Solomon.

The façade of Al Khazneh (the treasury)

Roman temple

Excavations taking place in front of the treasury seem to indicate that it had another storey below the current structure, which is now buried under debris washed down by the annual flash floods that created the *siq*. The treasury is fully bathed in sunlight for a couple of hours from around 9.30 in the morning, but looks pinker and more atmospheric when in shadow. A good, though officially unsanctioned, view can be had by climbing the rock face to the right of the *siq*, to a ledge level with the top of the treasury.

All the great façades, including the treasury, are, in fact, tombs. Dwellings have long since disappeared, but you can still see the 7000-seat theatre carved out of rock, and a temple built by the Romans when they governed the city. There is also a major stretch of

Nabatean road running past an old market area that would once have been thronged with shoppers and merchants trading goods and treasures brought to Petra from all over the Middle East.

It is no wonder that, tucked away in the middle of the desert, the city remained hidden and forgotten for 300 years after it was finally deserted, with only Bedouin living in its caves and tombs. It was 'rediscovered' for the West by Johann Burckhardt in 1812.

Although the Bedouin no longer live in the city they are still much in evidence, having been given sole rights to the various tourist concessions on the site in return for moving out to a nearby village.

Eroded carving of a man with a camel in the *siq*

Interior of the treasury

Building on the street of façades

Camels in front of the treasury with the *siq* behind

Petra is huge, and you will need a good few days to do it justice, especially if you are planning to visit some of the more outlying places, such as the monastery up in the adjacent hills. A good way to appreciate the size of Petra is to climb the steep steps to the High Place of Sacrifice, where you can see over most of the city and watch as the sun slides behind the camel-shaped mountain on the far side of the valley, before making your way back to your hotel through the rapidly darkening *siq*.

ⓘ

Petra is just a few hours' drive from the Jordanian capital Amman and is easily reached by bus or by car. There are a number of hotels in Petra, but the five-star Movenpick is just a few minutes from the site gate, making an early start a little easier. There are places inside the site that sell food and drinks but you should carry adequate water with you to avoid dehydration. The site is open from dawn till 6 p.m., although you can often linger longer to see the sunset. Passes for one, two or three days are available from the visitor centre. You can also hire a guide there.

Venice
Italy

Relief of Adam and Eve on the corner of the Palazzo Ducale

Gondolas moored in front of the church of Santa Maria della Salute

No city is more romantic than Venice, and no sight more essentially Venetian than gondolas bobbing on a misty Molo, the waterfront where the Piazza San Marco meets the lagoon. In the very early morning the square is quiet, with only a few commuters disturbing the handful of pigeons that strut imperiously on its worn flagstones. Soon the place will be thronged with both tourists and birds, but for now you can be virtually alone.

Piazza San Marco has been at the centre of the city since it was first constructed in the 16th century, although some of the buildings around it date from much earlier. At one end lies the Basilica di San Marco,

construction of which began almost 1000 years ago. Squat and strangely shaped, its domed roof looks more Islamic than Christian when seen from the soaring heights of the adjacent campanile, or bell tower. At sunset the façade of the basilica seems to come alive as the mosaics, and even the stone itself, glow in the warm evening light.

Stretching from San Marco down to the waterfront is the Gothic white edifice of the Palazzo Ducale, or Doge's Palace. The doges ruled the city from AD 697 until Napoleon's troops deposed the last of them in 1797. Although peppered with moralistic statues and carvings that depict such things as the fall of Adam and Eve, and a drunken Noah, the palace is best appreciated from afar, as it would

have been by visitors arriving by sea in the days of the doges. Seen from a boat on the lagoon, or even from the top of the campanile on the island of San Giorgio, the façade combines elegance with a feeling of fantasy.

If the doges wished to portray an impression of piety with the outside of their palace, the inside shows a much more worldly extravagance. Room after room is decorated with the finest gilding and paintings, including works by Titian and Tintoretto.

The doges were responsible for the judicial side of Venetian life, and many condemned people were led across the two-lane Bridge of Sighs to the prisons opposite.

Although not, strictly speaking, connected to the Piazza San Marco, the Grand Canal is linked with it. A lazy, sweeping 'S' shape, it

Façade of buildings around Piazza San Marco

Piazzetta San Marco

cuts through the city, defining it almost as much as the piazza does. The end of the canal opens into the lagoon where it meets the piazza, and the waterfront here is lined with the ubiquitous gondolas.

As all roads in Venice seem to lead to Piazza San Marco – virtually every street or alley junction has a signpost pointing in that direction – so all canals seem to lead to the Grand Canal. Now used mainly by tourists, gondolas still glide past the palazzos that line its sides.

Venice can be cold and damp during the winter, but this is a perfect time to visit. There are far fewer visitors, hotel prices are lower and, if you are lucky, you might even be there when the water floods Piazza San Marco, forcing locals and tourists on to raised walkways to keep their feet dry. Even in the winter you can experience blue skies and amazingly clear light.

Palazzo Ducale

A perfect winter day in Venice has to end with a warming hot chocolate or a typically Venetian spritz cocktail (white wine, lemon peel, a bitter aperitif and seltzer) at Caffè Florian. Founded in 1720, this elegant café, once patronized by Byron and Goethe, is decorated with mirrors and murals cracked by years of damp sea air.

From Marco Polo airport you can catch a *vaporetto* (water bus) or water taxi that drops you off at the Molo. Accommodation is expensive and can be hard to find in the peak summer months. The industrial town of Mestre is a short train ride away and offers cheaper options. The Regina and Europa Hotel is a luxury establishment in a converted palazzo, overlooking the mouth of the Grand Canal. A network of *vaporetti* ply the main canals and are a good way to get around. Otherwise, just walk and enjoy the experience of getting lost.

Palazzo Ducale

Palazzo Ducale from the top of the campanile

Façade of the Basilica di San Marco

Cloister at one end of Patio de los Arrayanes, Casa Real

The Alhambra
Granada, Spain

Patio de los Leones

Overlooking Granada, the Alhambra presents a hard and unyielding face to the world, its square towers displaying martial symmetry. This severity is softened when you approach from the back, as terraces of ornate gardens, interspersed with pools of running water, seek to emulate the shady, cool gardens of the Koranic heaven.

After the heat and dryness of North Africa the Moors must have thought they had reached heaven when they conquered Granada. The Sierra Nevada, snow-capped for much of the year, provided the conquerors with water for the fountains and pools that helped to make this corner of Spain paradise on Earth.

The Alhambra is a product of the wars between Christianity and Islam. The Moors of North Africa conquered Spain in 711, but by the beginning of the 13th century their influence had weakened and their 'kingdom' – just a few independent Muslim states in what is now Andalusia – was under pressure from Christian *reconquistas*. Prince Ibn al-Ahmar, who was driven south from Saragossa, decided to

create a new capital at Granada, and began building the fortifications that would keep it safe. For over 200 years the kingdom prospered, and subsequent rulers added to and refined the Alhambra. It was a period of peace that came at a price, however. During this time the Christian kings of Spain were in the ascendancy, and Granada was left in peace only because the Moors paid tributes and sometimes sent troops to fight on the side of the Christians against other, more troublesome, Muslim city states.

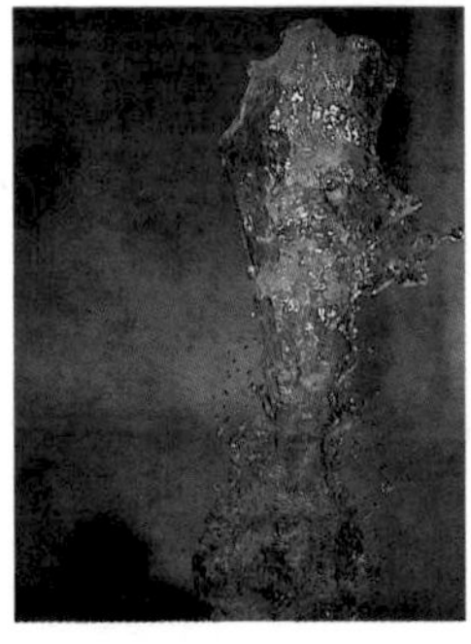

At the end of the 15th century the battlements of the Alhambra were called into use when the army of Catholic rulers Ferdinand and Isabella laid siege to Granada. Seven months later this last Muslim stronghold in Spain gave way, and it has remained in Spanish hands ever since.

Typical of Moorish architecture, the palace has a façade that is both commanding and utilitarian, yet hidden within its defensive walls is decoration of enduring beauty. The Alhambra consists of

The Alhambra floodlit at dusk with the Sierra Nevada behind

three main parts: the Alcazaba, or fortress; the Generalife, which was the summer palace and actually lies outside the main defensive walls; and the Casa Real, or Royal Palace. The last of these is without doubt the most beautiful part of the Alhambra, many of its rooms decorated with colourful tiles or richly carved stonework, the patterns based on stylized quotes from the Koran.

Gardens of the Generalife

Within some of these rooms you can still see the fountains or pools of water so prized by the Moors. Numerous small windows overlook shady gardens or the small white houses of the Albaicin district, the old Moorish quarter, parts of which are as old as the Alhambra itself.

Spring is a beautiful time to visit, with clear warm days and cool nights. The trees are newly green, the gardens are in flower and the

Bronze eagle on the exterior of the Palacio de Carlos V

Intricate Moorish decoration

Sierra Nevada, still snow-capped, stands watch over the city. Even better, the Casa Real is not crowded and you can generally get in without queueing or waiting for a slot, as you must in the height of summer, when all the timed entrance tickets are often allocated within an hour of the ticket office opening.

You might also be able to get a room at the Parador de San Francisco, a luxury, state-run hotel in a converted monastery within the gardens of the Alhambra – a tranquil retreat in the evenings when the crowds have gone.

There are many vantage points around the city from which you can get a different perspective on the Alhambra. From the Mirador San Cristobel you will see the Alcazaba against the backdrop of the Sierra Nevada. Walk through the rambling, cobbled streets of Albaicin to the Mirador de San Nicolas and you will see wonderful sunsets that bathe the Alhambra in glowing red light. From the top of the Sacromonte (the old gypsy quarter, where some gypsies still live in caves carved into the hillside) you will see how the Alhambra towers over the town from its perfect defensive position. And from the hill above the Generalife you can appreciate how much the gardens and water terraces contribute to the Alhambra. Also visible is the massive Palacio de Carlos V, built in the 16th century, after the Christian conquest, on the site of many lesser Moorish buildings. The grounds of this palace are so large that bullfights were once held in the courtyard.

Moorish decoration

Granada is easily reached by road from Seville or Málaga, two international airports that are well served by the Iberia airline from most parts of Europe. While the Alhambra is seen to advantage from many viewpoints around the city, you can enjoy it at close quarters by staying in its gardens at the luxurious Parador de San Francisco. However, you should book well in advance for the privilege, even in the low season.

Tha Alhambra seen from the hill behind the Generalife

Statues in front of the seventh pylon of the Precinct of Amun

Karnak Temple
Luxor, Egypt

The Precinct of Amun reflected in the Sacred Lake

Karnak Temple is a lasting tribute to the ancient Egyptian pharaohs' quest for immortality. And as a powerful religious institution it is arguably more representative of life in ancient Egypt than the Giza pyramids which, despite their impressive size, are ultimately tombs for the dead rulers of the Old Kingdom. The temple's influence, which lasted for more than 1300 years, was central to the power of numerous New Kingdom pharaohs, including Seti I and Rameses II.

The Great Hypostyle Hall, which is more than 3500 years old, covers an area of 6000 square metres and contains a forest of 136 stone pillars, each 23 metres tall and 15 metres in circumference. Many of these have been extensively renovated, but are still covered with deeply carved hieroglyphics and elaborate bas-relief depictions of Egyptian gods, especially Amun to whom this precinct of the temple is dedicated. Some of the pillars still bear traces of the original colouring, dating back to around 1300 BC.

In the days of the pharaohs the whole of the hall would have been roofed over, and the remains of some of the lintels that supported the roof can still be seen. The interior would have been in semi-darkness, punctuated by shafts of light from grilled windows along the central aisle. It is easy to imagine processions of priests passing through its hallowed halls, and even Pharaohs coming to admire the bas-reliefs of gods in their own image.

The Precinct of Amun is the largest and most complete of the three enclosures that make up Karnak Temple. The other enclosures, the Temple of Mut and the Precinct of Mont, are largely ruins. Whilst the Great Hypostyle Hall is Amun's most impressive structure, there is a great deal more to see in the complex. From the entrance, an avenue of ram-headed sphinxes leads up to the first pylon, a 43-metre-high wall with a gap in the middle to allow entry. Inside the courtyard beyond the wall is a colossal statue of Rameses II, and a small temple devoted to Rameses III. There are a number of sphinxes outside this temple and more tall statues inside. Beyond the next pylon lie the pillars of the Hypostyle Hall, and beyond that the rest of Karnak Temple, which you could easily spend a couple of days exploring. I would recommend employing the services of a local guide, if only to save you from the temple guards and their constant demands for baksheesh, a small tip.

Defaced bas-reliefs in a sanctuary in the Precinct of Amun

Karnak tends to get very crowded during the day, but if you arrive as it opens at six in the morning it is often deserted. Take the correct entrance money as the gate seldom has change at this time, and leave by 9 a.m. to avoid the worst of the crowds. If you can cope with the afternoon heat, it's worth returning after 3 p.m. when the tour

The Tuthmosid obelisk and pillars in the Great Hypostyle Hall

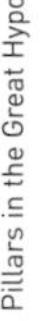
Pillars in the Great Hypostyle Hall

Bas-relief on the exterior wall of the Great Hypostyle Hall

groups have left and the temple is quiet again. You can sometimes use the same ticket in the morning and afternoon, especially if you mention at the gate when you leave that you will be returning.

You can return to town by walking along the Avenue of Sphinxes, once the route of a procession in honour of Amun. Nowadays, many of the sphinxes are missing and the avenue disappears briefly on the outskirts of Luxor. It can be picked up again at the back gate to Luxor Temple, where it joins a more impressive avenue of sphinxes linking the temples of Karnak and Luxor just as they were linked in the time of the pharaohs.

ⓘ

Luxor is easily reached by internal flights from Cairo or you can catch the very comfortable night train from the capital. The most famous hotel in Luxor is the old Winter Palace in the centre of town, but the Nile Hilton Hotel is more convenient for Karnak. Official guides can be hired from the ticket office but agree the price first. Taxis are very cheap but, as with everything in Egypt, haggle hard. You can also take a horse-drawn calèche, but choose only healthy-looking horses and stop the driver from galloping them. Do not leave Luxor without visiting the Valleys of the Kings and Queens across the Nile.

A sanctuary in the Precinct of Amun

The feet of the colossus of Rameses II in the Precinct of Amun

Galapagos Islands
Ecuador

Nesting pair of blue-footed boobies, North Seymour Island

Marine iguanas, Bartolome Island

It was on the Galapagos Islands, off the coast of Ecuador, that the process of evolution was first understood. Charles Darwin (1809–82) arrived at the Galapagos in 1835 and stayed for just five weeks, observing and collecting specimens of fauna and flora.

The diversity of life forms he encountered in this small area, and the adaptations they had made to local conditions, led him to formulate his theory of evolution. This was eventually published as *On the Origin of Species by Means of Natural Selection* in 1859, and remains one of the most influential books ever written.

As there are no natural predators on the islands it is still possible to see the diversity of wildlife that so inspired Darwin. Human interference has also been minimal, so the animals and birds seem quite unconcerned by the presence of visitors.

Each species has evolved to exploit the character of individual islands. The blue-footed booby on North Seymour Island, for example, feeds close to the shore, whereas the red-footed booby on more outlying islands, such as Genovesa, feeds a long way out to sea. These two birds are fine examples of related species adapting separately to their environments.

Pinnacle Rock, Bartolome Island

Sea lions playing, Isla Lobos

The 'signature' animal of the Galapagos for most people is the giant tortoise, which can be seen lumbering around the highlands of Santa Cruz, the second-largest island in the archipelago. Some of these creatures are so old that they might have been seen in their youth by Darwin himself.

Your time in the Galapagos will be remembered as a series of unique wildlife vignettes: snorkelling with sea lions that swim and play within inches of you, and continue leaping in and out of the water long after you have tired and headed for dry land; seeing dozens of sea iguanas clinging haphazardly to a rock; watching from just a few feet away the elaborate courtship ritual of the blue-footed booby; feeling small sharks touch your feet as you wade ashore; noticing a

Isla Lobos at sunset

sea turtle cruising majestically along the edge of a coral reef; and, most magically, seeing a humpback whale and her calf surface with a great gout of exhaled air.

The archipelago, which consists of 12 main islands and several smaller ones, is difficult to visit independently. The most practical way to get around is on a cruise of four, seven or even more days. The contrasts between the islands make them very special.

Cruising between them, just as Darwin did nearly 200 years ago, you will feel as though you are getting a privileged insight into an untouched world. At night you will sleep on board the cruise ship, leaving the wildlife in sole occupation of the islands, which are as unspoilt now as they have been since the beginning of time.

ⓘ

The only practical way to get around the Galapagos Islands is on a short cruise. Metropolitan Touring run a variety of trips but the most popular last from four to seven days. Tame Airlines flies to the islands from Quito, the capital of Ecuador, via Guayaquil, the country's largest city. Be sure to check that your tour operator's fee includes the park fee (your ticket will be stamped if it does) – if not, you will not be allowed to leave the airport until you pay *in cash.* Access to the islands by boats and tourists is strictly controlled by the government of Ecuador to minimize the environmental impact of tourism. You cannot wander freely on the islands and the planning of activities and timing is quite rigid. Despite these controls, each day is spectacular. The busiest times are Christmas, Easter and August.

Young great frigate, Genovesa Island

Sally Lightfoot crab

Giant tortoise, Santa Cruz Island

Marine iguanas, James Island

Sea lion, North Seymour Island

Lake Titicaca
Bolivia and Peru

View of the Bolivian Cordillera from Isla de la Luna (Island of the Moon)

Lake Titicaca has a haunting and desolate beauty. The intensity of the rich, dark blue of the water is unique among freshwater lakes and makes the wide expanses of sky and landscape look even more stark and exceptional. At more than 3800 metres above sea level, Lake Titicaca is the highest navigable lake in the world. The clarity of the air at this altitude, combined with the hues of the lake and its islands, produces a colour palette of intense vibrancy.

The lake, which is 176 km long and some 50 km wide, and straddles Bolivia and Peru, is considered to be sacred by many of the local people, who believe that spirits live in its deep waters. In Andean creation myths Lake Titicaca was the birthplace of civilization, and the sun, moon and stars rose out of it.

To really appreciate the lake and the people who live on it, you have to go out on to one of the islands, where the scenery and culture

Sailboat at the island of Taquile

Boats on the island of Taquile with the island of Amantani in the background

Drop-spinning wool thread to make traditional clothing on Taquile

Inca ruins on Isla del Sol (Island of the Sun)

are totally different from those of the mainland. Many tourists head straight for the floating islands of Uros, which are created from bundles of floating reeds. As the lower reeds rot and fall away new ones are added to the top to maintain the structure, a method of construction that dates back to antiquity.

Sunset seen from Copacabana, Bolivia

The islands of Amantani and Taquile, which are some three hours by boat from the town of Puno, are less affected by tourism. The people on these islands speak Quechua, the oldest living language in Peru, and their traditions survive largely unscathed by the 21st century. The people of Taquile still wear clothing that they weave from the wool of alpacas. The women wear layered skirts and shawls, whereas the men adorn themselves with embroidered waistbands and woollen caps.

Amantani, the larger of the two islands, is inhabited by about 800 families – fishermen, farmers and weavers. Ancient stone walls divide terraces that belong to different families. There are two peaks on the island; one topped by the ruins of the Temple of Pachamama and the other by the ruins of the Temple of Pachatata. These pre-Incan structures represent Mother Earth and Father Earth respectively. Every January the Fiesta de la Santa Tierra (Festival of the Sacred Land) splits the island, with half the people attending each of the ruined temples.

The high altitude makes the hike up to Pachamama strenuous, but the views across to the mountains of the Cordillera Real on the Bolivian side of the lake make it all worthwhile. The hill is also a perfect place to watch the sunset when the colours of the lake and the sky become even more vibrant and intense.

The snow-capped Cordillera Real is visible from most of the lake and forms a distinct border between the stark expanses of water and sky. Sometimes the vista is softened by a flock of flamingos strutting imperiously across the shallows of the lake. This incongruous smattering of pink brings some relief from the unyielding colours of Lake Titicaca.

Puno is the gateway city on the Peruvian side of Lake Titicaca. The train journey from Cuzco to Puno takes a day and passes through some beautiful high-altitude terrain. The town of Copacabana in Bolivia, on the southern half of the lake, can be reached from La Paz. The famous views of the snow-covered Bolivian Cordillera are best seen from the islands accessible from Copacabana: Isla del Sol and Isla de la Luna. Do not underestimate the effects of the altitude here, especially if you are planning strenuous activities such as hiking on the islands. The ferry that crosses the lake between Peru and Bolivia takes just 12 hours.

Island of Amantani, with the Bolivian cordillera in the background

Reeds at the edge of the Uros islands

Santorini
Greece

Church bell, Fira

Blue-domed church, Oia

Sitting in the peaceful town of Oia on the island of Santorini (known as Thira to the Greeks), watching the sun slip quietly into the sea, it is hard to imagine the colossal forces of nature that blew the island apart around 1550 BC.

This volcanic eruption is believed to have devastated an outpost of the advanced Minoan civilization, which had been established on the island before 2000 BC, leading to many theories that Santorini is in fact Plato's lost city of Atlantis.

The present-day island of Santorini is formed from the circular caldera of the volcano. The circle is incomplete in places and, flooded by the sea, forms a natural harbour so vast that visiting ferries and cruise ships are dwarfed by it.

A small island in the middle of the caldera is actually the centre of the volcano and can be reached by boat. You can even walk around its rocky 'moonscape' and stand next to the still-steaming mouth of the volcano that created Santorini in the first place. Like most smoking volcanoes, it seems to hold the threat of erupting at any

Town of Fira perched on top of soaring cliffs

time. (The last eruption happened in the 1920s and an earthquake devastated the island in 1956.)

The jagged walls of the caldera rise up to 300 metres above the sea. The highest cliffs are at Fira, the capital of Santorini, and the adjacent town of Firostefani, now all but swallowed up by Fira. These towns are built on the very rim of the caldera, overlooking the waters far below.

Each town has its own harbour at the foot of the cliffs, reachable by a zigzag path from the top. Fira now has a modern cable car, and it is only the tourists from cruise ships and ferries who make the long hike up. If you can't face walking, you can rent a donkey from one of the irascible old men who spend the day leading their mounts up and down the path. Come sunset, the donkeys leave Fira at a gallop, glad to be on their way home, and you have to take care not to be knocked over in the rush.

Santorini is renowned for its white-walled, blue-domed churches, which are often photographed against the dark blue waters of the

Aegean. In fact, there are so many churches on this island that you have to wonder who on earth goes to them. Is there some feud that prevents all the islanders attending the same one?

Many of the churches are still in use, and you will often see grey-bearded priests, dressed entirely in black, hurrying from church to church, presumably trying to find their flock in one of the numerous possible locations.

Cross on top of a church, Fira

Like so many other places Santorini has been comprehensively taken over by the tourist trade, and most of the fishermen's cottages have now been converted into hotels, restaurants or guest houses. Despite this, however, the island still retains much of its original character. Oia, especially, still has a sprinkling of locals living among all the tourist places, and outside some of the cottages, hung with

Small chapel, Firostefani

baskets of brightly coloured flowers, fishing nets await repair and scraggy cats doze in tiny front yards.

ⓘ

Santorini is easily reached by ferry, or internal flight on Olympic Airways, from Athens. There are even some direct flights from European airports during the summer season. Accommodation can be hard to find during the summer months, so it is advisable to book in advance. One of the best hotels in Fira is the Santorini Palace, which overlooks the caldera. The bus service around the island is fairly limited but there are taxis and car hire is quite easy. Most of the beaches are outside the main towns and, although the sand is volcanic black, they are ideal spots to while away the day.

Traditional houses in Oia

Traditional blue-domed church, Oia

Priest with an ancient bible outside the Asheton Maryam monastery

Lalibela
Ethiopia

Mystery and myth surround the creation of the carved stone churches of Lalibela in the remote highlands of Ethiopia. Some say that the churches were built by crusaders returning from the Holy Land, but Ethiopians believe that they were created with the help of angels by King Lalibela over 1000 years ago.

The most magnificent of the churches is Bet Giorgis, the House of Saint George, named after the patron saint of Ethiopia. Carved out of solid rock in the shape of a cross, the church is a structural marvel. Builders would first have created the 6-metre-deep courtyard to form the 'exterior' of the building, before carving the doors and windows into it, and then hollowing out the rock beyond to make the interior. The immensity of this task, and the precision it required, is almost inconceivable, especially bearing in mind that all the work was done by hand.

In all there are 11 carved churches at Lalibela, including Bet Medhane Alem (the House of Emmanuel) which, at 800 square

Bet Giorgis

metres, is the largest carved monolithic structure in the world. Its great bulk is supported by a total of 72 pillars, half of which are inside and half outside.

Although the churches would be evocative as deserted ruins, they are still in constant use and each has a resident priest who, with a little prompting, will bring out a church treasure to show you. Sometimes this might be an ancient Bible, perhaps 700 years old, handwritten in the ancient religious language of Ge'ez on goatskin pages. More usually, the priest will produce the church cross. In various intricate shapes, some crosses date back to the days of King Lalibela himself.

Looking down into the courtyard around Bet Giorgis

Bet Giorgis

Pilgrim reading an old bible

Pilgrims seem to come to Lalibela from all over Ethiopia, and can often be seen praying in the churches. There are also a number of semi-permanent ascetics, who stay in Lalibela praying and can be seen sitting around the churches reading well-worn bibles.

On 19 January Timkat (Epiphany) is celebrated at Lalibela. This is a tremendously colourful festival when the holy *tabots* (which are believed to be replicas of the Ark of the Covenant) are taken from each church and paraded through the town.

The official religion of Lalibela is Ethiopian Orthodox, a form of Christianity that the country adopted in the 4th century. This choice was freely made by the people, unlike in the rest of Africa where Christianization was the result of missionary work, centuries later.

Although synonymous in the West with famine and disaster, Ethiopia is steeped in ancient and biblical history. The Queen of Sheba is believed to have come from here, a native of the northern city of Aksum, at that time the centre of a great and powerful civilization. It was the break-up of the Aksumite Empire that caused King Lalibela to flee south and set up a new capital, where he built his churches.

Many Ethiopians believe that Haile Selassie, Emperor of Ethiopia from 1930 to 1974, could trace his lineage directly to the illegitimate

Pilgrim praying outside Bet Medhane Alem (the House of Emmanuel)

son of King Solomon and the Queen of Sheba. This son was said to have brought the Ark of the Covenant back to Ethiopia, and it is believed to reside in Aksum.

A worthwhile excursion from Lalibela is up to the Asheton Maryam monastery carved into the rock on a desolate, windswept plateau a couple of hours' walk from Lalibela. Here you can see a fascinating collection of paintings and relics, and also observe the harsh conditions in which many local people live.

ⓘ

Ethiopian Airlines flies from airports around the world to the Ethiopian capital, Addis Ababa and offers internal flights to Lalibela. (The alternative is a hard two-day drive.) It is also possible to get a flight pass on the so-called 'historic route' service that takes in Aksum, Bahar Dar, Gonder and Lalibela. Accommodation in Lalibela can be basic. One of the best hotels is the Roha, part of the government-run Ghion chain. Book in advance, especially during the Timkat celebrations. A ticket costing about $20 will get you into the site and is valid for the duration of your stay. A local guide is useful – especially to translate when you meet priests. Most hotels can provide guides, but make sure their English is up to the job.

Painted interior of a church at Lalibela

Pilgrim at Lalibela

Priest of Bet Giorgis

Hills in the Giant's Castle area

The Amphitheatre
Drakensberg, South Africa

Sunrise near Cathedral Peak

Stand by the edge of the 850-metre cliffs of the amphitheatre of the uKhahlamba-Drakensberg Park and you will be dwarfed. The cliffs are a massive horseshoe of rock, often filled with swirling clouds that appear to change their mood as you watch. Sometimes they fill the basin, making the view of a few seconds ago seem like a mirage. At other times they just disappear, revealing the valley below.

The cliffs of the amphitheatre drop vertically down to a green valley and offer commanding views of the Devil's Tooth rock formation. Part of the way along the upper rim of the amphitheatre the 'bridal veil' Tugela Falls spills 850 metres over the edge to form the source of the Tugela River.

Drakensberg is Afrikaans for 'dragon mountain' and uKhahlamba is Zulu for 'barrier of spears' – fitting names for the 320-km escarpment of harsh and jutting rock that forms the border between Lesotho and the Republic of South Africa.

At the top of the escarpment is a tableland plateau. In Lesotho, the 'Kingdom of the Sky', this is a unique and fragile habitat for wildlife and many rare plant species. In the beautiful alpine landscape of mountain streams and lush grasses are small wild flowers that have adapted to the climate, which can turn from fine and bright to cold and stormy in minutes. In fact, the plateau's great height means that the temperature there can be freezing while the parklands at the bottom can be warm and sunny.

The best way to reach the plateau is to drive to the Golden Gate Highlands National Park (a park within the Drakensberg area). From here there are two ways to reach the top of the escarpment: a two- to three-hour hike up a steep trail, or a climb up a notorious chain ladder. Whichever route you choose, it is wise to make a very early start as mists often sweep in during the late morning and can completely obscure the view.

View of Devil's Tooth from Golden Gate Highlands National Park

Hills in the Giant's Castle area dappled with shadow

Tucked away in numerous caves around the Drakensberg are some of the finest examples of rock art in Africa. In the Drakensberg area alone there are hundreds of sites with thousands of rock paintings. They were painted by the San people who used to roam over much of southern Africa but are now confined to a few pockets around the Kalahari Desert in Botswana. Diminutive in stature, they are often (erroneously) known as the Bushmen of the Kalahari. Their rock paintings, which are usually found in shelters or overhangs, record the life and history of the San people but, more importantly, are thought to have a spiritual significance as openings to the spirit world. The oldest paintings are about 25,000 years old and the most recent may be just 200 years old. Pigments were ground from iron oxides for the reds and yellows, manganese oxide or burnt bone for black and fine clay for white. The artists often painted over earlier images or added to existing ones.

A variety of terrains in the park are worth exploring, and you could also visit the Cathedral Peak and the Giant's Castle, the latter involving a five-day trek along the escarpment, or a day's drive.

The Drakensberg escarpment is about two hours' drive from Pietermaritzburg and a scenic five hours' drive from Johannesburg. The various locations and lodges along the escarpment are relatively close to one another as the crow flies but you should use the main roads. Do not be tempted to use more direct routes as these are rougher, carry very little traffic and have no services. The parks are administered by KwaZulu-Natal Wildlife, which runs a number of lodges and camps that make access to the various sections of the park easy. Getting to the top of the uKhahlamba escarpment involves an arduous hike from the Golden Gate Highlands National Park. You should make a very early start to avoid the late morning mists that often obscure the views.

View of Devil's Tooth from Golden Gate Highlands National Park

View below Giant's Castle; the Giant's Castle formation is in the background, towards the left

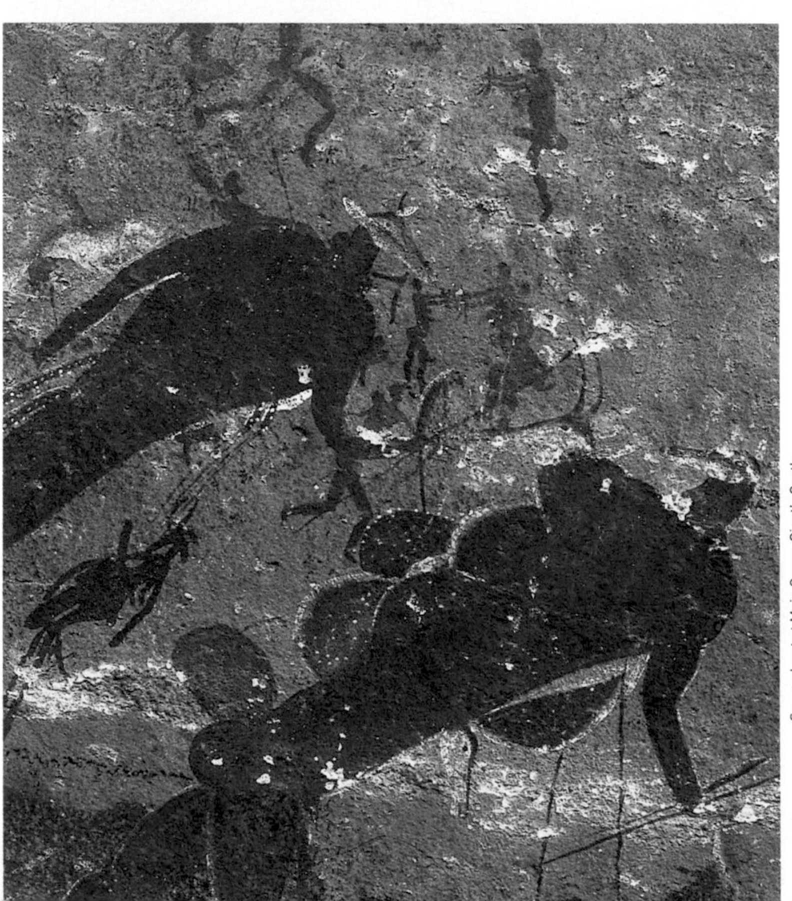

San rock art at Main Caves, Giant's Castle

Machu Picchu with Huayna Picchu in the background

Machu Picchu
Peru

Ruins seen from the summit of Machu Picchu peak

Everything about Machu Picchu makes you marvel that it ever came to exist. The lost city of the Incas is built on a saddle-shaped ridge slung between two giant peaks. Near-vertical slopes drop away on either side, down to a massive bend in the Urubamba River. What could have motivated the Incas to undertake such a construction at this remote location in the Andean cordillera?

Machu Picchu, built over 700 years ago and hidden by jungle since the 16th century, was rediscovered in 1911. It consists of about 200 buildings, which include dwellings and temples, a central plaza and a royal palace, all flanked by terraces for farming.

The stone for the buildings was mined from a quarry and shaped using bronze tools, then smoothed with sand in order to fit tightly together. No mortar was used in the construction. Even after many centuries of wear and tear, the precision is amazing; it would be impossible to slide a piece of paper between many of the blocks.

Machu Picchu is notable for the way that existing rock features were incorporated into the design. Inevitably, the craftsmanship on sacred buildings is the finest.

For spectacular views, make the steep climb up to Wayna Picchu, the mountain behind Machu Picchu. Alternatively, climb to the top of the less crowded Machu Picchu peak, which catches the first rays of the rising sun. Both mountains overlook the entire site, down to the river below, which puts the Incas' great achievement of construction into perspective.

The Incas worshipped the sun god Inti, so the summer solstice was the most important day in their calendar, and the Temple of the Sun their most important building. In fact, all their temples and

Royal Tomb, a cave under the Temple of the Sun

Double doorway

Sunrise over Machu Picchu

sacred sites were designed to mark solar and astrological events. A stone, Intihuatana ('Hitching Post of the Sun'), is the focus of a major religious site where a ritual was performed, in the shortening days before the winter solstice, to prevent the sun disappearing. Similar stones were at other Inca sites, but were damaged or destroyed by Spanish conquistadores. The one at Machu Picchu survived because the site was never discovered.

The population of Machu Picchu is believed to have numbered over a thousand, and the people were so distant from other settlements that they would have produced much of their own food. This accounts for the intricately terraced fields, which have survived remarkably intact thanks to the care and skill that went into their construction. Maize and potatoes were grown, and advanced irrigation techniques were used to ensure that rainwater didn't just run off down the hill to the Urubamba River far below.

No-one knows for sure why Machu Picchu was built. Some surmise that it was a royal or religious retreat for one of the Inca rulers. Certainly its remote location and altitude of nearly 2500

Dwellings near the Temple of the Sun

Terraces below the Intihuatana

metres would seem to rule out any trade or military function. Whatever its use, the obvious effort that went into its construction indicates that it was considered important and held in high regard by those who created it.

ⓘ

All trips to Machu Picchu begin and end in Cuzco. The train journey from Cuzco to Aguas Calientes, the town in the river valley below the ruins, takes four hours. Buses go to and from the town to the ruins from 6 a.m. until 5.30 p.m. The trains from Cuzco arrive mid-morning and leave late in the afternoon, so the least crowded times at the ruins are the beginning and the end of each day. The fitter and more adventurous can take the three-day Inca Trail to reach Machu Picchu. There is plenty of accommodation in Aguas Calientes. However, the best place to stay for access and proximity to the ruins is the Machu Picchu Sanctuary Lodge, an Orient Express Hotel. It is the only hotel next to the ruins and a stay there is a unique experience.

Dwellings on eastern side of the site

Pilgrims walking the Nangkhor

The Potala Palace seen from the roof of the Jokhang

Lhasa
Tibet

It is not just the altitude that makes Lhasa a dizzying experience, although at nearly 4300 metres you get only get 65 per cent of the oxygen you would get in each breath at sea level. That light-headed feeling comes in part from the deep spirituality of the place, and from the heady mix of juniper smoke and the ever-present smell of yak butter.

Expansion and modernization characterize the Chinese part of the city, but the old Tibetan quarter still has an ethereal, almost medieval atmosphere, especially in the network of small streets that surrounds the Jokhang Temple. The centre of Tibetan Buddhism, the Jokhang was completed in AD 647, although it has been continually restored and expanded ever since – most recently following damage caused when the Chinese brought their Cultural Revolution to Tibet.

There are several distinct pilgrimage circuits around the Jokhang. The outer one, called the Lingkhor, runs around the entire city. The Barkhor, or middle route, is a circular road that runs round the outside of the temple. Throughout the day and long into the night pilgrims process in a constant stream – always clockwise – around the Barkhor. Fearsome-looking Khambas (people from the eastern

Pilgrim with prayer beads

highlands), notable for the red threads braided into their hair, mingle with scarlet-robed monks and Golok nomads who wear huge sheepskin coats. Most spin prayer wheels as they walk, or mumble prayers which they keep count of on long strings of beads. Some stroll and chat, while others display penitence by repeatedly prostrating themselves along the route. Protected by leather aprons and with wooden paddles on their hands, they throw themselves across the paving flags, making a skittering sound that echoes around the Barkhor.

In the square in front of the Jokhang are two large braziers where pilgrims burn offerings of juniper: its pungent fragrance will for ever remind you of Lhasa. Also here is a small market, selling everything that the pilgrims might need for their devotions: yak butter, prayer flags, prayer wheels and, of course, fresh juniper.

Pilgrims taking a break outside the Jokhang

Woman on the pilgrimage circuit around the Potala

Within the main porch of the temple are two giant prayer wheels, kept in constant motion by the streams of pilgrims. On the patio in front, pilgrims of all ages prostrate themselves time and again in a repetitive ritual, seemingly inured to the discomfort.

Yak-butter lamps in the 1350-year-old Jokhang Temple

Inside the Jokhang, a double row of prayer wheels skirts the outside of the main prayer hall. This inner pilgrimage route is called the Nangkhor, and pilgrims walking around it attempt to spin each of the prayer wheels by hand to release their prayers up into the sky.

Inside the dark main hall of the Jokhang the air is heavy with the smell of yak-butter lamps, and the occasional low, rhythmic chanting of monks imparts a hallowed atmosphere that threatens to overwhelm the emotions. Pilgrims walk round the outside of the main hall – the centre being the exclusive preserve of monks, statues of former abbots and a giant golden Buddha image – past a number of small shrines and statues.

Towering above the whole city of Lhasa is the Potala Palace. The former home of the Dalai Lama, the spiritual leader of Tibetan

Pilgrim on the Barkhor

Gilded roof of the Jokhang

Buddhism, it is now little more than a museum. I had feelings of both guilt and sadness as I walked through the private quarters, realizing that the Dalai Lama, rather than I, should have been there. Once situated on the outskirts of Lhasa, the Potala is now somewhat isolated in the middle of the modern part of the city. Around the base there is another pilgrimage route of prayer wheels which, like the Barkhor, is in constant use.

The Dalai Lama, who fled Tibet in 1959, following the Chinese invasion in the early 1950s, has recently stated that he never expects Tibet to be liberated. While Tibetans enjoy more religious freedom than they originally did under the Chinese, pictures of the Dalai Lama are still banned and any dissent is strongly suppressed. Migration from China means that Tibetans are now in a minority in their own country, so even if there were to be a referendum on the nation's future it would probably preserve the status quo.

ⓘ

Tibet is a politically sensitive area, so the rules on visiting are subject to change without notice. You will need a special permit as well as a Chinese visa. The easiest way there is to take a tour from either Kathmandu or the city of Chengdu in China, although travellers from Nepal are often unable to change the duration of their permit once they arrive. Travellers from Chengdu can change the date of their return flight and effectively stay in Lhasa for the duration of their visa. Tours from both places can be arranged with other travellers in a couple of days. At the time of writing (2003) it is possible to travel independently from Chengdu only. Shigatse Travels, a travel agency based in Lhasa, can help and advise with arrangements. Most of the cheaper accommodation is in the Tibetan quarter. Many travellers feel that they should support Tibetan, rather than Chinese-run, businesses and are prepared to sacrifice comfort for atmosphere.

Entrance to the main prayer hall of the Jokhang

Khamba women on the Barkhor with the Potala Palace behind

The bridge at the eastern end of the water-lily pond

Monet's Garden

Giverny, France

Monet's house

For anyone with even a passing knowledge of the work of Claude Monet (1840–1926), his gardens at Giverny in Normandy, France, will be instantly familiar. The tranquil pond of water lilies inspired some of the greatest paintings of the 19th century.

Monet first saw Giverny from a train window. He moved there in 1883 and started to create the gardens, which he came to regard as his greatest achievement. They are places of light and shadow, where subtle reflections of foliage and flowers in the cool green waters are fleetingly transformed by the fluctuating light of the changeable Normandy weather.

The gardens, intersected by many small gravel paths, slope gently down to the lily pond, which is surprisingly small but very atmospheric. A path skirts their perimeter, offering a range of views and variations in light as you walk along it. Some of the views are open, others punctuated by weeping willows.

Monet's house at Giverny is large and rustic, and visitors can walk around it and look out on to the views that inspired him so much. He watched the colours gradually change as the seasons passed and woke up each morning to look at them from his bedroom window.

The largest of the garden paths – the Grande Allée – leads from the house to the Japanese bridge, well known from Monet's numerous depictions of it. The gardens are now divided by a road, but both parts are connected by a tunnel.

Since his earliest days as a painter, Monet worked in the open air rather than a studio. He believed in trying to 'capture the moment' in his paintings, which meant that he had to work fast. This technique created an impression of the subject matter, rather than a detailed description, and led to its exponents being called 'Impressionists'.

A painter at the water-lily pond

The water-lily pond

During his time at Giverny Monet was often visited by his artistic contemporaries, including Cézanne, Renoir, Matisse and Pissarro, few of whom enjoyed recognition during their lifetimes. It is now staggering to imagine so much talent gathered in one small place. Monet died at Giverny in 1926 at the age of 86.

Monet's gardens in the village of Giverny are 65 km north-west of Paris, off the A13 motorway. The nearest English Channel ferry ports are Le Havre and Dieppe. Vernon, 8 km from the A13 and 5 km from Giverny, is the nearest useful town and has good accommodation and restaurants. The gardens get extremely crowded in the middle of the day, so aim to arrive as early as possible. They are open daily except Mondays (to allow select artists to paint) from 9.30 a.m. to 6 p.m. from 1 April to 1 November. The most popular months to visit are July and August, when the water lilies flower. Accommodation in Giverny itself is limited. A website (www.giverny.org) has information about where to stay, transport and flowering times.

Monet's bedroom

Water lily

Poppy seed heads

Uluru
Australia

Uluru at sunset (Uluru-Kata Tjuta National Park is a World Heritage area)

From whatever angle you look at it, Uluru (commonly known as Ayers Rock) dominates the surrounding landscape. Seen from afar, it is the only feature that breaks an otherwise flat horizon, while up close – such as on the approach road from the cultural centre – it looms above you, completely filling your vehicle's windscreen.

Uluru is the largest monolith (single piece of rock) in the world. Composed of sandstone, which is normally grey, it has become red through a process of oxidization (in effect, rusting).

As you get closer to Uluru, its brooding mass yields up a wealth of detail. Follow the walk that skirts the base of the rock and you will see great flutes that spawn torrential waterfalls when it rains, which

The western side of Uluru

Muṯitjulu waterhole

is quite often despite the parched landscape round about. Elsewhere are caves and crevices eroded into the rock – many of which have been woven into Aboriginal creation tales – and right up close the rock is stippled and textured in a variety of ways.

Aṉangu (local Aboriginal people) are the Traditional Owners of Uluṟu, which has great cultural significance to them. Two of the walks on the rock illustrate Aboriginal respect for natural places, and pass by apparently insignificant features in the landscape that they hold deeply sacred.

The Muṯitjulu Walk takes you through an area that has been inhabited by Aboriginal people for thousands of years to the Muṯitjulu waterhole. Various features along this walk are said to have resulted from a great fight between two ancestral snakes, Kuniya and Liru.

The Mala Walk takes you around some of the places used by the Mala (hare-wallaby) people for a religious ceremony (Inma), which involved their menfolk climbing to the top of Uluṟu. At one time, following a route to the top was a 'must' for tourists. Though many still do, this is now discouraged because it causes offence to Aṉangu.

Uluṟu from the south

The southern side of Uluṟu near Muṯitjulu Walk (Uluṟu-Kata Tjuṯa National Park is a World Heritage area)

While no-one actually prevents you from climbing, Anangu request that you don't do it.

Balancing the needs of Anangu and the tourists shows the difficulties of resolving the differences between a culture that pretty much values and reveres everything with a culture that seems to revere almost nothing.

Some 45 km away from Uluru lie the domed peaks of Kata Tjuta (the Olgas). Some of these are even taller than Uluru and are also held sacred by Anangu. Like Uluru, the peaks are spectacular at sunrise and sunset, and you should aim to spend at least a day exploring them and walking the sacred Valley of the Winds.

The images in this book have all been taken under the strict rules governing commercial photography in the Uluru-Kata Tjuta National Park, which are intended to prevent pictures of sacred sites being published and offending Anangu. This does, however, effectively rule out photographing almost half the site, including views of the sunrise when Uluru glows iridescent orange – a phenomenon that on its own makes a visit worthwhile.

Uluru seen from Kata Tjuta

Kata Tjuṯa (Uluṟu-Kata Tjuṯa National Park is a World Heritage area)

ⓘ

Connellan Airport is just a few kilometres from the small town of Yulara (Ayers Rock Resort). The only airline that flies there is Qantas and to get reasonable fares you should book well in advance. There are organized tours around the park, but hiring a car at the airport is hardly more expensive, even for a single traveller – though you should book in advance. A range of accommodation is available at Yulara, from a campsite to the new luxury Longitude 131° complex, and the town has a number of restaurants and shops. It is all run as a monopoly by one company so don't expect too much competition. The entrance fee gives access to the park for up to three days.

Uluṟu in the setting sun

Uluṟu silhouetted at sunrise

Dome and minaret of Bibi Khanum Mosque

Samarkand
Uzbekistan

Dome of Tillya Kari Madrasa

The great city of Samarkand lies on the so-called Silk Road, the ancient trading route that led from China through the Middle East and into Europe. The city grew rich through trade, and constructed some of the finest buildings to be found in the Islamic world.

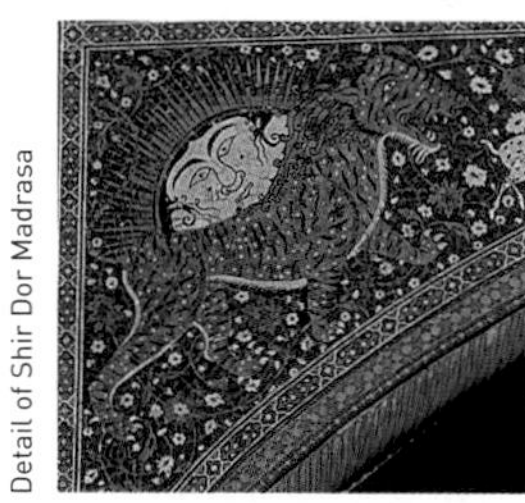
Detail of Shir Dor Madrasa

Its strategic position has led Samarkand to be conquered and sacked many times throughout its long and bloody history. The first settlement there was constructed in the 6th century BC and was first conquered by Alexander the Great some 200 years later. As trade routes built up over the next few hundred years, the city grew in power and wealth despite being captured by both the Turks and Hun tribes. Indeed, it continued to flourish, as recorded by the Buddhist monk and traveller Xuan Zang when he arrived there in AD 630.

At this time Samarkand followed the Zoroastrian religion of Persia, but the city fell to Islam when Qutaiba ibn Muslim invaded it in 712. This was the start of the first great period of Islamic development, which was curtailed at the beginning of the 13th century when the city was sacked by the Mongols of Genghis Khan, who slaughtered much of the population.

By the time another great traveller, Marco Polo, arrived at the end of the 13th century the city had been rebuilt, and he sang its praises. The Uzbek national hero, Tamerlane, chose it as the capital of the relatively small region of Transoxiana in 1370 and then proceeded to

expand his empire until it reached as far as India and Syria. He was responsible for several great buildings, most notably the Bibi Khanum Mosque. His grandson, Uleg Beg, ruled the city until it fell to nomadic Uzbeks. Uleg Beg's great-grandson, Babur, retook the city in 1512 but was later driven out to India where he founded the Mogul Empire. This was the end of a golden era. Ravaged by earthquakes, looting and changing trade routes, Samarkand eventually succumbed to the Bolsheviks and became part of the Soviet Union in 1924.

The ancient centre of Samarkand is the Registan. This square, one of the finest in Asia, is surrounded on three sides by madrasas, or Islamic colleges. Uleg Beg constructed the square and the first madrasa in the 15th century. The fronts of the madrasas are towering façades that lead into ornate courtyards ringed with two storeys of small cells where the religious students lived and studied.

Ironically, for all their anti-religious sentiment and public denigration of Islam, it was the Soviets who restored much of the Registan, straightening precarious minarets and reconstructing the characteristic turquoise-tiled domes. These still shine with an

Detail of Bibi Khanum Mosque

Shir Dor Madrasa

Cell where Islamic students would study

Shir Dor Madrasa

Shir Dor Madrasa

iridescence that perhaps suggests the cool water that is often lacking in this dry land.

Islam forbids the representation of living things, so each of the madrasas is covered with ornate patterns (none symmetrical, as this too is forbidden), intricate Kufic quotations from the Koran and inscriptions extolling the magnificence of the buildings. Bizarrely, though, the Shir Dor Madrasa on the eastern side of the square has two representations of lions in front of suns with shining human faces. This apparent heresy is attributed in part to the ego of the governor who built the madrasa and also to the continued influence of the Persian Zoroastrians who revered the power of the sun.

The Uleg Beg and Shir Dor madrasas are flanked by minarets, used more for decoration than for calling the faithful to prayer as the buildings were primarily colleges rather than mosques. In Tamerlane's day, however, they were also used for public executions: a favourite way of dealing with criminals was to throw them from the top in a sack.

For a couple of dollars, one of the uniformed guards might let you climb the crumbling steps to the top of the north minaret at Ulug Beg Madrasa for one of the most impressive views across the city to the Bibi Khanum Mosque. Tamerlane constructed this vast mosque from the finest materials after sacking the city of Delhi in 1398.

In the adjacent bazaar life and trade continue much as they did when the Silk Road brought spices, gold and fabrics to be traded here. You can still buy the round hats worn by many of Uzbekistan's Muslims, decorated flat breads and exotic spices that hark back to the days when peppercorns and saffron were more valuable than gold.

Detail of Registan Square

ⓘ

Samarkand is easily reached by bus or air from the capital Tashkent. Several airlines fly to Tashkent, including British Mediterranean. Uzbekistan Air has a remarkably modern fleet and a fairly good worldwide network. Buying a domestic ticket overseas can be difficult, so you will probably find it easier to attach it to your international flight. Hotel accommodation is plentiful in Samarkand, including the four-star Hotel Presidential Palace.

Shir Dor Madrasa

Ngorongoro Crater

Tanzania

Common zebra Opposite: Looking down into the caldera

The Ngorongoro Crater feels so cut off from the outside world that you almost expect to see long-extinct dinosaurs, not just teeming wildlife, roaming within its steep, forbidding walls. Veined by the forces that created them, these walls rise 600 metres above the flat floor.

Ngorongoro is actually a caldera, not a crater, formed when a volcano collapsed millions of years ago. At more than 20 km across, it is the largest complete, unflooded caldera in the world. As you look down from the rim you could be forgiven for thinking that Ngorongoro is completely deserted and rumours of its bounty exaggerated. But closer inspection through binoculars reveals signs of life. Those ant-like dots moving slowly across the caldera floor are actually bristling Cape buffalo, arguably the most dangerous animal in Africa. Only then does the true scale of the caldera become apparent.

Ngorongoro is so large that it has its own distinct weather patterns. Mist and cloud often coat the densely forested flanks of the

caldera, sometimes spilling over the edge. Occasionally, these clouds are so dense that they fill the bowl of the caldera. Leaving the comfort of your lodge and journeying down to the caldera floor in these conditions can become something of a leap of faith. The weather can be quite localized. It can be cloudy, even raining, on one side while the other side is bathed in bright sunshine.

Clouds rearing up over the walls of the caldera

For all the beauty and majesty of Ngorongoro, it is the wildlife that is the greatest draw. The walls act as both refuge and restraint, trapping and protecting a surprising amount of big game. The caldera is home to some 30 black rhino – the largest concentration of the species left on the continent. In the dry season they can be remarkably difficult to spot, as they spend much of the day asleep in the long grass; but when the grass is short and green they virtually litter the caldera floor, bringing back memories of a bygone age when they used to stomp and snort their bad-tempered way across the whole of Africa.

Ngorongoro is also famous for its lion population, much filmed for television documentaries, but apparently chronically inbred. The isolation of the caldera prevents fresh blood from wandering in from the nearby Serengeti.

In the middle of the caldera lies Lake Magadi, a vast soda lake frequented by flamingos. The population fluctuates from a few

Wildebeest on the caldera floor

Female ostrich on the caldera floor

thousand to literally hundreds of thousands in June, when the flamingos flock back from their migration to the Great Rift Valley.

Most common African wildlife is found in the caldera, with the notable exception of giraffe which find the walls too steep. Most of the animals are permanent residents, although elephants and buffalo are often to be found feeding on the upper rim, especially at night.

The caldera officially opens just after dawn. The tracks on the north rim are vertiginous, requiring a four-wheel-drive vehicle. The track on the south rim, servicing the Sopa Lodge, is much less steep, allowing quicker and safer access to the caldera floor.

Looking down from the caldera rim

Wildebeest

Don't be surprised if you see Masai *morani* (warriors) bringing cattle down into the caldera. Although the Masai often come here to make money by posing for tourist photographs, they also have grazing and watering rights for their cattle. If you wonder at the wisdom of bringing a potential food source into lion territory, you will be told that after generations of experience the lions have a healthy fear of the Masai, and tend to disappear as soon as they arrive – much to the chagrin of the safari guides.

ⓘ

The Ngorongoro Crater is about six hours' drive from Arusha in northern Tanzania. You can fly to Arusha from Dar es Salaam or Zanzibar with Air Excel. Accommodation can be found in lodges overlooking the caldera. Most are on the relatively crowded north side but Sopa Lodge, which offers fine views of the sunset and uses the much safer access road, stands in splendid isolation on the south side. Safari guides can be hired from Abercrombie & Kent, the oldest established travel company in Africa. For the full safari experience you could combine Ngorongoro with the nearby Lake Manyara National Park, or even the world-famous Serengeti National Park.

Elephants on the caldera floor

Makalu

Himalayas, Nepal

High in the Himalayas, amid mighty peaks encrusted with glaciers, is Makalu, the fifth-highest mountain in the world. Although less well known than other peaks in the region, notably Everest and the Annapurna range, Makalu has arguably the most stunning scenery. Set in the remote Makalu Barun National Park, it has the added advantage of being away from current centres of political unrest.

Like many of the peaks in the Himalayas, Makalu is considered a holy mountain. Its name is said to be derived from the Sanskrit word 'Mahakala', the personification of death and rebirth, which, for Tibetan Buddhists, represents the power of the Lord Buddha's protection. The mountain is believed to be the kingdom of Mahakala.

The Himalayas are built on a massive scale, and there is little to prepare you for their immensity and beauty. But it is not a stationary beauty. Distant avalanches can occasionally be heard, thundering like

View of Everest from the glaciers at the foot of Makalu

Opposite: Lake scene on the Makalu trek

Trail through a farm near the Arun River valley

express trains, and the mountains appear to alter in shape, colour and mood as the light and cloud formations change throughout the day. This is a transfixing sight that you can sit and watch for hours. Sometimes whole sections will be illuminated by the golden afternoon light, casting great shadows into valleys and crevasses. At other times vast swathes of mountains will turn blue or be completely obscured by swirling clouds.

The air is so clear at this height that it is always possible to make out the shape of the snow-capped peaks, and you can almost read by the light of the stars that fill the night sky.

To visit the beautiful and remote Makalu takes both time and effort, as the trek is not easy and takes nine days from the airstrip at Tumlingtar. Much of the trek is done at altitude, which is debilitating until you become acclimatized.

The trek takes you over many passes, through verdant farmland and past many steeply terraced hillsides. *Khambas* (farms) within just a few hours of the base camp remind you that people actually live

Makalu peak

Mountain seen from Makalu base camp

High mountain lake on the Makalu trek

Makalu peak

in this harsh environment – a humbling thought when you grow weary of the regular downpours that leave the paths littered with leeches. However, along these ancient and well-travelled routes are a number of tea shops and it is easy to meet and talk to the local farmers and porters over a refreshing cup of chai (tea).

From the Makalu region you should be able to see four of the five highest mountains in the world: Everest (8848 metres), Kangchenjunga (8586 metres), Lhotse (8516 metres) and, of course, Makalu itself (8463 metres). (The world's second-highest peak is K2 on the Pakistan border.)

If you have the energy you could trek to the Everest base camp which lies just west of Makalu. It is also possible to follow the

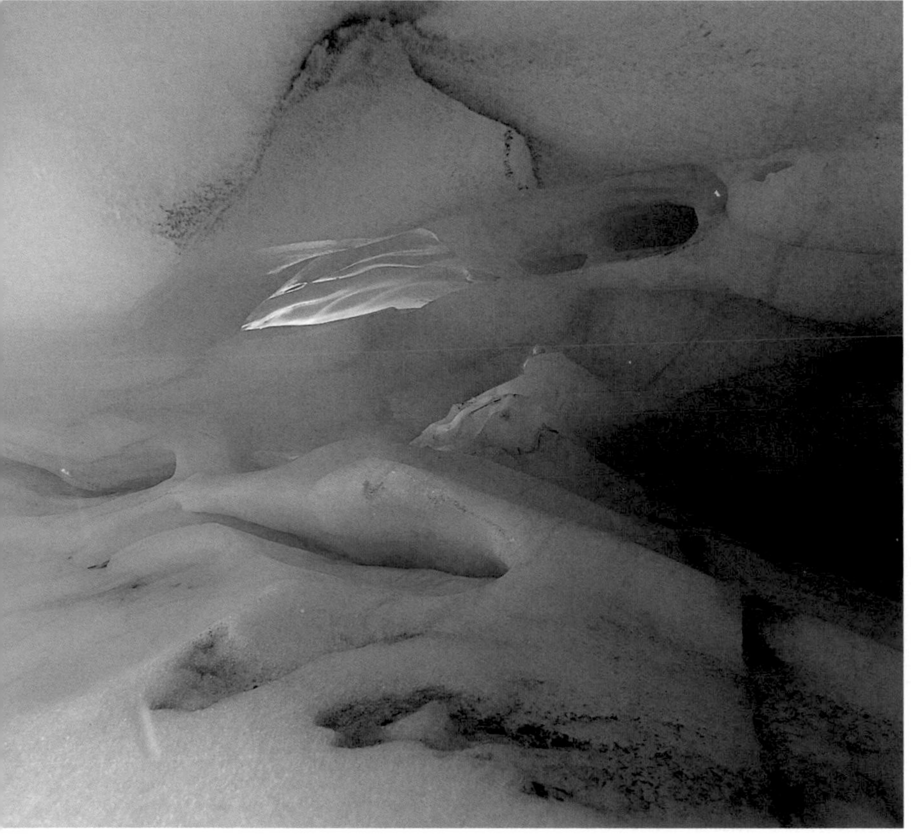

Glacial ice

View from the glaciers at the foot of Makalu

standard Everest trek back to Lukla and then catch a flight back to Kathmandu. Although it follows a much more well-trodden route and doesn't enjoy the quiet solitude of the direct route to Makalu, it does at least avoid trekking back the way you have come.

ⓘ

The trek to Makalu starts from the airstrip at Tumlingtar, which can be reached from the Nepalese capital, Kathmandu. From here it is an arduous nine-day trek to the mountain and, of course, nine days back again. Unless you are an experienced trekker you would be wise to organize this with a local trekking company in Kathmandu and take a guide with you. Nepal is currently suffering from a Maoist insurgency and you should make yourself aware of local conditions before undertaking the trek. The best times to trek are April and May, and late September through October.

Yellowstone National Park
USA

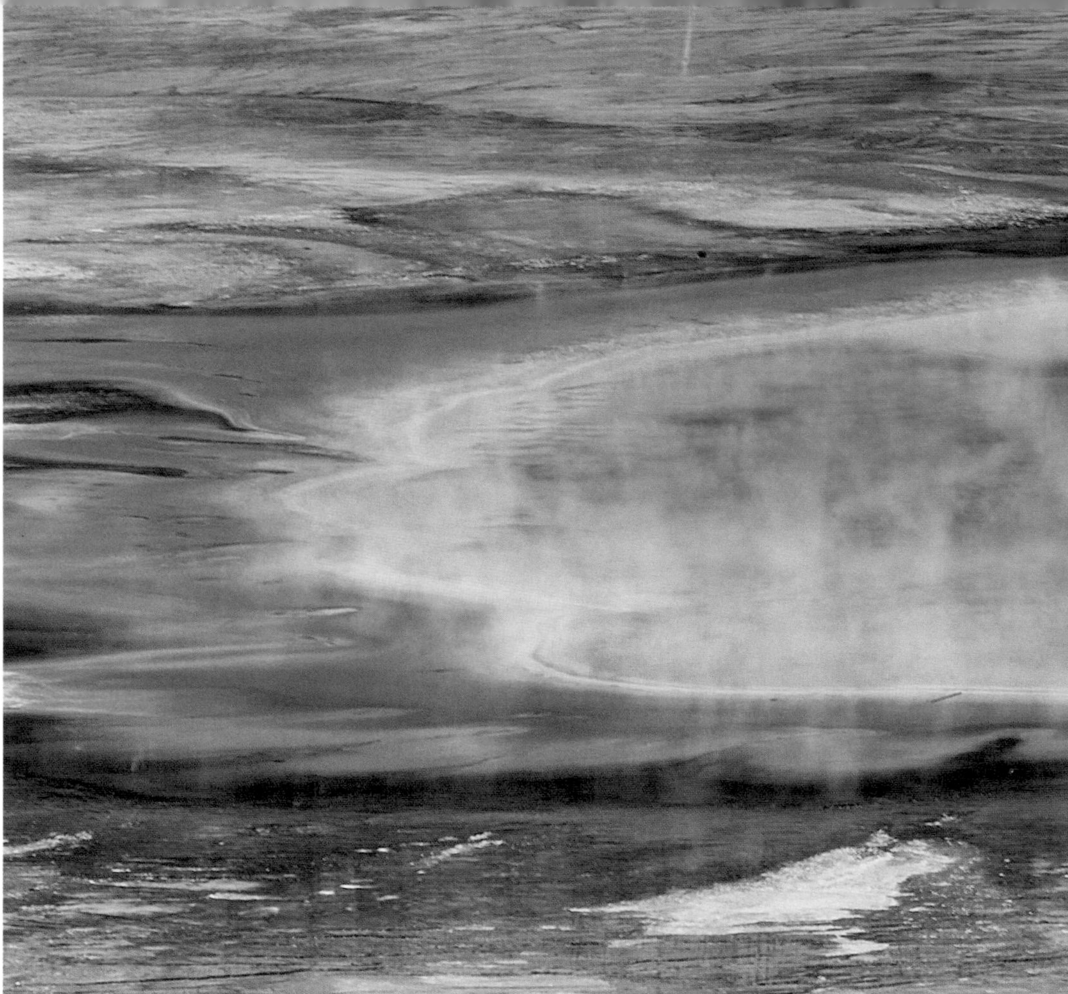

Steam swirls above Grand Prismatic Spring

In the centre of one of the world's largest-known volcanic calderas, Yellowstone National Park is a bubbling, hissing, surreal landscape teeming with iconic North American wildlife. From sweeping plains, high mountains and deep canyons to boiling rivers, explosive geysers and thundering waterfalls, its geographical variety is perhaps without equal – and its extensive network of trails, for both day walks and longer backcountry trips, make it a hiking wonderland.

Established in 1872, following several exploratory expeditions and lobbying of Congress, Yellowstone was the world's first national park and is more popular now than at any stage in its history, with around three million visitors a year. Thankfully, most of these don't venture far, if at all, from their cars, which makes walking the perfect way to explore, and get a feel for, the truly wild Yellowstone.

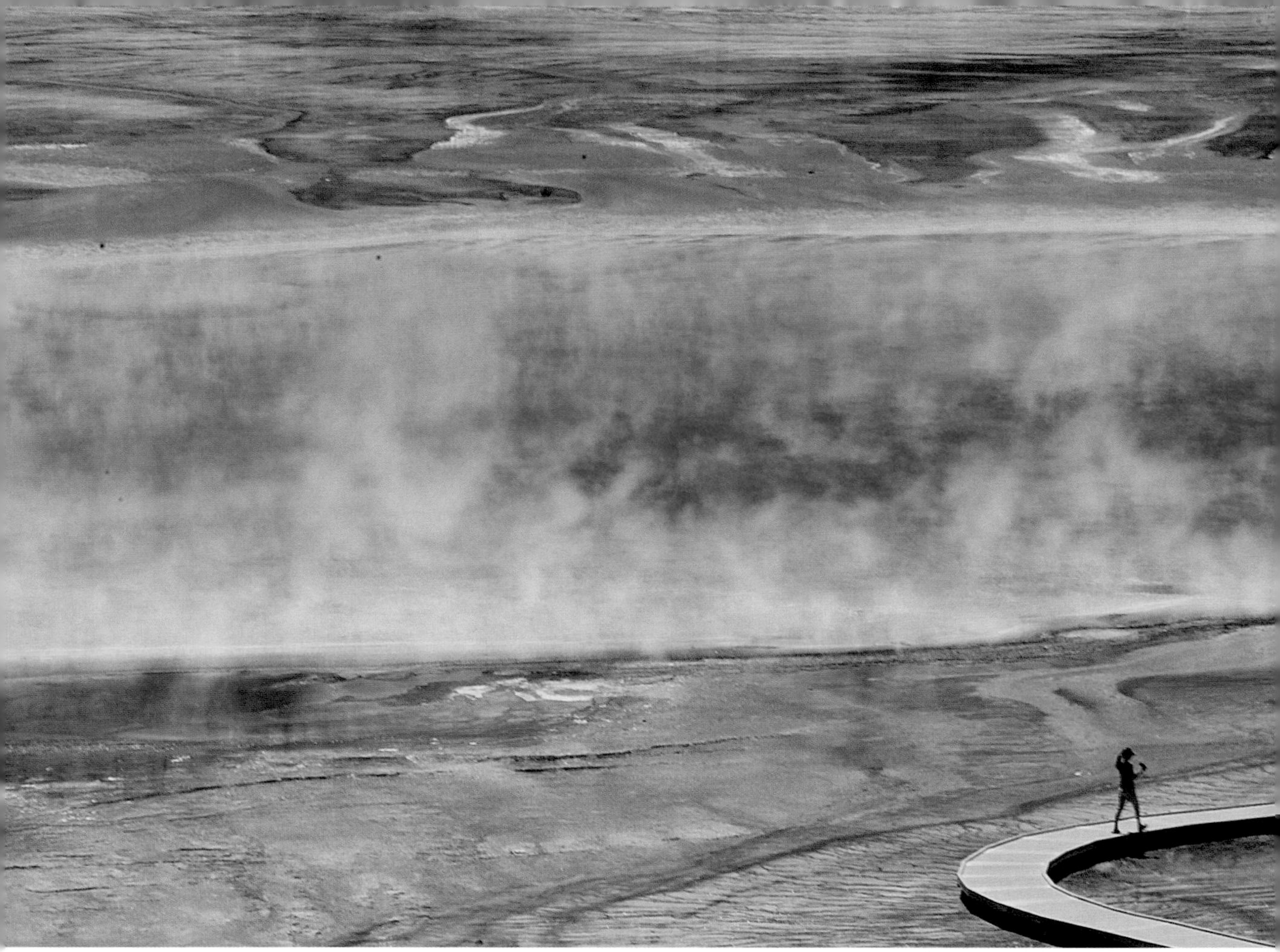

Throughout geological history there have been three major eruptions in the Yellowstone region; the most recent was 600,000 years ago and created the 72 km by 48 km caldera. These cataclysmic events were powered by the same heat and energy that today fuel over 300 geysers inside the park – two-thirds of all those on the planet – as well as numerous hot springs, mud pots and other geothermal features.

A gentle introduction, especially if you enter Yellowstone from the north entrance at Gardiner, is to take a walk around the Mammoth Hot Springs area. One of the park's multi-tiered boardwalks – common features on its more accessible trails, these reduce environmental impact and allow access to otherwise dangerous geothermal areas – winds its way up through an extravagant cascade of brilliant white, travertine terraces and steaming, thermal springs.

On the trail to Fairy Falls

Rainbow at Upper Falls on Yellowstone river

Bison are a common sight around Yellowstone

One of the most dramatic features in the park is the Grand Canyon of Yellowstone – a vertiginous, 366-metre-deep, 32-km-long fissure, carved largely by the Yellowstone river and otherwise by glacial action. The South Rim Trail makes for an exciting and relatively easy half-day hike and gives sensational views of the canyon's two pounding waterfalls: Upper Falls and Lower Falls. The path at first weaves its way through open forest. As it nears the Upper Falls there are viewpoints where, on a sunny afternoon, rainbows can be seen dancing across the plumes of spray thrown out from the cascade.

If you are reasonably fit, a side trip, Uncle Tom's Trail, will take you down an almost vertical set of 328 steps into the base of the canyon for incomparable close-up views of the Upper Falls. The testing return ascent is definitely one to take slowly. From the top of the steps, the main trail continues to Artist Point. This is the most famous place to view the canyon and the Lower Falls, a thunderous torrent that plunges 94 metres through a V-shaped cleft into the canyon. It is a lost world, where lone trees cling for life to the cliff face and the steaming azure and emerald river glows in the late afternoon with reflected light from the golden walls.

If you venture further south in the park, there will probably be encounters with bison and elk, especially around Firehole river and Geyser Basin where flatlands prevail. In the Midway Geyser Basin, another excellent and relatively easy half-day trail passes the outrageously coloured Grand Prismatic Spring en route to Fairy Falls, an enchanting, wispy cascade near the head of Fairy Creek. Soon after the start of the walk the spring comes into sight – a dense curtain of pink and blue steam rising on the horizon. Surrounded by blindingly white flats dotted with skeletal trees, Grand Prismatic is the third-largest hot spring in the world. It is an experience to see it from the ground, but to see it at its most spectacular it is necessary to work a little. Along the trail there is a series of small hillocks with indistinct, steep paths that take you up for a staggering aerial view of

Boiling pool in Firehole river basin

Desolate landscape at Mammoth Hot Springs

Boardwalks allow access on to fragile areas at Mammoth Hot Springs

the blue waters and the brilliant green, yellow, orange and rust-red fringes of the spring – colours created by bacteria growth.

Beyond the spring, the trail to Fairy Falls narrows and passes through young lodgepole pines overshadowed by legions of towering charred, black trunks. This area was badly damaged in 1988 during extensive wild fires that destroyed over one-third of the park. Tucked away in a scalloped alcove of grey rock, Fairy Falls tumbles serenely from the lip of the Madison Plateau. In free fall for much of its 60-metre descent, it eventually splashes gracefully on to darker rocks below, spreading across them into countless ephemeral rivulets.

Previous pages: Grand Prismatic Spring

Dusk over Geyser Basin

A more remote geyser experience than the park's perennial favourite, Old Faithful, can be found along the road to West Thumb. The trail to Lone Star Geyser, an 8-km return hike, passes through lush, old-growth forest, untouched by the 1988 fires, and alongside the upper reaches of the tranquil Firehole river. It is a beautiful and easy walk, starting at Kepler Cascades, and if you time it right you may see the geyser in action. Every few hours it erupts into a 14-metre-high jet of boiling water. And here, unlike at Old Faithful, the chances are you will be alone, seeing the wild heart of Yellowstone.

ⓘ

In Yellowstone it is necessary to be alert for the presence of bears and other wildlife, such as bison and elk. Full guidelines are available at the ranger stations. Much of the park is accessible only from June to September, as snow covers the ground and roads for the rest of the year. Backcountry trails require permits to access and take several days to hike; they are very committing and require experience. If you only have a few days in the park, the day-hike trails, which don't require permits, are the best way to sample Yellowstone's various features. Accommodation inside the park is very limited and usually booked up many months in advance. There are more options in the towns around the four park entrances.

Evening light at Grand Prismatic Spring

Sakura at Nanzen-ji Temple

There is no better way to delve into the ancient, eastern spirit of Kyoto, Japan's majestic, imperial capital, than strolling around the city's exquisite Buddhist temples and shrines. If you venture there during springtime, you may catch the very brief sakura season when the cherry-blossom trees bloom, lining the footpaths with an extravaganza of ephemeral floral beauty.

Situated about 370 km southwest of Tokyo on the island of Honshu, in a narrow waist of land between the Sea of Japan and the Pacific Ocean, Kyoto – originally known as Heiankyo, or 'capital of peace' – is extraordinarily well preserved. For over 1000 years, from the end of the eighth century, it was the imperial, religious and intellectual capital of Japan. Although it lost its political power to Tokyo in 1868, it has remained a major centre and almost 2000 Buddhist temples and Shinto shrines testify to its continuing role at the heart of Japanese religion.

Temples of Kyoto

Japan

Osawanoike Pond at Daikaku-ji Temple

The temple walks are spread around the cardinal points of the compass, and it is worth spending a day or two exploring each direction. In the east lies one of the city's most popular walking trails, the Philosopher's Path, which runs from Ginkaku-ji Temple to Nanzen-ji Temple along a beautiful waterway lined with cherry-blossom trees. The path, named for the renowned Kyoto philosopher Nishida Kitarô, who used to frequent it, is a hugely popular place to witness the ethereal, white and pink sakura blossoms making their brief appearance. Within two weeks at most, the spring rains and wind send the delicate flowers falling gently to the ground.

Zen garden at Ginkaku-ji Temple

Cherry blossom on the Philosopher's Path

The Zen temple of Ginkaku-ji was originally built as a villa by the Muromachi shogun Ashikaga Yoshimasa in 1482. Twirled around a small stream and several ponds at the foot of a wooded, mossy hill, the temple complex has a large Zen garden of carefully swept, light grey stones, arranged in dynamic stripes, and a perfectly sculpted mound. Nanzen-ji Temple, at the path's southern end, is entered through a mammoth Sanmon gate. Established in 1291 by the emperor Kameyama, it is the headquarters of the Rinzai school of Zen and one of the most important Zen Buddhist temples in the world. With its stunning location, at the base of the forested Higashiyama Hills, it is a

Temple slippers at Fushimi Inari Taisha shrine

Gravel mound at Ginkaku-ji Temple

fitting finale to the Philosopher's Path. The vast and peaceful Maruyama Park, where the cherry-blossom displays are exceptional, is a short stroll southwest from Nanzen-ji.

A five-minute train ride to the south of Kyoto takes you to one of the city's most iconic shrines, Fushimi Inari Taisha; a wonderful place to spend half a day exploring the unique trails around the hillside grounds. The shrine boasts thousands of torii gates, which are erected so close together that they create surreal, brilliant orange and vermilion tunnels around the footpaths. Inari is the Shinto god of rice and the numerous fox figures around the site represent his messengers. Relatively few people venture out on to the paths furthest from the main shrine, where a tree-shrouded lake and bamboo trees await.

Some of Kyoto's most enchanting temples are to the west of the city in the Arashiyama Hills. An excellent half-day walk takes you from Tenryu-ji Temple, with its ornate gardens, to Seiryo-ji Temple in

Lake at Fushimi Inari Taisha shrine

Tunnels of torii gates line the trails at Fushimi Inari Taisha shrine

the beautifully preserved, tranquil district of Sagano. From Saga-Arashiyama station, a 40-minute rail journey from Kyoto, it is a brief walk to Tenryu-ji, the 'temple of the heavenly dragon'. Established in 1339, its halls and temples are linked by raised wooden boardwalks. Adjoining it is the exquisite Sogen Garden, one of the oldest Zen gardens in Japan. En route to Seiryo-ji Temple, it is possible to take a stroll through a giant bamboo forest and visit several other temples, including Nison-in, where maple trees are an impressive sight during autumn. From Seiryo-ji, the walk can be extended by a couple of kilometres or take a short taxi ride to the beautiful Daikaku-ji Temple, set around the idyllic Osawanoike Pond. It is off the beaten tourist track but much favoured by local people.

Foxes are regarded as messengers in Shinto

Just to the northwest of the centre of Kyoto are two of the city's most popular temples: Kinkaku-ji – the Golden Pavilion – and Ryoan-ji with its strikingly simple Zen rock garden. Be warned, though, you will be hard-pressed to find a Zen-like peace at either, as both temples are constantly overcrowded with tour-bus groups. A little further west, and easily reachable on foot from Ryoan-ji, is Daitoku-ji Temple. Accessed via another impressive Sanmon wooden gate and broad steps, the open spaces of its main courtyard will be a welcome relief.

Sunset over the delta from Macatoo Camp

Driving along Route 66

Arizona, USA

Rolling hills near Seligman

Hackberry gas station

Dubbed 'America's Main Street', Route 66 crosses the country from Chicago to Los Angeles and is probably the world's most famous road. Interstate highways have replaced many parts of the old route but the spirit of 66 is still alive and kicking, and one of the best ways to get a true taste of it is to drive the original section between Williams and Topock across the wild expanses of Arizona.

The story of Route 66, all 3600 km or so of it across eight states, is infused with the characters, landscapes, lifestyles and even songs that epitomized the Great American Dream of the 1940s through to the 1960s. Given its official name in 1926, the road soon after gave

Twisters Soda Fountain

Road sign in Williams

passage to the large-scale migration of Midwestern farmers and their families fleeing drought for the lure of California – immortalized in John Steinbeck's Pulitzer-Prize-winning book *The Grapes of Wrath*.

It took until 1937 for the entire route to be paved – the first cross-country highway to be completed – and it was only after the end of the Second World War that the road really caught the imagination of the American public. With car ownership soaring, Route 66 became a favourite holiday drive; and California continued to be a magnet for people who were looking to change their lives after returning from the war. Songwriter Bobby Troup was doing just that, heading for the bright lights of Los Angeles, when in 1946 he wrote the now legendary 'Get Your Kicks on Route 66' – just try not singing it as you're driving along the road.

On the verge of being buried under the new network of interstate highways in the 1980s, the old road has recently experienced a strong

Corvette at Hackberry gas station

revival. There are original sections in most of the states, but Arizona is home to the longest continuous section. Some 40 km west of Flagstaff is the small town of Williams. Gateway to the not-to-be-missed Grand Canyon just over an hour's drive or train ride north, its streets are lined with classic 1950s diners, gas stations and soda shops. Walking into Twisters Soda Fountain, with its pink Cadillac parked outside and interior filled with chrome fixtures, is like stepping back to a time when nobody hurried, everybody chatted and the days slipped by as easily as the ice-cream sodas and fresh coffee slipped down.

Old gas bowser, Seligman

With your car windows wound down and some good old, steering-wheel-thumping rock and roll music on the radio, set off west to the nearby village of Ash Fork, where Route 66 says goodbye to Interstate 40 for almost 260 km. Immediately, the stresses of driving begin to ease as the relatively traffic-free old highway begins to stretch its way

across the open plains and low-lying hills towards Seligman. Every now and again a Harley-Davidson, with its deep, window-rattling roar, will pass you, the wind flowing through the hair of its almost invariably heavily suntanned rider. It is an *Easy Rider* image of freedom, adventure and the seemingly eternal American Dream that somewhere along the road there is a better life.

Seligman is an iconic Route 66 town, rising out of the plain and consisting of one overly wide main street and a host of classic diners, motels and general stores. Old Chevrolets, Cadillacs and Ford Dodge trucks line the way or can be seen, rusty, parked in backyards. Seligman is also home to Angel Delgadillo, the town's now-retired barber and one of the most fervent campaigners to revive the mother road – he founded the association to preserve it as Historic Route 66. His barbershop, with its walls decked out with the business cards of clients, is an attraction for all who pass by. If you stop overnight at the Historic Route 66 Motel somebody famous, whether a Motown

Angel Delgadillo's barber chair

The renowned barbershop in Seligman

artist or a Hollywood actor, is almost certain to have stayed in your room before you.

Further west, the old highway passes through magnificent undulating country where sweeping views open up at every crest on this roller-coaster drive. At the characterful Hackberry gas station, every surface is decorated with Route 66 memorabilia. The rusty wreck of a very old Ford leads on to the seductive lines of the owner's red-and-white Corvette up front. Neon signs light up the forecourt while behind the station a fascinating collection of old pick-ups and other dilapidated cars reflects the glory of Route 66's heyday.

As beguiling as the open road is, perhaps the most classic section of Route 66 lies ahead to the south-west of Kingman. Soon after leaving the town, easily the biggest on this continuous stretch, the old highway begins to climb into the Black Mountains towards Oatman, a quirky Wild West gold-mining village straight out of a B-movie western. The narrow and precipitous road twists, curves and

snakes its way upwards and demands the utmost concentration. In the early days of Route 66, when brakes overheated and power steering wasn't even a pipe dream, there were drivers who found this section so frightening that they hired locals to drive it for them. It is exhilarating. En route several parking spots allow you to stop and admire the stunning views.

Oatman itself, with its creaky wooden walkways and restaurants, gift shops and lopsided saloons, was one of the first Route 66 villages to be bypassed by a new interstate highway. These days its most famous inhabitants are the wild donkeys that wander the street looking cute in an attempt to solicit food from travellers, although feeding them is prohibited. As the road begins its long descent out of the mountains towards Topock on the California border, the

Twisting route through the Black Mountains to Oatman

Heading to the Black Mountains from Kingman

landscape becomes dry and is dotted with cacti. The other traffic is even less frequent and you can slide your elbow out of the window, crank up the volume on your stereo and sing along to 'Get Your Kicks on Route 66' all the way to the sunshine coast.

ⓘ

Driving the entire length of Route 66 would take at least three weeks and allow only minimal time to see places en route. The Arizona section from Williams to Topock could be done in a couple of days, but it is worth spending four days or so savouring places along the road and heading up to the Grand Canyon. Although there are gas stations, make sure you plan your fuel stops to avoid running dry, especially on the section from Kingman to Topock. There are plenty of motels along the way for accommodation. If you have a motorbike licence, several companies in the region rent out Harley-Davidsons.

Following the reindeer migration

Lapland, Sweden

Lap dogs are small but effective reindeer herders

Riding pillion on a skidoo while trying to herd some two hundred reindeer during their spring migration has got to be one of the more exhilarating ways to travel through the vast Arctic tundra. It also allows you to get close to a very special and ancient way of life as you join the indigenous Sámi people on a 200-km journey across Sweden's Lapland. Just like their ancestors before them, they take their animals from the lowland winter feeding grounds through an extraordinary landscape, where frozen lakes, fir trees still laden with winter snow and wide open lowland valleys lead ultimately to mountains and summer pastures.

Neck tags enable wandering females to be monitored

Skidoos are a fun way to travel

The traditional home of the Sámi people, Lapland includes the northernmost parts of Norway, Sweden and Finland, and also the Kola peninsula in Russia. For would-be herders, the migration most typically begins in the small northern town of Gällivare in Sweden, about a three-hour drive south-east of the airport at Kiruna. Here you climb aboard a skidoo then slowly weave your way towards higher ground, fertile grazing and the 1810-metre Kallaktjåkkå mountain, where the first calves are born at the beginning of May. This is part of Stora Sjöfallets (Great Lake Falls) national park, a World Heritage Site.

This journey is an intrinsic part of life for both herders and reindeer, bonding them in a special relationship. Come spring, the animals would naturally begin to head west, instinctively picking a route through snow-filled valleys and upwards to the mountains. However, alone they would be vulnerable to bad weather, lack of food and even attack by predators. For the Sámi, a safe migration is essential as the reindeer are central to their lives, providing them with food and income through the sale of meat and fur – so they head into the tundra to herd the animals on this crucial journey. It is something the Sámi have undertaken for thousands of years and remains a carefully preserved tradition, handed down from generation to generation.

Keeping away the chills at overnight camp

One dominant reindeer always leads the herd

Sámi herders now use skidoos rather than skis

The migration was once an even tougher job than it is today. Before the use of modern skidoos, the herders set out on cross-country skis. Now the distance can be covered much more quickly, but some of the age-old traditions haven't been forgotten – not least where you rest your head in the evening.

You will find yourself bedding down for the night in a *lavu*, the traditional herder's tent, made now of tough canvas rather than reindeer skins and erected on the snow. While this may sound chilly don't be put off – skins cover the floor and are used on top of sleeping bags for extra warmth. It may just begin to get too comfortable, especially when it comes to getting up to help with the early morning job of rounding up the reindeer and collecting food for them. But you can take on as much or as little of the work as you want. The 'real'

Sunset over a *lavu* tent

herders are there, rising early and jumping on to their skidoos to race off and find the reindeer – which don't stay still for long. Following their natural instinct to head west to the mountains, these gentle animals just keep moving.

Even in spring the roots, lichens and moss that they like to feed on remain hidden under snow, so the Sámi collect and lay out food for them, including their favourite *sláhppu*, a wiry moss that grows in tree branches. Before you know it you will probably find yourself wanting to be out there with the herders, doing the work rather than watching from a distance.

Participating fully means bashing branches to get at the moss and frantically flailing and waving your arms as you join in the daily round-up. This is one of the slightly more chaotic parts of the day, when break-away reindeer have to be coerced back into the herd – and the sight of a herder lying flat on his face in the snow after an unsuccessful chase is not unusual. There are people, arms and animals almost everywhere. Then, almost magically, the wonderful, blissful peace is skilfully and sublimely restored and the journey can begin again, across yet more untracked snow.

It's hard not to get drawn into the life of the herd and this migration. Every reindeer has its own unique character, from the toss of a head to the shake of a tail, and the animals become absorbing to watch and get to know. A white reindeer – a particularly rare colouration – is considered spiritually special by the Sámi, and if a family has one it is highly valued.

Each day for a week, as you follow the animals, direct them, regroup them and even guard against the possibility of a wolverine or lynx attack, you become closer to them. And covering ground means getting them to new pastures where they will grow and prosper. The moment when you look out on the herd grazing contentedly on high ground is one you will savour; and the one when you know you have become an honorary reindeer herder.

A couple of airlines, including SAS Airlines, fly into Kiruna in Swedish Lapland. The reindeer-migration experience can be organized by Vägvisaren – Pathfinder Lapland, a Sámi family-run ecotourism company set up to provide sustainable tourism in Lapland. Their trips are certified as 'Nature's Best' by the Swedish Eco-tourism Society, whose ecotourism certification system is one of the first in the world. You will need warm clothing for the journey, but outer snow suits and shoes are provided. Traditional Sámi herders will guide and drive you. There may be an opportunity to drive your own skidoo, and full training in driving and herding is given.

Sunset over the western hills

Tracking mountain gorillas

Parc National des Volcans, Rwanda

View from Virunga Lodge

Trekking high up on volcanic slopes in the dense bamboo forests of the Parc National des Volcans (Volcanoes National Park) in Rwanda's Virunga massif, you may have the privilege of meeting one of our closest living relatives: the mountain gorillas. Catapulted into the limelight by the work of Dian Fossey, these animals are highly endangered and coming face to face with them is among the most highly prized and moving wildlife encounters on the planet.

Sign at the park's head office

Trekking towards Sabinyo volcano

Getting to see the gorillas' kingdom is an adventure in itself, as you travel deep into Central Africa from Rwanda's capital, Kigali, to the region where the country's northern border connects with Uganda and the Democratic Republic of Congo (DRC). Thankfully, Rwanda is now well on the road to recovering from the terrible genocide that scarred it so deeply in the mid-1990s. The renewed peace and stability allow you to see the real nature of its people, who invariably greet visitors with big smiles, excited waves and the endearing cry 'Misungu!'

Once you arrive in Kigali it is a spectacular three-to-four hour drive north to the town of Ruhengeri. The lush, dramatic mountains are striped with terraces and patchworked with fields where, among other crops, sorghum, tea, bananas, potatoes and maize grow. Accommodation options in the region are fairly limited, but the most spectacularly located is undoubtedly Virunga Lodge. Perched on a high ridge, it is surrounded by volcanoes and overlooks two vast lakes: Bulera and Ruhondo. Every morning and evening, as the villagers in the valley light their fires, a wispy blanket of smoke extends a further layer of mystery to the enchanting landscape.

An early morning drive to the national park office takes you along very rugged tracks to the village of Kinigi, 15 km north-west of Ruhengeri. Anchored along a ridge of six volcanoes, the Parc National

Members of Susa Group on Karisimbi volcano

Susa Group is the largest in Rwanda

des Volcans is part of a unique conservation initiative that links it with adjoining parks in Uganda and the DRC to create an extensive 650-sq.-km protected habitat for the mountain gorillas. It also became home to Dian Fossey, who fell in love with these animals during a visit in the 1960s and lived among them for about 20 years, conducting ground-breaking studies and protecting them from poachers. The Dian Fossey Gorilla Fund continues her work in the park and a lengthy trek up the Bisoke volcano leads you to her grave – she was mysteriously murdered in 1985.

Park guides explain about gorilla life

Our tracking experience started after another short drive, from the park office up towards the 3634-metre Sabinyo volcano. Soon after leaving our vehicle and the throngs of children and other villagers keen to bid us farewell, we swapped agricultural fields for thick stands of bamboo as we climbed further into the park. Unseen ahead of us, trackers were hunting for the trail the gorillas would have left when they moved on from where they had nested the evening before. We were looking for 13 Group, one of five gorilla groups in the park, which is led by a particularly successful silverback male called Munane. As with any wildlife trip, there are no guarantees – tracking can take

anything from an hour to a day depending on what the gorillas are doing and how fast they are moving.

Seasonal rains had turned the narrow trail into a mess in places, and after slipping and sliding around the first few pools of mud we realized that the best way was the straight way. Ducking and clambering through the bamboo thickets was great fun and the sense of adventure grew the further up the volcano we climbed. Eventually, our trackers appeared ahead. The gorillas, we assumed, were still a little way off.

Chilling out with Susa Group

Leaving our backpacks behind – they could scare the gorillas – we left the main trail and scrambled through dense undergrowth. To our surprise we saw our first gorilla, the immensely powerful-looking Munane, almost immediately, sitting in the grass of a small clearing and staring intently at us. It was an incredible moment, and slightly unnerving too, as we knew he held the only rule book for the encounter. We hardly dared to breathe while the trackers made soothing grunting noises to assure him that we were not out to cause him problems, and he seemed to accept our arrival in his kingdom. In front of him, nursing a curly-haired five-month-old baby, was one of Munane's nine females – an unusually high number of admirers.

All gorilla encounters are limited to one hour, but that hour seemed to last a lifetime as we watched the daily life of 13 Group: the baby intent on eating anything around him, clambering over his mother or simply climbing bamboo shoots until they snapped, sending him tumbling to the forest floor and us into muffled giggles. It was like watching a human family out for a Sunday picnic. As the rains came down again, we slid our way back down the trail and returned to Virunga Lodge to dry out.

Dominant male silverbacks lead the gorilla groups

The following day we went in search of the 40-strong Susa Group – a wonderful trek up the flanks of Rwanda's highest peak, the 4507-metre Karisimbi volcano. The drive there took us through a succession of villages where children played with sticks and hoops while older people carried unfeasible loads of chickens, beer and grass on rickety bicycles. Eventually, the rough four-wheel-drive track petered out and the trek began in earnest, up through steeply terraced fields.

An hour and a half later, the trackers appeared and we scrambled down a steep, overgrown slope to be greeted by the mesmerizing sight of about 20 gorillas in a large, open clearing. In contrast to 13 Group, who had been at rest, Susa, which boasts four silverbacks, nine females and an array of youngsters, was busy feeding and playing. For a magical hour we watched as the young gorillas fought and tumbled while the older ones moved slowly around, crunching their way through bamboo shoot after bamboo shoot. Memorably, the group gave us a momentary glimpse of their new two-week-old baby. Any wildlife encounter brings a sense of wonder, but meeting the gorillas is different. It is like stepping back millions of years to find an ancient mirror reflecting an image not too unlike yourself.

Village in the foothills of Karisimbi volcano

Permits to track the gorillas are tightly controlled and are often booked well in advance, so plan ahead. Visitor numbers are strictly limited. There are five gorilla groups, each of which can be tracked by a group of up to eight people each day. Physical contact with the gorillas is strictly forbidden. A significant percentage of the permit fee goes back into conservation and development projects in villages surrounding the park. Several companies, including UK-based Discovery Initiatives, organize full gorilla tours to suit your own itinerary and can arrange accommodation at the lovely Virunga Lodge. Kenya Airways offer the best flight options to Kigali from Nairobi, with connecting international flights.

Pyramid of Kukulcán
Mexico

The stone serpent's head near Kukulcán's pyramid

Sitting at the centre of the ancient Mayan site of Chichén Itzá on the Yucatán peninsula in Mexico, the pyramid of Kukulcán has a pleasing symmetry and an imposing bulk, but perhaps its true majesty lies in the secrets of its construction – over 1000 years ago.

The pyramid is a giant calendar. It consists of nine levels faced with a total of 52 panels – the number of years in the Mayan–Toltec cycle. The staircases on each face of the pyramid have 364 steps. Add the square platform at the top, and you have 365 – the number of days in

Kukulcán's pyramid

the solar year. Most impressively, at the spring and autumn equinoxes the shadow cast by the sun on the northern staircase appears to cause a massively long 'snake' to crawl down the building and link with the stone serpent's head at the foot of the staircase.

The pyramid of Kukulcán has other secrets too. Hidden deep within it is another, much older pyramid. A small door takes you to a narrow passage that appears to run up what would have been the outside of the original structure. Cramped and oppressive, it leads to the original sanctuary, where a large *chac-mool* – the characteristic reclining Mayan figure – and a jaguar-shaped throne are for ever entombed, the jade inlay of the big cat's coat shining dimly through the gloom.

Detail of cladding on Kukulcán's pyramid

North staircase on Kukulcán's pyramid

You will have to get up early to appreciate Kukulcán properly because by 10.30 a.m. it is swarming with visitors. If you are among the first through the gate at 8.30 in the morning, you should manage an hour of near-solitude. A good way to achieve this is to stay at the Mayaland Hotel, just a few metres from the quiet east gate. Here you will be so close that you can see the ruins of the ossuary, or bone sanctuary, silhouetted by the setting sun and filling the doorway of the hotel bar.

From the top of the pyramid the whole site seems to be completely surrounded by a sea of trees stretching as far as the eye can see, and obliterating almost all signs of human life. Only the tops of some of the lesser ruins and the open grassed ceremonial area are visible.

Observatory in a sea of trees

A number of other ruins make up the ceremonial area of Chichén Itzá, including the Temple of the Warriors, a large structure surrounded by intricately carved stone pillars and topped with a reclining *chac-mool*. Sadly, visitors are no longer allowed to mount the steps to see this statue, so you will have to make do with looking down on it from the top of the pyramid of Kukulcán.

The other most impressive structure is the ball court, once the scene of a complicated game in which teams of players attempted to pass a rubber ball through a stone hoop high up on the wall using only their elbows, knees and hips. It often took hours to achieve this and consequently the game was won on the first score.

The pyramid is visible from many of the outlying structures on the site, which gives you the chance to appreciate its harmonious proportions from a number of perspectives: through dense trees, from the top of carved pillars and even appearing between the jaws of a stone serpent's head.

Head of *chac-mool*

Every evening there is a sound and light show at the complex, which is included in the ticket price. Although the show is garish, it's worth attending on nights when there is a full moon because if you linger afterwards you will get a unique view of Kukulcán's pyramid illuminated only by the moon, and glowing in its incandescent light.

ⓘ

The airport nearest to Chichén Itzá is at Cancún, and the site is reachable by bus or hire car. If you are staying at the Mayaland Hotel you should get off at the park gate and walk through the site. Many tourists visit Chichén Itzá on a day trip, but you should aim to stay at least overnight so that you can see the site in the quiet mornings and afternoons. The interior of Kukulcán's pyramid is only open in the middle of the day so you will have to brave the crowds at least once.

Wall of skulls on the Tzompantli, a sacrificial altar

Dead Vlei

Sossusvlei National Park, Namibia

In the parched landscape of the Namib Desert, the golden-orange light of dawn starts by illuminating the very tips of the dead camelthorn trees that point skeletal branches at the lightening sky. It then moves down their trunks and onwards, just as it has done every morning of their 600-year existence, until it reaches the drought-crazed white surface of Dead Vlei. Then everything appears to speed up, as the sunlight pushes aside the shroud of shadow and sweeps across the pan of the former lake. The contrast between the cracked white of Dead Vlei and the red sand dunes that surround it is stark. There is literally a hard line where one finishes and the other begins.

Shadows sweeping across Dead Vlei at sunrise

A vlei is a lake pan, and there are three main ones in the Sossusvlei National Park. Although Dead Vlei is smaller than the more famous Sossusvlei that gave the park its name, it is more atmospheric and has a more impressive location. (The third is the even smaller Hidden Vlei.)

Sossusvlei is part of the great Namib Desert from which Namibia takes its name. As public transport links to the park aren't good, travellers generally find it much easier to stay at one of the luxury camps that run their own transport into the park. If your budget won't stretch to this, cheaper accommodation is available near the park gate at Sesriem.

Dunes in the valley of the Tsauchab River

Driving across the desert terrain is difficult. There is a car park for four-wheel-drive vehicles about 4 km away from Sossusvlei. However, drivers of two-wheel-drive vehicles must use a car park situated along a dirt track about 60 km from the park gate and take a shuttle bus to the four-wheel-drive car park. It's then a hard, 20-minute uphill hike to Dead Vlei.

Despite the almost complete lack of water in the area – Sossusvlei was last flooded in 1997, but Dead Vlei has not flooded in living memory – you can still see some forms of life. Gawky ostriches stalk around, and oryx stand motionless in the heat haze, as if waiting for the day to cool before they deign to move. On a smaller scale, look down at the sand and you will often see the erratic trails of beetles.These creatures spend most of their time burrowed in the sand, and survive by tilting their bodies to catch the morning dew that sometimes sweeps in from the sea many kilometres away on the Atlantic coast, their heads down to catch and drink the condensation that forms on their hard shells.

The national park is also famous for its sand dunes, which are reputed to be the tallest in the world: Big Daddy, the tallest at Sossusvlei, is over 300 metres high. The dunes are a deep red colour, which is especially intense when lit by the rising or setting sun.

You should definitely try to climb at least one of the dunes, but make sure you take plenty of water with you, as it's a hot and draining experience. From the top you will have spectacular views of the

Hiking across the ridge of Dune 45

Camelthorn tree in Dead Vlei

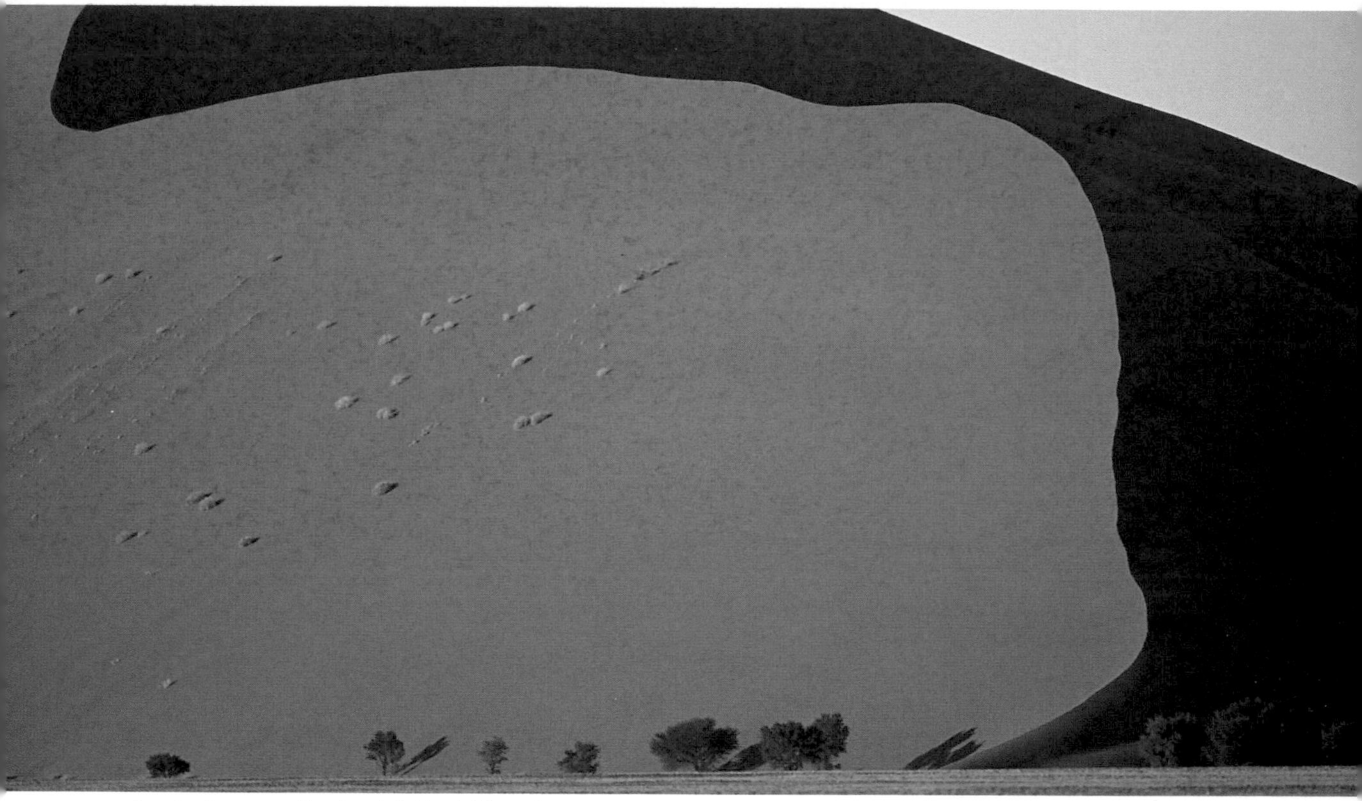

Dunes looming over camelthorn trees in the Tsauchab River valley

desert, with endless series of dunes stretching out in front of you – a sight that is both humbling and awe-inspiring.

While you are visiting Namibia you should aim to take in the Skeleton Coast, a desolate stretch of the Atlantic seaboard where shipwrecks, whale bones and even the occasional lion can be found on the beach.

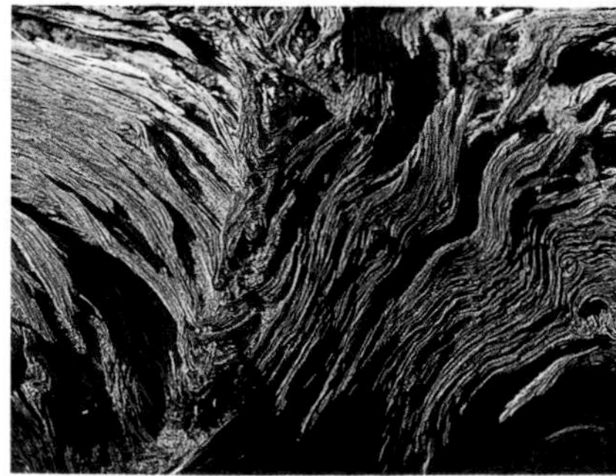

Camelthorn tree

ⓘ

Sossusvlei can be reached by road from the Namibian capital, Windhoek, or from Cape Town – a long drive across the South African border. Accommodation close to the park entrance at Sesriem is limited, but there are several luxury camps and lodges about an hour from the main park gate. The desert is best appreciated from the top of one of the dunes, but if you decide to climb one do make sure you take more water than you think you'll need. Have plenty of cash, too – petrol stations in Namibia do not take credit cards.

St Petersburg
Russia

If the mention of a place can bring to mind a season, then St Petersburg conjures up winter – deepest winter. Snow-covered statues, breath rising in clouds and the Winter Palace seen through mist across the frozen River Neva.

Winter is not an easy time to visit Russia – the biting cold might restrict your sightseeing – but it is the time of year that defines both the city and the Russian people. It is also the season when the tsars used to visit St Petersburg. The Winter Palace was built to house and amuse the Russian royal family during the long dark winter months. From inside you can gaze out upon the same frosty scenes that Catherine the Great once saw, the views distorted by a covering of ice on the windows.

View of the Hermitage, the Admiralty and St Isaac's Cathedral

St Petersburg was founded by Peter the Great in 1703, and the Winter Palace was completed in 1762. The founding of a European-style city on the western border of the country, and the moving of the capital from 'Asiatic' Moscow in the east, marked a Europeanization of Russia. The House of Romanov became one of the great ruling dynasties of Europe, rivalling even the Bourbons and the Habsburgs. The Winter Palace is probably their greatest creation.

Statue of Catherine the Great

St Petersburg itself has been at the centre of European history for 300 years. Revolution was fermented in the city, and the tsars were overthrown when the Bolsheviks stormed the Winter Palace in 1917, ushering in more than 70 years of Communism for Russia. St Petersburg was renamed Leningrad by the new regime and became

The gate from the river jetty into Peter and Paul Fortress, with the River Neva in the background

Winter Palace

Tikhvin cemetery

one of the bulwarks that held up the spread of Nazism during the Second World War; a heroic defence that saw the city all but destroyed. Reverting to the old name of St Petersburg following the fall of Communism was a gesture that marked the demise of the old Soviet Union and the re-emergence of Russia.

Throughout all this history, the Winter Palace has endured. It is a massive structure, stretching some 200 metres along the riverfront. Other buildings, notably the Hermitage and the Hermitage Theatre, were added by Catherine the Great, a ruler whose excesses and love of power were to help to bring about revolution and the end of a dynasty.

A palpable sense of history pervades every part of the Winter Palace. It is easy to imagine the Russian royal family residing here, cocooned from the harsh realities of daily life experienced by most of their subjects. Or the monk Rasputin, who held such sway over Tsar Nicholas's wife, Alexandra, that he was poisoned the year before the dynasty fell. One can also imagine the amazement of the Bolsheviks who stormed the palace in 1917, seeing for the first time the opulence in which their rulers lived.

The Hermitage is notable among the riches of the Winter Palace, housing one of the greatest collections of art in the world – an astonishing 2.8 million exhibits. Get there early and you could have works by Monet or Picasso all to yourself.

Despite the Byzantine paperwork required to get a visa, St Petersburg is a relatively easy city to visit. Seemingly unaffected by the long years of Communism, it retains the atmosphere of imperial Russia, especially during the long hard winters when, like the tsars of old, you can seek refuge from the cold amid the warmth and grace of the Winter Palace.

Although Communism has long since gone, the visa application process has changed little. It is time consuming and there is a lot of paperwork. A visa agency will help to smooth the process. A number of European airlines fly to St Petersburg. Alternatively, you can take the train through Europe. The city is well served by rail connections and it is possible to get a train all the way to Vladivostok or even Beijing. Try to book a central hotel – the city is big and spread out and you will maximize your sightseeing by minimizing travel time. Intourist, the old state travel company, can organize hotels and tours. The metro is an interesting experience and very efficient, but keep track of where you are – station signs are difficult to read and it is easy to miss your stop.

Pavilion Hall, Gallery 204, the Hermitage

Ceiling of the Jordan Staircase, the Hermitage

Large Hermitage, Gallery 241

Assumption of Mary Cathedral seen from the city walls

Dubrovnik
Croatia

View of the city from the north

Looking down on to the red-tiled roofs of the Old Town of Dubrovnik as it nestles quietly alongside the cool waters of the Mediterranean, it is hard to credit that its history is steeped in political intrigue, war and destruction. But appearances are deceptive, and Dubrovnik has a more violent and colourful past than most cities in Europe.

For most of its long history Dubrovnik was an independent city state. It came under the protection of Venice in the 13th century, and Hungary some 150 years later. The city preserved its independence by careful diplomacy and payment of tributes. Under these conditions it grew into a wealthy democracy with a wide network of trading outposts. As the importance of the city increased many civil construction projects, such as the city walls, were undertaken, and Dubrovnik proved attractive to writers and artists.

Although the sovereignty of Dubrovnik passed to the Ottoman Empire in the 16th century the city continued to flourish until it was

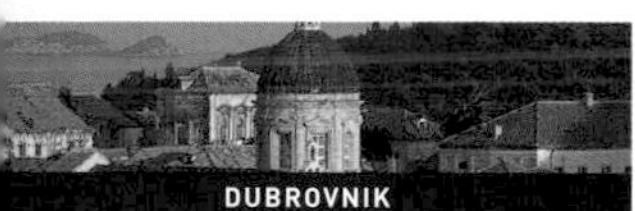

all but destroyed by an earthquake in 1667. It was rebuilt in 1683, but the shifting trade allegiances and wars that rocked Europe during the 18th century weakened its power. The final death blow came in 1808, when Napoleon formally abolished Dubrovnik's tenuous independence, prompting a bombardment by British forces.

The city languished through subsequent wars and European politicking until it once again shot to prominence during the 1990s' Balkans War, following the break-up of Yugoslavia. During a siege which lasted seven months, before finally being lifted in May 1992, over 2000 shells slammed into the city.

Despite past violence and destruction, Dubrovnik is still a beautiful city. Indeed, the depredations of the siege have been

View of the city and the harbour

View from city walls with Lokrum Island in background

repaired so successfully (with financial assistance from UNESCO) that visitors could be forgiven for thinking that war had never touched it.

The best way to get orientated in Dubrovnik is to walk around the towering and immensely thick 13th-century walls that surround the Old Town. At the highest point of the walls on the landward side of the city is the distinctive Minceta Tower, which has the best panoramic views of the city, Lokrum Island near the harbour mouth and the Mediterranean beyond. The battlements at the top of the tower give great views down into the narrow streets and courtyards. Church domes and spires reach above the expanses of red-tiled roofs, and at sunset golden light skims these roof tops and casts the skyline into relief against the surrounding landscape.

The main thoroughfare, the Stradun, divides the city into two halves and extends over 200 metres, from the Pile Gate in the west to the clock tower at the harbour entrance. Once a marsh that separated the Roman and Slavic halves of the city, the Stradun is now paved with stones polished by years of pedestrian traffic, and lined with shops.

The city walls dropping down into the Mediterranean

City walls and street below

As you wander the narrow streets away from the Stradun, you get a sense of the tightly knit community. The houses in the Old Town are small and close together, with laundry strung between them, children play in the streets, and neighbours sit on front steps or lean from windows chatting and watching the world go by.

Positioned in the middle of some of the most beautiful coastline in Europe, Dubrovnik is the perfect place to while away a few days. Although it lacks the grandeur of Venice, and the power and influence it enjoyed in the 15th and 16th centuries has long since passed away, this small and modest city has a beguiling charm of its own.

ⓘ

Charter flights to Dubrovnik are available, but if you want the flexibility of a scheduled service your options are more limited. Alitalia fly there with a connection in one of three Italian cities. Alternatively, you can to fly to Belgrade and then take a domestic flight on Croatia Airlines. Dubrovnik offers a wide range of accommodation, but you should try and book during the summer months. Most of the better-quality accommodation is outside the city walls.

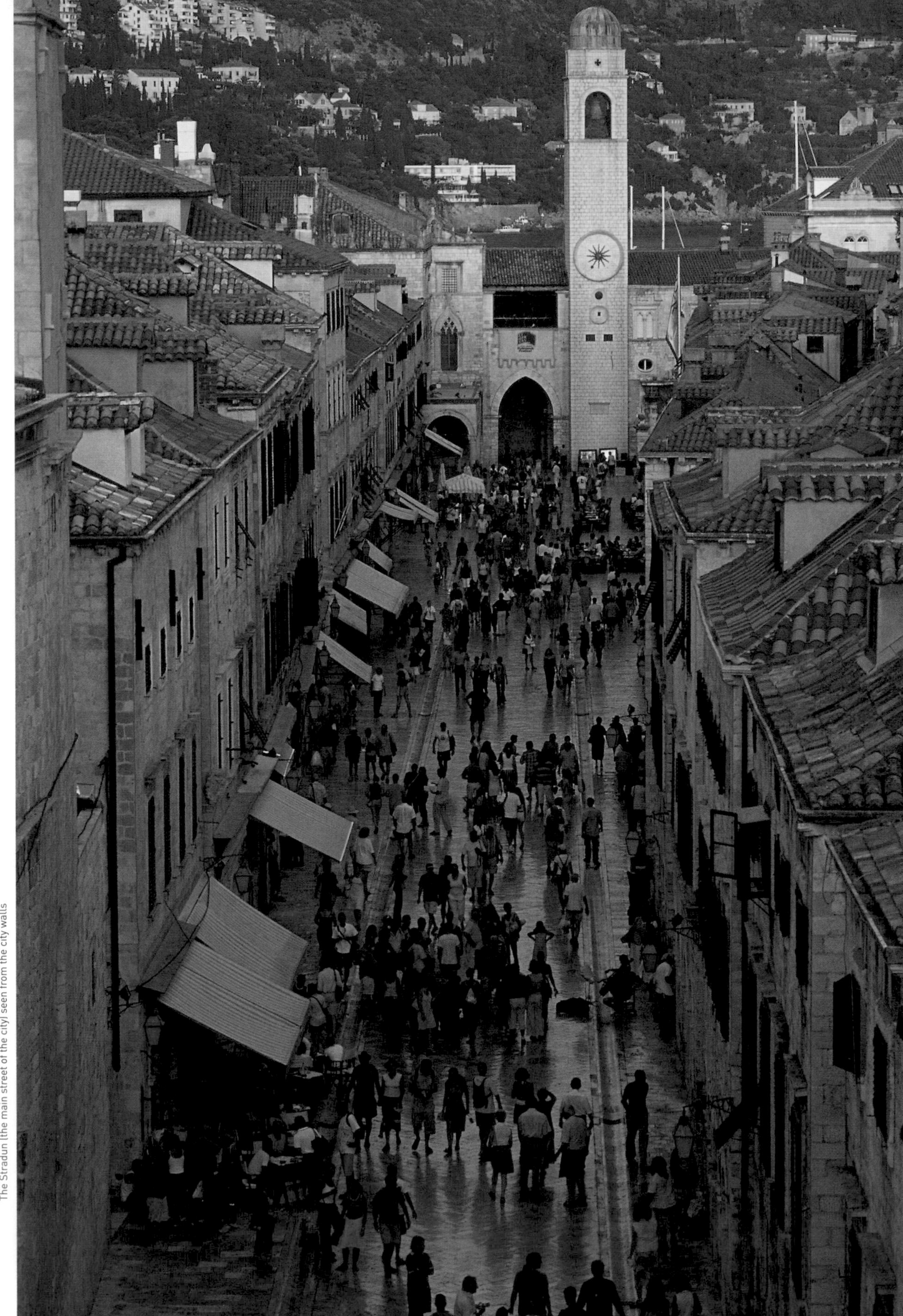

The Stradun (the main street of the city) seen from the city walls

The Bund

Shanghai, China

Pudong, the Bund and the Huangpu River from the top of the Peace Hotel

There are few cities in the world that have given rise to a verb, but it seems wholly appropriate that the frenetic city of Shanghai should have done so. 'To shanghai' originally meant to kidnap a drunken man and press him into work as a sailor, but it eventually came to mean compelling someone to do something by fraud or by force.

The verb fits the city that was once central to the commercial exploitation of China and much of Asia but had an underbelly steeped in vice, gambling, prostitution and opium. The British were granted

Building on the Bund

the first trading concession in 1842 after the First Opium War, when the Chinese government was forced to relegalize the import of the drug. The commercial exploitation of China by Europe had begun. Great fortunes were made in trade and lost on the spin of a roulette wheel. Shanghai thrived on intrigue, catered to every kind of perversion and allowed criminal gangs to roam the streets. Not for nothing was the city known as the 'Whore of the Orient'.

Other countries – notably France – were later granted concessions, and soon a virtual European city existed. European Shanghai laid a

Shopping by bicycle in the old streets of Shanghai

thin veneer of respectability over the city with the creation of the Bund, an imposing stretch of buildings along the Huangpu River. Many were the head offices of great trading companies, insurance houses and banks. The most imposing, however, is the Customs House, one of the few buildings on the Bund that retains its original function. Another place worth checking out is the Peace Hotel, formerly the Cathay Hotel, once the most fashionable place in European Shanghai. The art deco interiors have recently been restored, and the hotel is probably the most atmospheric and historic place to stay in the city.

Although the vice and intrigue of Shanghai were suppressed by the Communists when they took charge of the city in 1949, they are now making a comeback. Walk along the Bund and you will continually be offered fake Rolexes and even, occasionally, sex. (The

View across to the Bund

Looking down to the city from the top of the Oriental Pearl TV Tower

first sex shop in China opened recently on the main Nanjing Donglu.)

In a uniquely Chinese demonstration of one-upmanship, the city authorities didn't demolish evidence of the colonial era – they merely dwarfed the buildings of the Bund, making them look insignificant. On one side of the Huangpu River, the Pudong New Area has been reclaimed from marshland, and since 1990 has become a massive area of tower blocks. The most spectacular are the Oriental Pearl TV Tower and the 88-storey Jinmao Tower, the top 35 floors of which house the Grand Hyatt Hotel. A new skyscraper currently under construction is expected to become the tallest building in the world.

As you look down from the top viewing-stage of the Oriental Pearl TV Tower or the Cloud Nine Bar at the top of the Hyatt Hotel, the sprawling towers of Shanghai seem to threaten the buildings of the Bund and push them into the river. Nonetheless, the Bund remains one of the most potent symbols of Shanghai, and from ground level it retains some of the gravitas and presence that it enjoyed in the past.

Outdoor laundry in the backstreets

View of Pudong New Area from the Peace Hotel

It also remains the centre of Shanghai life. From the early morning, when it is thronged with kite flyers, old people practising t'ai chi and *qi gong*, and couples ballroom-dancing before work, to the daytime, when tourists from all over China flock to be photographed against the backdrop of the Bund and Pudong, through to the evening, when locals emerge to stroll in the cool breeze coming off the river, this stretch of waterfront is always packed and bursting with life.

The old streets of Shanghai can still be found in the Chinatown area of the city. Peculiar as it seems to have a Chinatown in a Chinese city, this area is a throwback to the days when Europeans ruled the roost and locals were restricted to certain parts of the city. A sign on the old British public gardens at the end of the Bund used to ban, among other things, dogs and Chinese.

Many of the old streets have been demolished to make room for the tower blocks of new Shanghai, and the rest are probably under threat in the headlong dash for progress. Among the surviving streets,

some of the most atmospheric are between the old Yu Yuan (Jade Gardens) and the river. The gardens themselves are typically Chinese, created in the mid-16th century during the Ming dynasty. Shady pools, rock gardens and pagodas form a haven of peace in the noisy city, the atmosphere only slightly compromised by the Yu Yuan Bazaar, a sprawling 'old' themed shopping complex next door.

Life in the old streets of Shanghai seems to have remained unchanged for generations, and it is easy to imagine European sailors or traders staggering down alleys such as these in search of women or opium, never to be heard of again. The present, though, is less dramatic as daily life unfolds at a slow pace, punctuated by the constant chirruping of crickets kept in small bamboo cages for good luck.

Shanghai is one of the main international gateway cities of China and can be reached by air from most countries. Although there are many places to stay, the choice really comes down to the old – the atmospheric Peace Hotel right on the Bund – or the new, skyscraping Grand Hyatt Hotel. The city sprawls for miles, but most of the main sights are along the river – either along the Bund or in the reclaimed area of Pudong. There is a modern underground railway or you can catch a ferry across the river. A visit to see the famous Shanghai acrobats is a 'must'.

Morning exercise on the Bund

The Bund

Heron Island

Great Barrier Reef, Australia

The Great Barrier Reef is a series of interlocking reefs and islands that stretch for over 2000 km in the waters off the coast of Queensland, Australia. It is the most extensive coral-reef system in the world, and the largest structure made completely from living organisms: tiny coral polyps.

Between 50 km and 300 km away from the shore, the reef comprises more than 2500 individual reefs (strips of rock or coral) and 600 islands. There are basically three types of island: continental islands

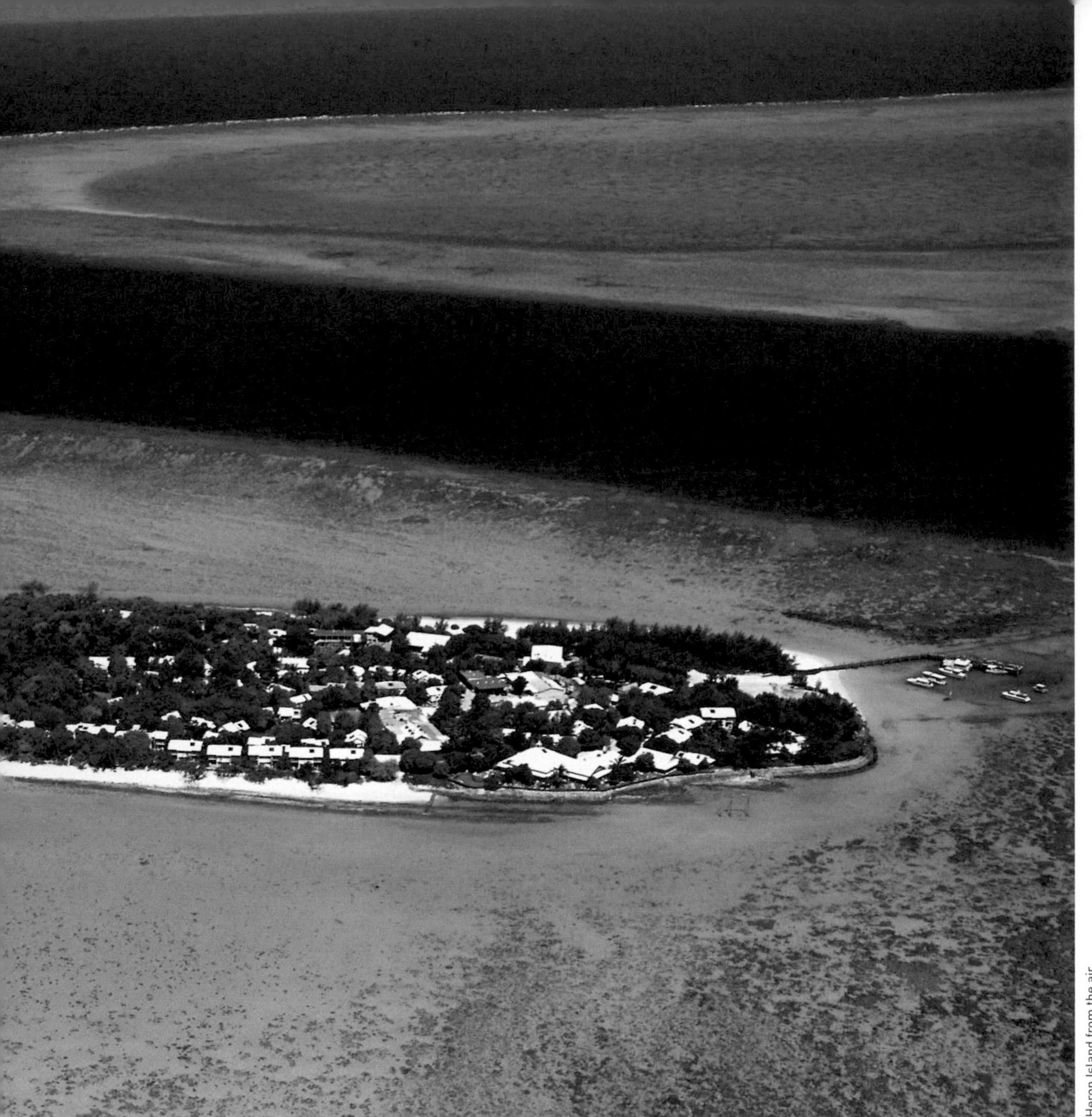

Heron Island from the air

(the peaks of sunken mountain ranges), sand islands and coral cays. Many of these islands have coral reefs nearby, or even mini-reefs fringing them, but Heron Island and the nearby Wilson Island are unique in that they are true coral cays that offer accommodation and actually form part of the reef. This means that you can simply swim from their beaches to dive or snorkel on the Great Barrier Reef itself.

The diving around Heron Island is reputed to be some of the best on the whole reef, attracting people from all over the world. The island has been leased out to the Heron Island Resort, which

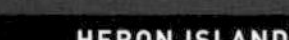

Wilson Island fringed by reef

provides a range of accommodation, as well as diving and snorkelling excursions. Wilson Island is administered by Heron, and just 10 people are allowed to stay on it at any one time. Those with a scientific interest in the reef can stay at the research centre on Heron Island, which is run by the University of Queensland.

From ground level, the barrier reef appears unexceptional. The sea might be a luxurious blue and the islands' sandy beaches creamy white, but little else is revealed unless you go up or down. From the air the true extent and colours of the Great Barrier Reef become apparent. Within waters of the purest turquoise, reef after reef seems to stretch away as far as you can see, and dotted around are tiny, white-fringed coral cays surrounded by their own reefs.

Diving or snorkelling on the reef is a truly magical experience, and no superlatives can do it justice. It's like experiencing a completely new world, where sight is the only sense you need and

The reef near Heron Island

Underwater coral

gravity seems irrelevant. Stick to shallow waters if you want to see the colours clearly, as deeper water filters out most of the red and green wavelengths, giving everything a deep blue tinge.

The coral is home to a wealth of life forms: multicoloured fish dart around at lightning speed, while green turtles and loggerheads take things at a more leisurely pace. At the top of Heron Island, in the aptly named Shark Bay, you will have a very good chance of being able to swim with the small and relatively friendly reef sharks.

If you don't fancy getting wet, the Heron Island Resort has a semi-submersible – basically a boat crossed with a submarine – where you can sit in the glass keel and view this underwater world in comfort.

You don't always have to go beneath the waves to see marine wildlife. Coming back from Wilson Island by boat, I came across a couple of migrating humpback whales. In the shallow waters of this part of the reef they were unable to dive deep, so I could hear them

communicating with their haunting 'songs'. You are most likely to see migrating whales in September, while January and February are good times to see turtles laying eggs and the young eventually hatching.

Qantas offer regular flights from Brisbane to Gladstone. From there, you can reach Heron Island by ferry or helicopter transfer – a good way to combine travel and seeing the reef from the air. There is one ferry daily, but it is available only to guests of the Heron Island Resort or to those staying at the research centre. Prices at the resort include all food and the quality is exceptional. Try to be there for the Saturday night seafood buffet. If you are not staying on the Island the only way to visit it is by charter boat. As it is a marine park, diving and snorkelling among the reefs around the island are allowed.

Beach at Heron Island

Herons on the beach

Coral on Wilson Island

Ephesus
Turkey

Columns on the way up to the Temple of Domitian

Sunset over the amphitheatre

The ruins at Ephesus are the best preserved of any Roman site in the Mediterranean. Although only 10 per cent of the city has been excavated, the wealth of surviving detail makes it easy to imagine the lives of the people who lived there: the latrines in the public baths are communal and packed close together; the brothel is across the street from the Library of Celsus; the agora, or market area, is vast, showing the importance of trade to the city; temples occur at frequent intervals; and a cemetery for gladiators has provided much information about their lives.

The ruins are spread along the slopes of two hills, with two level sites in between connected by the sloping Street of Curetes. The lower site, closest to the ancient harbour, has a vast amphitheatre that can seat 25,000 people. Concerts are still held here today.

Also on the lower site is the Library of Celsus, the single most impressive ruin at Ephesus, which is best seen at sunrise. All that remains is the front façade, with its entrances to the original building, and two huge storeys of pillars, statues and windows. Constructed using subtle techniques to manipulate perspective,

the building, when viewed from ground level, appears much larger than it really is.

The Street of Curetes climbs upwards from the library, its wide pavement concealing sophisticated sewerage and water systems. On either side are columns and façades – the ruins of terraced housing, public baths with rows of latrines, a brothel, shops and temples.

Temple of Hadrian

Ephesus was founded by the Greeks, who arrived in the 10th or 11th century BC. Under their influence it became a mighty city and sea port, with a population of some 200,000 people. The Temple of Artemis (Diana), built during their time, was one of the Seven Wonders of the World. The present-day ruins, now about 5 km away from the coast, date from a city that was founded in the 3rd century BC by

Library of Celsus

View down the Street of the Curetes, from the Monument of Memmius (lower right) to the Library of Celsus

Library of Celsus

Lysimachus, one of Alexander the Great's generals. The city came under Roman control in the 2nd century BC, and it later became an important centre of Christianity. (St Paul visited several times, and St John is said to be buried here.)

The Ephesus Museum in Selçuk has a great collection of artefacts and statues from Ephesus that will enhance your understanding of how the city must have looked, and what it might have been like to live there.

ⓘ

The airport closest to Ephesus is at Izmir, which is 30 km away from the nearby town of Selçuk. The ruins are open from 8 a.m. which is just before summer sunrise strikes them directly. The gates close at 7 p.m. but you can generally wander around for at least another hour. The ruins are occasionally lit at night for special events, so it is worth finding out if your visit coincides with this impressive sight. Many people visit the site on day trips from beach locations such as Kusadasi, but if you want to really explore Ephesus you should stay in Selçuk, 3 km away. The best accommodation here is at the Hotel Kalehan.

The Agora near the Library of Celsus

Statue in the façade of the Library of Celsus

Library of Celsus

Jaisalmer Fort

India

The fort at dusk

Gadi Sagar tank flooded after the monsoon

Jaisalmer Fort sits in the Thar Desert in the westernmost part of Rajasthan. Located on a former trade route used to transport spices and silks between Arabia and India, Jaisalmer, more than anywhere else in India, appears to have stepped out of the *Tales of the Arabian Nights* – a collection of ancient folk tales. This is partly due to its location in a remote and inhospitable desert, and partly because of its appearance. Made rich from trade, its merchants built havelis, or merchants' houses, with finely detailed windows and balconies that owe more to Arab style than Indian.

There are bigger and more impressive forts in Rajasthan – such as that at Jodhpur – but few have such an isolated and atmospheric location. Jaisalmer is also reputed to be the only inhabited fort in the world. The maze of tiny streets still rings with daily life, and visitors

will often have to push past sacred cows which, unsurprisingly after generations of veneration, act as if they own the place.

The fort, built when the city was founded in 1156, is made up of 99 bastions (projections) linked by battlements that are two walls thick in places. It has seen action a number of times in its history and stone missiles – intended to be hurled down on besieging armies – still sit on top of the battlements. Various city states seemed always to be at war, but the fort was first sacked by Muslim invaders in 1294. Rajput warriors would never surrender, preferring to ride out to their inevitable death in battle – an act of mass suicide known as *johar* – while their women and children threw themselves on to fires to preserve their honour.

Although the main attraction of Jaisalmer is the fort itself, there are several things you should aim to see before leaving. Taking up

two sides of the main square of the fort, the Rajmahal (city palace) of the former maharaja is seven storeys high and from the top you can look out over the town below and far out into the desert.

There is also a group of exquisitely carved Jain temples, some dating back to the 12th century when the fort was built. Within those it is possible to enter there is a subtle play of light and shade on the carvings, making them even more impressive than those on the outside.

Detail of balcony carvings

Built almost 700 years ago, the Gadi Sagar tank used to be the sole source of water for the town. Now often completely dry, it sometimes fills during the monsoon season (around September), and you might be rewarded with the rare sight of the fort seemingly perched above a vast lake.

Although it has endured for nearly 900 years Jaisalmer Fort is currently in danger of collapse. The city authorities blame this on soil shrinkage arising from the excessive use of water by the guest houses in the fort. Hoteliers deny this claim and blame the city authorities for using drainage pipes that are too small for the job. Whatever the cause, there are moves afoot to ban all business from the fort, which will

Havelis in Jaisalmer town

mean that tourists must stay in the town outside and pay to visit the fort for sightseeing. Whether or not you agree with this strategy, it will certainly change the atmosphere of the place for ever.

Although the camel trains have long gone Jaisalmer remains a trading town, and people come to its market from the villages nearby. Camels, however, still contribute to the town's prosperity as a number of tourist operators offer camel safaris into the surrounding desert.

On the outskirts of the town are the Barra Bagh *chatris* (royal cenotaphs). These have commanding views over to the fort and offer

Jain temples inside the fort

Detail of carvings in a Jain temple

good vantage points from which to watch the sun set, its last rays turning the town and the fort from the uniform yellow of daytime to a glowing golden hue.

During the peak tourist season (November to January) you can fly to Jaisalmer direct from New Delhi. Outside of these times the airport is closed and you will have to take a night train or a bus from Jodhpur. (There are at least three flights a day from Delhi to Jodhpur.) There are two Heritage hotels in Jaisalmer, the Jawahar Niwas and the Naryan Niwas Palace. The latter has phenomenal views of the fort from its roof. If you fancy a camel safari, you should book with Mr Desert – the face of Jaisalmer.

Sacred cow in the narrow streets of the fort

Elephant statue outside Nathmal ki Haveli

Great Ocean Walk
Australia

The Twelve Apostles at sunset

Few countries, if any, can match Australia when it comes to magnificent wild beaches and awe-inspiring coastlines. Sandwiched between the Otway Ranges and the often tempestuous waters of Bass Strait and the Southern Ocean, the 91-km Great Ocean Walk on the coast of Victoria takes you on an invigorating journey through tangled forests to remote bays and deserted beaches. Along the way you will be reminded of the early days of European settlement, and encounter koalas and kangaroos. The finale is the extraordinary Twelve Apostles – towering sea stacks sculpted by the pounding surf.

Waves crash ashore at Castle Cove

Inaugurated in 2006, this long-distance route takes eight or nine days to complete and runs from Apollo Bay, a two-and-a-half hour drive southwest of Melbourne, to near Glenample Homestead. The rather inexplicable and inglorious official end point – the homestead is no longer open to the public so the route terminates in an isolated car park – means that most people continue to the Twelve Apostles, a kilometre further on, and Loch Ard Gorge, about another hour away, for a more fitting climax to their walk.

Shortly after leaving Apollo Bay, the route skirts around the Marengo Reefs Marine Sanctuary, and takes you past Storm Point and on to Shelly Beach. Although the Great Ocean Walk primarily follows the coastline, there are several sections that detour inland, and the climb from Shelly Beach to Elliot Ridge and back down to Blanket Bay is the longest at around three hours. The trail passes through a beautiful twist of coastal shrub entangled with ancient myrtle beeches before following Parker Road, an old 4WD track amid

Parker Road forest trail

Koala and joey

giant ferns, mountain ash and soaring gum trees. Black wallabies – also known as swamp wallabies – can sometimes be seen bounding through the bush, as you begin the descent back to Blanket Bay, the end point for day one.

An inspiring place to spend a night or two is the Great Ocean Ecolodge, a 20-minute drive from the bay – the hosts pick you up and

take you back to the trail. Owned and run by dynamic young ecologists Shayne Neal and Lizzie Corke, it is an environment research centre and refuge for injured wildlife. With acres of eucalyptus forest in its grounds, it is ideal for spotting koalas, and at dawn and dusk you can sit in the lodge and watch kangaroos and wallabies foraging near by.

Back on the trail, the 3.5-km section to Parker Estuary skirts high above the sea through more enchanting forest, before descending quickly back to the shoreline. After crossing the Parker

Cape Otway lighthouse

river, the low-tide route has you scrambling over rocks and boulders, and along pristine beaches, before climbing to reach Cape Otway lighthouse. The combination of stormy seas and rugged coastline was disastrous for many ships during the early years of Australia's exploration by Europeans. Rounding the cape to reach Melbourne was notoriously difficult and the lighthouse, the first in Victoria, was

built in 1848 in an attempt to reduce the number of shipwrecks. The prominent white tower has become an iconic image of both the state and the Great Ocean Road – the motoring equivalent to the walk. A telegraph station was also built on the site in 1859, allowing direct communication between the mainland and Tasmania. The lighthouse beam was eventually extinguished in 1994, but it is still possible to climb the 18-metre tower for spectacular views over Bass Strait to the left and the Southern Ocean to the right.

Kangaroos at Great Ocean Ecolodge

The highlight of the following day's hike to Castle Cove is walking along lengthy Station Beach, which is pounded by a relentless march of swells and waves. At its southeastern end is Rainbow Falls, a tumble of fresh water over colourful mosses. Walking through sand is slow going, but it allows you more time to be awed by the power of the ocean, as it

Anchor of the *Marie Gabrielle*, Wreck Beach

Surf at Station Beach. Overleaf: Twelve Apostles at dusk

crashes on the shore just metres away. After crossing a bridge over the Aire river the trail narrows, and rises and falls over a series of small headlands below striking orange cliffs to delightful Castle Cove. Another excellent place to overnight, in nearby bed and breakfast accommodation, the cove can be magical at both dawn and dusk.

The walk continues on to Johanna Beach. Wild, remote and at the mercy of the ocean's wrath, it is one of the highlights of the route and wandering along it for an hour or two, watching the full fury of Mother Nature, is a revitalizing experience. After traversing Milanesia Beach and ascending steeply to Moonlight Head, the trail heads inland again before emerging on the coast at the Gables lookout.

The next day, you encounter some remarkable reminders of the fates met by many sailors and passengers who ventured to these parts during the nineteenth century. At the suitably named Wreck Beach, there are anchors from the *Marie Gabrielle*, which floundered in 1869, and the *Fiji*, which hit the rocks in 1891. From the beach, the trail follows a sandy 4WD track to Princetown before entering Port

Walking along Johanna Beach

Previous pages: Giant bamboo forest near Seiryo-ji Temple in Arashiyama district

Garden at Sanzen-in Temple

Venture further from the city to the surrounding countryside and you get a taste of what Kyoto was like in bygone times. At Ohara, about a one-hour bus ride north, the pace of life drops considerably and the enchanting, ancient temple at Sanzen-in is a mossy, green paradise of calm. Rarely visited by tourists, it is a hidden gem with beautiful, wooded gardens ripe for exploring on foot. Half-emerging from the lawns are beguiling, tiny stone figures with childlike, innocent faces, which cannot help but bring a perfect Zen moment of unbridled joy.

ⓘ

Many airlines, including ANA, offer international flights into Tokyo, from where it is a thrilling two-and-a-half hour Shinkansen (bullet train) journey to Kyoto. The Japan National Tourist Organization can supply a wide range of information on visiting Kyoto and the temples, including an excellent brochure of walking routes. It can also advise on the availability of volunteer student guides, who ease the way if you don't speak Japanese. There is an excellent and cheap system of buses and metro trains for getting around Kyoto and its environs. Taxis often take far longer because of heavy traffic. The sakura season shifts from year to year but generally arrives in Kyoto in late March or early April. Autumn is also a beautiful time to visit the city.

Lake at Sanzen-in Temple

Mediterranean Sea from path to Ravello

Amalfi Coast
Italy

Positano clings to the cliffs

Clinging precariously to the steep cliffs and terraces of the Lattari Mountains, villages along the Amalfi coast seem to need only a gentle nudge to send them tumbling into the Mediterranean Sea below. Soaked in Roman, Greek and Byzantine history, and with an inexhaustible supply of gourmet food and wine, the coastline is a relatively little-known walking delight.

Stretching for around 70 km from Sorrento, south of Naples, to Salerno, the coast is renowned for its dramatic road, which twists its way above precipitous drops. The severe terrain you pass through hardly suggests walking as a pleasurable way to explore, but a network of ancient, stone stairways and paths threads its way along the coastline, through the villages and above the cliffs into the beautiful green hinterland.

Amalfi, the pretty little port that gives its name to this part of the coast, is an ideal hub from which to access some of the area's best walks. Strung out along the mouth of a deep gorge and up its sides, the town is riddled with contorted passages and stairways, which in themselves make for intriguing exploration. The main street is dominated by the glittering, gold and columned façade of Sant'

Andrea Cathedral, from where narrow steps lead below the broad cathedral steps on to a balcony walkway to Atrani, the neighbouring village. Far quieter than its popular neighbour, it is set along a narrow beachfront and punctuated at its eastern end by the Santa Maria Magdalena Church set high upon a rocky outcrop jutting into the sea.

From the church, an impressive stone staircase leads ever upwards towards the village of Ravello, which makes for a good half-day round-trip walk from Amalfi. Perched atop a long promontory,

Lemons on sale in Amalfi market

Mules are used to transport goods to villages

Ravello is widely considered to be the most cultured pearl of the Amalfi coast. Its spacious, cobbled main square is a hive of activity by late morning and the swanky cafés around its fringes are the places to be seen. There are several options for walking back to Amalfi, or buses and taxis await anyone with weary legs.

For those with bundles of energy, an excellent extension to the walk – making it a full day – takes you into the beautiful nature reserve at Valle delle Ferriere, inland from Ravello. The path contours below spectacular cliffs, through enchanting woodland and past streams and small waterfalls before it emerges in the village of Pogerola.

Amalfi port

Santa Maria Magdalena Church, Atrani

Sunrise between Amalfi and Atrani

Sant' Andrea Cathedral, Amalfi

Ravello has an enviable ridge-top location

Door at Sant' Andrea Cathedral, Amalfi

To the west of Amalfi the Via Maestra dei Villaggi, an old mule track that dates from the ninth century, leads through lemon groves and idyllic villages far from the tourist trail. Matriarchs returning from local markets patiently and steadily climb the endless steps back to their homes. Mules are still used to transport goods between the main roads and villages, and goat herders run their animals along the track to pastures new.

The most famous walking trail along the Amalfi coast is the fancifully named Footpath of the Gods (Sentiero degli Dei). Running from the mountain village of Bomerano, it snakes its way high up along the coastal cliffs to the village of Nocelle, from where there is a popular trail extension down to the seaside town of Positano. It is an outstanding walk, not simply because the views of the Mediterranean coastline and the island of Capri are majestic, but also because it is relatively easygoing as it descends gradually the entire way. From Bomerano, the footpath skirts around terraced lemon groves and ancient, ruined mountain huts, and above thrilling drops down to Praiano at the foot of the steep, forested slopes below. From Nocelle, a short section along a quiet mountain road leads to the village of Montepertuso and on towards a lengthy, knee-pounding set of steps that takes you all the way down to Positano.

Picturesque, with pastel-coloured houses that seem to be almost stacked on top of each other as they climb up the steep cliff walls, Positano arcs around a small beach and cove. A powerful centre of trade during the twelfth century, the town then fell from grace. Today, it is packed with chic Italian stores and boutique hotels – during the busier seasons visitors fill the narrow streets and it can be a struggle to walk around. For many people, Positano is the only taste they get of this stunning coastline, but by wandering the Amalfi coast's trails and passageways you will discover that the ancient character of the region remains intact.

Footpath of the Gods, near Bomerano

ⓘ

Although it is possible to walk year-round on the Amalfi coast, from late June through August the high temperatures are probably too extreme for most people. The nearest international airport is Naples, from where it is a two- to three-hour journey by a combination of bus and train or taxi to Amalfi. There is an excellent SITA bus network for getting around the coastal villages and towns. Hiring a car is not necessary. Parking space is severely restricted around the towns on the coast, another good reason to use the buses. Julian Tippett's excellent walking guidebook, *Landscapes of Sorrento, Amalfi and Capri – Car Tours and Walks* by Julian Tippett (Sunflower), gives detailed descriptions and maps of many of the possible walks.

The Footpath of the Gods descends gently to Nocelle

Tour du Mont Blanc

France, Italy and Switzerland

Trient village, Switzerland

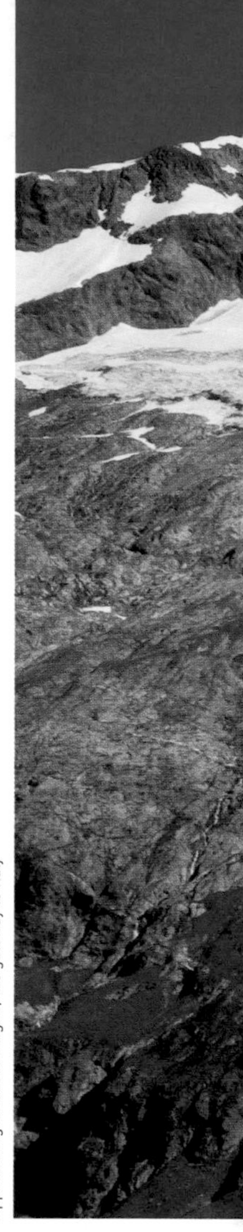

Approaching Col de la Seigne, the gateway to Italy

Snow-capped mountains, lush meadows, wooded valleys, tumbling rivers and the tinkle of cowbells are the sights and sounds of this altogether Alpine experience. Taking in three different countries in roughly 14 days, the Tour du Mont Blanc (TMB) marches across the roof of western Europe, circling its most famous and highest peak.

Europe's most popular long-distance walk, with an estimated 10,000 hikers embarking on it each summer, the TMB was first undertaken in 1767 by Horace-Bénédict de Saussure. Some 170 km long, it winds in and out of valleys linked by a succession of high passes, following an

oval route around its grand mountain epicentre. Although there is an accumulated height gain and loss of roughly 10,000 metres, the highest pass is only 2665 metres, so no technical skills or equipment are needed to complete a circuit during the summer months.

The TMB can be walked in either a clockwise or anti-clockwise direction and there are a number of starting places. The traditional departure point is Les Houches in the Vallée de Chamonix.

A cable-car ride to Bellevue can short-cut the initial hard slog of the first day, after which there is plenty of climbing to be done on the steady ascent to the Col de Tricot at 2120 metres. A Nepalese-style

Torrent de Bionassay, on the trail in France

Alpine meadows ring to the sound of cowbells

suspension bridge that spans the turbulent waters of the Bionnassay must be crossed before the gradual climb upwards continues in earnest, past the sometimes rumbling Glacier de Bionnassay.

A series of switchbacks leads down to the clustered hamlet of Chalets de Miage, serenely positioned next to a burbling river bedecked with Alpine blooms. The path then climbs across the shoulder of Mont Truc before descending through deep green woodland to the pretty ski town of Les Contamines, your first overnight stop, where wood-fronted chalets line the high street.

The next day delivers another steady ascent that initially takes you along a paved mule track and rises through a striking hanging valley, which was formed by glacial erosion, to the Col du Bonhomme. The following lofty traverse to the Col de la Croix provides lengthy vistas of rolling mountain peaks. A popular descent option is to the Vallée des Glaciers and the tiny hamlet of Les Chapieux.

At the head of the valley is the Col de la Seigne; the gateway to Italy. At 2516 metres this pass offers the first potential view of mighty

Mont Blanc, set amidst the grand limestone slabs of the Pyramides Calcaires and the sweeping Vallon de la Lée Blanche. Further down, the pretty Rifugio Elizabetta nestles beneath the sweeping ice of Trélatête and Glacier de la Lée Blanche.

The next town is Cormayeur, where it is worth wandering down the high street if only to admire the chic style of its residents and savour a truly frothy cappuccino or a bowl of home-made pasta. The lush green Val Veni then leads into the Val Ferret, carrying the route onwards and gradually upwards to the 2537-metre Grand Col Ferret; take a backward glance here for the last sweeping views over Italy.

This is where you enter Switzerland and descend through typically rolling Alpine meadows. As you pass the barns and summer pastures of La Peula you will hear the unmistakable clatter of cow

Glacier de la Lée Blanche, Italy

Val Ferret, Italy

bells. Pretty wooden chalets, adorned with the vibrant red Swiss flag, dot the hillside as the path eventually winds into the small town of La Fouly. Set beneath the jutting, frozen cascade of the Glacier de l'A Neuve this is the obvious place for an overnight stay with a view.

Overlooking Champex, a village on the Swiss section of the TMB

The route then meanders enjoyably along the Swiss Val de Ferret, closely following its tumbling river, the Drance de Ferret, its banks lined with pink flowers. Later it slaloms through the chalets of Praz de Fort and the rustic farm buildings of Les Arlaches before ascending, through woodlands awash with wild mushrooms, to Champex. Set around a gracefully curved lake presided over by an intriguing modern sculpture of geese, this village is a popular base for walkers.

Val Ferret, Italy

Glacier de la Lée Blanche and Rifugio Elizabetta, Italy

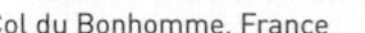

Col du Bonhomme, France

Col de Tricot

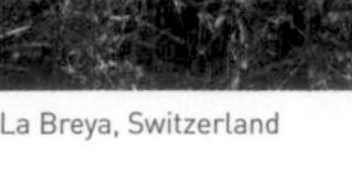

La Breya, Switzerland

Aiguille du Midi overlooks Mont Blanc

A climb through ravined woods, across three different river beds, leads to the barns of Bovine and views down the Vallée du Rhône and to the distant Bernese Oberland mountains. At the 1526-metre Col de la Forclaz you can enjoy one of the local specialities, *tarte aux myrtilles* (blueberry tart), before an easy descent to the small village of Trient clustered around its church.

Vallée de Chamonix, seen from the Aiguille du Midi

From here it's a steady upwards pull to the Col de Balme, where the route crosses back into France and the grand U-shaped Vallée de Chamonix stretches ahead, separating the Aiguilles Rouges and the Mont Blanc massif. After the village of Argentière the path along the Grand Balcon offers airy views to the tumbling, crevasse-strewn Argentière glacier.

At the heart of the valley is the buzzing town of Chamonix, the Alpine capital of mountaineering, where climbers waiting for good weather drink coffee in pavement cafés and the towering mass of Mont Blanc is rarely out of sight. If you want to get even closer to the mountain, the Aiguille du Midi cable car glides upwards to a viewing platform at 3842 metres, from where the snowbound summit can be seen.

On the final section of the route some of the best views of Mont Blanc are from Le Brevant, before the path descends and winds its way through woodland back to Les Houches – making your circular tour of Europe's premier peak complete.

ⓘ

June to September, when most cable cars and the mountain huts are in service, are the most popular months for undertaking the Tour du Mont Blanc. There is no fixed way to walk the route, and accommodation can vary, from camps, mountain refuges to hotels or B&Bs in towns. Sherpa Expeditions offers a two-week escorted tour with hotel accommodation. Bags are transported daily, so you only have to carry a light daypack.

Tiger Leaping Gorge

China

Spectacular night-time illuminations on Wanga Lou Temple, Lijiang

Widely regarded as one of China's best treks, the two- to three-day walk through Tiger Leaping Gorge offers magnificent views of the Yangtze river and the Jade Dragon Snow Mountain range.

Ascending Tiger Leaping Gorge above Walnut Garden

Chinese lanterns, Lijiang old town

The gorge is located about 70 km north of the delightful ancient city of Lijiang in China's remote Yunnan province, close to the border with Tibet and Myanmar. It is the principal capital of the Naxi tribe's autonomous county, and its old town dates back over 800 years – the old cobbled streets, lined with pagoda-roofed houses and restaurants separated by small, winding canals are captivating to explore.

Pleasant in the daytime, the city becomes particularly atmospheric at night, with a surreal mix of dimly lit shops quietly trading much as they have done for centuries butting on to the raucous karaoke scene along Xinhua Jie street, which leads off Sifang Square. Dominating the town in all directions is Lion Hill, crested with the elaborate, multi-tiered Wanga Lou Temple. At night both are illuminated to give one of the most striking city skylines you are ever likely to see.

En route to Halfway Guest House

Village in the clouds, near Daju

Clear streams tumble into the Yangtze river

Although most trekkers access Tiger Leaping Gorge from Qiaotou, an uninspiring, small market town on the main road from Lijiang to Zhongdian, it is possible to start from its other end, at Daju. Setting off from here means you avoid the gruelling ascent up the notorious 'twenty-four bends' section. It is sometimes referred to as 'twenty-eight bends', but both names fail to reflect the reality – that it is a steep, constantly weaving, energy-sapping climb.

The journey to Daju from Lijiang is in itself memorable, as you drive along a rough track through the high peaks of the Jade Dragon Snow Mountain range. Clouds swirl in and out, cloaking and revealing

Narrow canyon near Halfway Guest House. Overleaf: Rockfalls often tumble into the gorge, partly blocking the Yangtze river

the valley far below, with its small villages and the snaking Yangtze. From tiny Daju – which has no facilities – it is a short walk down the steep bank of the river to reach the ferry. Banish all thoughts of a Yangtze cruise – this mini-ferry is purely functional: slightly battered and powered by two tractor engines complete with steering wheels. When you look at the swift currents of the caffelatte-coloured Yangtze you will wonder whether the life jackets should be worn rather than kept in a plastic bag behind steel bars in the driver's cabin.

Once across the river, a winding road traverses the relatively flat valley floor before gradually ascending into the gorge, to the small

village of Walnut Garden. This is a good place for lunch with several restaurants boasting terraces that overlook the chasm. The Yangtze reaches its narrowest point here in the gorge – at the 25-metre-wide spot where, according to legend, a tiger leapt across the raging water to escape a hunter. This funnelling of the water flow creates rapids so powerful that only one of the attempts to traverse this part of the river, by a Chinese team who in 1986 rafted the entire Yangtze from source to sea, has been successful; all the others have ended in catastrophe.

Around 20 minutes from Walnut Garden the road walking ends and the high trail proper begins, just opposite Tina's Guest House. It gently climbs across open slopes with ever improving views down along the Yangtze – this section is known locally as Golden Sands river. The gorge is sandwiched between two imposing peaks, 5596-metre Jade Dragon Snow Mountain, which gives its name to the

Buddhist prayer flags flutter at a trail shrine

Several small villages are located in the gorge

entire range, and Haba Mountain, not much less a colossus at 5396 metres. The summits are often shrouded in cloud, but the sheer 2000-metre-high dark rock walls of the gorge ensure that the scenery is always spectacular.

The ascent eventually eases and the path traverses, passing a couple of waterfalls, some isolated Naxi family houses and a shrine bedecked with fluttering Buddhist prayer flags. It then reaches your overnight stop: the appropriately named Halfway Guest House, set in an enviable location in Ben di wan village. You can sip a beer or green tea on the terrace and enjoy the beckoning silence of nature, as dusk casts its subtle blue and pink light across the cliffs opposite.

High waterfalls bisect the trail en route to Halfway Guest House

If you are on a two-day schedule, the second day's walk is a couple of hours longer than the hike on day one. The trail is fairly easy-going for the first couple of hours, following a wide track before it leaves the open slopes and ascends through delightful forest towards a 2660-metre knoll that heralds the descent along the 'twenty-four bends' section. The downward path is tricky to negotiate, but you will be thankful you aren't one of the many poor souls you pass who are having to ascend it. All too soon, the altitude of the high trail is lost and the path emerges alongside the Yangtze river. The road walk out to Qiaotou will give you plenty of time to savour the memories of your enthralling trek on the high trail of this impressive gorge.

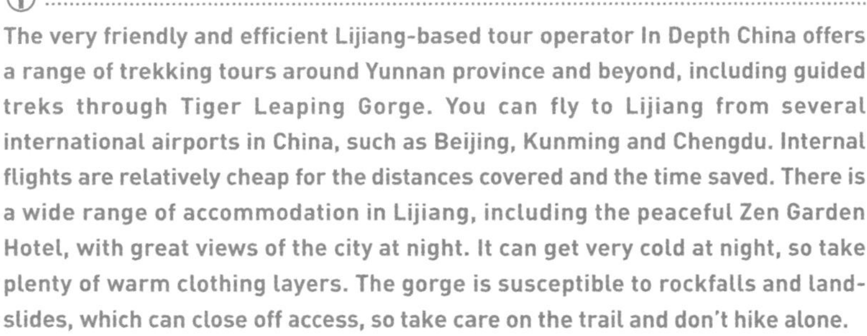

The very friendly and efficient Lijiang-based tour operator In Depth China offers a range of trekking tours around Yunnan province and beyond, including guided treks through Tiger Leaping Gorge. You can fly to Lijiang from several international airports in China, such as Beijing, Kunming and Chengdu. Internal flights are relatively cheap for the distances covered and the time saved. There is a wide range of accommodation in Lijiang, including the peaceful Zen Garden Hotel, with great views of the city at night. It can get very cold at night, so take plenty of warm clothing layers. The gorge is susceptible to rockfalls and landslides, which can close off access, so take care on the trail and don't hike alone.

Morne Trois Pitons
Dominica

The Caribbean conjures up images of white sandy beaches, luxury resorts, relaxation and overdressed cocktails, but Dominica is different, very different. With merely a handful of volcanic black-sand beaches, one five-star hotel and pristine rainforests perfect for action-packed hiking, only cocktails survive the comparison. After tackling the best trails the Caribbean has to offer, those fancy drinks will taste sweeter than ever.

Nestled between Guadeloupe and Martinique, about halfway along the crescent-moon-shaped chain of the Lesser Antilles, Dominica is the Caribbean island that progress left behind. With no direct international flights, getting there requires a modicum of effort, which thankfully is enough to deter the tourist masses. Even the cruise ships that stop by every now and then rarely stay overnight. This relative isolation combined with a progressive government initiative to protect natural parts of the island, as reserves and national parks, means Dominica is more authentically Caribbean than almost any other island in the region: tranquil, green and as easy-paced as a lazy Sunday morning.

Nearing the island, the view from the plane window is of precipitous valleys, heavily cloaked in steaming, impenetrable

Middleham Falls

Boiling Lake

Thermal stream, near Roseau

rainforest leading up to the ragged, dark peaks of Morne Trois Pitons National Park. Such is the immediate allure and mystery of the place, it is easy to understand why the *Pirates of the Caribbean* movies were filmed on the island.

One of the appeals of hiking on Dominica is that your days don't have to be all about walking. Up in the foothills behind Roseau, the capital, there are spectacular, natural hot springs with massage treatments and holistic healing on tap to ease your mind and soothe those weary feet and shoulders. Fruit and vegetables, which have probably been grown within a stone's throw of the restaurant table, are so succulent and tasty they stir memories of how food used to taste before global markets became the norm. Hummingbirds flit skilfully among vibrantly green broad leaves looking for nectar, lizards scurry across the soft, moist ground and the humid warmth wraps itself around you like a comfort blanket. In Dominica, everything feels right with the world.

Contrary to first impressions, the intimidating terrain of Morne Trois Pitons National Park, which covers around 6880 hectares, offers a range of excellent walks to suit just about any ability. One of the easier options, and a good choice for initially stretching your legs, is the two- to three-hour return hike up to Middleham Falls. The trail winds its way through dense rainforest, barely giving a hint of the powerful cascade ahead. After an hour or so, the increasing roar heralds your arrival and soon after a blanket of fine spray drenches everything. The 60-metre fall plummets from a small cleft among the trees and, barely touching a rock en route, splashes into the large, green plunge pool far below.

Morne Trois Pitons, after which the national park is named, is the island's second-highest mountain, and there is no gentle warm-up if you decide to hike to its summit. From the start the route follows steep and often slippery steps and muddy paths – compensated for by great views over the entire eastern side of the island.

Exotic flowers are found all over the island

A bizarre twist comes near the summit, where the trail winds its way among and through a dense tangle of giant tree roots: a dark, dank and utterly fascinating underworld. Then, with little warning, you pop your head out of a gap and find you are at the top – a unique approach to a summit. The views over much of the island and out to the Caribbean Sea are outstanding.

Tangled rhododendron roots near the summit of Morne Trois Pitons

The most renowned trail on Dominica, and quite possibly the best trek in the entire Caribbean, takes in pristine wilderness and surreal geothermal areas on the way to Boiling Lake. Although it is only a six- to seven-hour return hike, it is not for the faint hearted. The trail starts out easily enough, easing its way gently upwards through thick rain-forest from dramatic Titou Gorge, where early returners may get a chance to cool off with a swim.

After crossing Trois Pitons river, tagged Breakfast river by the guides and the only accessible place to drink refreshingly chilled

Descent into the Valley of Desolation

Roseau Bay

rainforest water, the trail climbs steeply and incessantly up the flank of Morne Nichols on to a breathtaking knife-edge ridge. All around, lush green tree tops rise and fall with valleys that few people have seen at ground level. After cresting the ridge, where blustery weather conditions can exaggerate the effects of exposure, the trail takes a hair-raising dive into the spectacular Valley of Desolation. Near the bottom there is the first whiff of sulphur, and wispy puffs of steam from the geothermal springs can be seen.

As the trail descends into the steam, the valley floor sparks into life, bubbling and hissing as you pass fumaroles and mud pots. Beyond the springs, the trail constricts and continues high above the sulphur-filled waters of a stream, before a stiff climb leads up to the dramatically located Boiling Lake.

Set deep in a steep-sided mountain bowl, backdropped by soaring green peaks, the milky-blue lake boils and threatens to erupt into something much bigger but never does. The size of the lake has fluctuated drastically over time and it has even drained away completely before refilling itself, sometimes with cold water that slowly comes back to the boil. It is a wondrous and wild sight on this idyllic island, and it makes the ascent back out of the Valley of Desolation seem fully worth it.

ⓘ

The Dominica Tourist Office can supply information about all aspects of visiting the island and walking there, including recommending local guides. There are no direct international flights, so it is necessary to reach Dominica via Antigua or one of the other nearby Caribbean islands. British Airways offers direct flights to Antigua and other Caribbean destinations. There is a wide range of accommodation on offer, from seafront hotels in Roseau to spa retreats in the hills above.

Goatherd Leap (Salto del Cabrero)

Drovers' Roads
Andalucia, Spain

Step on to the drovers' roads of Andalucia and you will find yourself walking through a way of life that has defined the landscape for centuries. These well-trodden routes are the natural corridors used by shepherd, muleteer and goat herder alike. Thankfully, today you don't need a herd to explore them.

Whitewashed village of Grazalema

The roads can be found throughout Andalucia – the alluring deep south of Spain and heartland of flamenco, sherry and the grand sierras. The region is famous for its pueblos blancos (white villages) and one of them, Grazalema, is among the many places from which drovers used to depart.

Located in the northwest and a two-hour drive from Malaga, in a high valley in the Sierra del Endrinal, it clusters beneath the dominating rocky mass of Peñón Grande in the heart of Andalucia's first designated natural park: Sierra de Grazalema. The village itself is a twist of cobbled streets, where colourful flowers tumble from window pots; the high sierras rear above the houses and verdant valleys trail below them. This is one of Spain's most ecologically outstanding

regions. Rare griffon vultures soar on warm thermals and over 30 different species of orchid as well as unique Pinsapo fir trees can be found.

A twist of different paths, worn into the landscape after years of use by sheep, goats and mules, lead from Grazalema to surrounding villages like lofty Zahara de la Sierra, roughly five hours' walk away, with its Moorish castle precariously seated atop a craggy cliffside. The fortress is one of the area's most distinctive sights with the

Embalse de Zahara, a vast man-made lake, near Zahara de la Sierra

Late afternoon light in the streets of Grazalema

whitewashed houses beneath it spilling out to offer ringside views over the brilliant azure waters of the lake, Embalse de Zahara. Close by, Goatherd Leap (Salto del Cabrero) preserves the legend of the broken-hearted herder who flung himself from the 80-metre high walls of the chasm.

An ideal walk through this pastoral landscape links Grazalema to the neighbouring village of Montejaque, 17 km away. The rough, cobbled track of the Camino Medieval (medieval road) skirts out of town beneath towering limestone cliffs. The tinkling of a lead goat's bell may still be heard, an echo of both past and present as the path remains a working route, still used by modern-day herders.

The route goes south through rolling grassland then weaves through the corkwoods. Here, harvested trees reveal glowing orange trunks where strips of cork have been freshly cut. The path emerges from the dense woods into a clearing known locally as the cork patio.

The lofty village of Zahara de la Sierra

Below, lush, open plains, speckled with plump, rounded tree tops, hum with birdsong and the occasional buzz of a dragonfly. It was here that the drovers would put their animals out to graze for a while. It is not hard to imagine them stopping beneath the shady bowers of a tree for a brief respite from the midday sun.

While journeys between villages could sometimes be long, and may even have required drovers to camp out overnight, huddled down

Tumbling wildflowers and packhorse bridges are typical of Andalucia

Wild iris

at the nearest watering hole, they were not always lonely. The roads they travelled on were the natural highways, busy routes that followed valleys and streams, and avoided mountain ascents. They were the only way to get to market.

The main trail continues roughly northeastwards, towards what was once a bustling *finca* (farm) and is now a ramshackle ruin. The remains of the stone threshing floor can be found among the jumble of grasses and wild flowers, a hint of what were very different times.

Further down the track, orderly lines of olive trees cut stripes across the hillside and the rich brown earth glows with reddish hues in the afternoon light. The route now winds its way through the groves, a sign once more of the continuing relationship between the fertile land and its people; another crop carefully tended to produce an annual harvest.

Wild flowers scatter the banks, a confused sea of colours with yellows and pinks lapping at its edges. The track climbs a little higher towards a rocky pass amid the towering Sierra de Montalate. The limestone rock has been carved into deep notches and rough boulders, which line the drovers' route as it heads towards the valley floor. Up here in the peaceful solitude, the distant buzz of machinery

Flower box window, Grazalema

Evening stroll around the streets of Benaocaz

Ancient threshing floor on the Montejaque drovers' road

Various drovers' roads lead through Sierra de Grazalema National Park

from the sheep farm below is the only clue that life has moved on in any way.

The route now contours gracefully along the valley edge, then curves its way downwards on a good path. Slowly Montejaque comes into view. Chickens scratch for seeds in the verges and a terrace of squat, stone cottages lines the road into the village, where old men gather in the cobbled streets to catch up on the day's events.

Dawn mist over an Andalucian farm

Sheep flocks on an ancient route to Grazalema

With the exception of the hot summer months, Andalucia has an ideal climate for walking. One of the best times to visit the region is during spring (May) when its wild flowers are abundant. The nearest international airport to Grazalema is Malaga, approximately a two-hour drive away. Andalucian Adventures provides guided walking tours throughout the region, with a specialist wild-flowers tour based in Grazalema. Their walking programme includes many opportunities to explore the drovers' roads in this area.

King Ludwig's Way
Germany

King Ludwig's Way skirts the foothills of the Alps near Wildsteig

Eccentric and colourful, Ludwig II ruled Bavaria for 22 years until his early death in 1886 – and left a legacy of fanciful castles as well as an enduring mystery about his demise. Walking King Ludwig's Way, a 120-km national trail, is a sumptuous week-long stroll through the landscapes and traditional culture that helped to shape him.

In the south of Germany, bordering the Alps, Bavaria is the country's largest region and also its wealthiest and most egalitarian. The trail begins at Leoni, near Starnberg, on the edge of the Starnbergsee, the

lake where the king met his death, and ends at Füssen, close to Ludwig's greatest masterpiece: the fairy-tale Neuschwanstein Castle.

The king's dreamy, peaceful character and his style of rule, which included extravagant building projects and substantial financial support for the composer Richard Wagner, caused unrest among his powerful political enemies. In 1886, with no solid medical evidence, he was declared insane and was deposed. Three days later, Ludwig went for a walk around the Starnbergsee with his physician, and later that night their bodies were found in the lake. Many theories, from

Farm fields en route to Wessobrun

Monastery at Wessobrun

suicide to murder, have been expounded to explain why they died, but the truth remains an intriguing mystery.

Although most daily sections of the trail involve about 20 km of walking, the first day's effort after arriving in Starnberg – a 90-minute train journey from Munich airport – is a gentle 7 km from Leoni back to Starnberg. You reach Leoni by cab or ferry, and the main reason for this loop is to visit the tiny Votiv Chapel on the lake shore, which was erected to commemorate Ludwig's death.

Next morning, you head from Starnberg towards Diessen, on the edge of a vast lake, the Ammersee. The trail, consistently signed with a blue crown and K symbol, wends its way through the woodlands of the Maizinger ravine before crossing open farmland to the pretty village of Aschering. Another section of tranquil forest emerges on to rolling hills and a shrine-lined path to the hill-top monastery town of Andechs.

Founded in 1455 by Benedictine monks, the monastery is renowned both for its baroque church – built after the original buildings were destroyed by fire in 1669 – and the monks' on-site brewery. The astounding rococo frescos on the church ceiling will have you craning your neck, but a tipple of the monk's potent brew

The hill-top monastery town of Andechs is famous for its beer-brewing monks

A view from Diessen, which sits on the shores of Lake Ammersee

Church tower at Andechs

will be more than enough to ease any aches en route to Herrsching, the lake port for the ferry-crossing to Diessen.

Set on the southern shore of the Ammersee, the small town of Diessen has a charming waterfront park, where old fishing nets hang from wooden boathouses and sailing boats are moored to rickety jetties. The town centre features a couple of traditional restaurants or Gasthofs, where you can indulge in delicious Bavarian fare, such as goulash soup or Wiener schnitzel. On your way out of Diessen, you can visit the city's cathedral: the Marienmuenster. The whitewashed walls sit proudly on the skyline and it is one of Bavaria's most impressive baroque buildings.

The route continues through idyllic woods and open pastures, with views to the distant Alps, and along quiet back roads to the monastery at Wessobrun, another spectacular rococo gem. You will see blue-and-white striped maypoles in many of the towns and villages along the way, and the one at Wessobrun, just outside the Gasthof zum Post, features an array of figures that reflect Bavarian rural life.

The high point of the trail is at Hohenpeissenberg, before the overnight stop at Unterbrau. The climb is not too strenuous and the astounding views, across the forested valley to the high peaks of the Alps, from the terrace of the Gasthof at the top of the ascent are worth the effort. From Unterbrau, you enter the most dramatic part of the route as you negotiate the Ammerschlucht traverse, a breath-taking path through an enchanting beech forest in a sheer-sided glacial gorge. Where necessary, wooden boardwalks span precarious drops and ladders go up rocky outcrops.

Following an overnight stay in Rottenbuch, a delightful monastery town set around a cobbled square reached via a stone gateway, the route heads towards Buching. Along the way, it passes through the

Rococo ceiling at Rottenbuch church

Wies church attracts many pilgrims

A view of the Alps en route to Buching

Overleaf: Neuschwanstein Castle sits atop a dramatic ridge overlooking Forggensee

popular village of Wies with its ornately decorated baroque church – a pilgrimage site famed for its statue of Christ, which is reported to have cried tears in 1738 – and on through serene pine forests to Steingaden. As you approach Buching, at the base of the Alps, the towers of Neuschwanstein Castle can be seen on a distant hill.

Although there are buses up to the castle, the most fitting way to arrive is via the awe-inspiring ascent through the steep and narrow

Dusk over a small lake near Füssen

Evening light on a church at Buching

Pöllat Gorge. As striking as this part of the route is, it cannot eclipse the impact of the view from the exposed, gravity-defying bridge at its top. Neuschwanstein Castle, with its fairy-tale turrets, is perched on a precipitous ridge high above Ludwig's more reserved Hohenschwangau Castle and the green plain around the Forggensee and Füssen. The king built Neuschwanstein in 1869 as a temple to Wagner's genius. Ludwig's demise may be shrouded in uncertainty, but there can be no doubts about the majesty and vision of his architectural legacy or the richness of this walk through his much loved Bavaria.

ⓘ

Sherpa Expeditions, based in the UK, offers tours along King Ludwig's Way. It arranges accommodation en route, daily luggage transfers, so that you only need to carry a daypack, and international flights if necessary. The nearest international airport is Munich. From there it is a 90-minute train journey to Starnberg. The walking is fairly easy for most of the route. The best time to go is between May and early October.

Ascending Pöllat Gorge

Forest trail between Wies and Steingaden

King Ludwig's Neuschwanstein Castle (left) and Hohenschwangau Castle (right) at sunset

Fallingwater
USA

Over the last century human interaction with the natural world has all too frequently led to devastating consequences. This only serves to accentuate the pinnacle of perfection achieved by renowned American architect Frank Lloyd Wright when he integrated his architectural masterpiece, Fallingwater, into the Pennsylvania landscape. This iconic building, set among forest-clad slopes criss-crossed with a network of hiking trails, is proof that it is possible for us to live in balance with nature.

Nature and architecture mix on the cantilevered decks

Located near the town of Ohiopyle in the Laurel Highlands, part of Pennsylvania's Allegheny Mountains, Fallingwater is now owned by the Western Pennsylvania Conservancy. It was commissioned in 1934 by the Kaufmann family, who wanted a summer house at their favourite picnic spot, near a waterfall on their Bear Run property. Edgar Kaufmann Jr, had read Lloyd Wright's *An Autobiography* and been instantly won over by his holistic approach to blending architecture with nature. He told his father about him and Fallingwater resulted, reaching completion in 1939. It became famous almost immediately, when it was featured on the front cover of *Time* magazine.

Fallingwater was built across the Bear Run river waterfall

Stream, Fallingwater

Arbutus Trail in Bear Run Nature Reserve

Frank Lloyd Wright's inspiration for his organic architecture flowed from many sources, but some of his earliest influences date back to the summers he spent working on his family's farm near Spring Green in the Wisconsin river valley. He observed the subtle nuances of light throughout the day, and how the landscape changed as the sun marched across the sky; he watched the dappled rays as they filtered through the tree canopy on to the earth. Surrounded by woodland and rocky outcrops, he saw at first hand how natural structures provide enduring support for each other and form unlikely shapes and patterns. Later, Henry David Thoreau's and Ralph Waldo Emerson's writings about nature struck a chord deep inside him. All these influences came together perfectly in Fallingwater, widely acclaimed as his finest achievement.

While it is tempting to make straight for the house itself, to see it in context it is best to head first into the Bear Run Nature Reserve, just a few minutes' drive north of Ohiopyle along Highway 381. Also

Curvaceous tree form

Tree and rock colours merge, Bear Run Nature Reserve

owned by the Western Pennsylvania Conservancy, this 2020-hectare area on the west slope of the Laurel Ridge features about 32 km of trails, which can be followed individually or linked together to form longer hikes. Whatever your choice, exploring the reserve demands a slow walking pace. The more relaxed it is, the more remarkable this undulating terrain becomes.

There are 16 marked trails ranging from the 500-metre Kinglet Trail to the 4.1-km Peninsula Trail, which takes you to a lookout high above the Youghiogheny Valley. The Arbutus Trail is recommended as

Bear Run river runs into the Youghiogheny river, seen at dusk

Stone cairn, Youghiogheny river

Bear Run stream

a gentle introduction, as it heads along relatively flat terrain through a tangle of rhododendron bushes and mountain laurel. Amble along and your eyes will steadily become attuned to the subtle beauty of the forest: the splash of sunlight on the warped trunk of a hemlock tree, the shadow of a plant falling on a sandstone boulder. The sounds of the forest begin to sink in, too: the rustle of leaves as a breeze blows through the canopy, the flutter of a bird's wing.

For a full day out you can link the Arbutus and Wintergreen trails, climb on up the wilder Bear Run Trail, and then loop around the Laurel Run Trail on to the Peninsula Trail. If you tire, there are quicker alternative routes back to the car park. To see the Youghiogheny river up close, take one of the easy trails around the Ferncliff Peninsula, near the railroad crossing in Ohiopyle, which lead to lookouts over its most impressive rapids – a worthwhile two-hour hike.

Once you have an appreciation of the surrounding landscape, your visit to Fallingwater itself will be enriched. When you walk into its grounds, past a rocky outcrop, you soon hear the waters of Bear Run stream flowing towards the property over a tumble of bedrock. When the Kaufmanns told Lloyd Wright they wanted a house that would take full advantage of a dramatic rock ledge and waterfall, they couldn't have dreamt that he would build one that spanned them. It is an astounding and daring piece of design that brings the water through the middle of the structure before it cascades below large cantilevered terraces.

Cantilevered tree on Ferncliff Peninsula

Curved tree, Bear Run Nature Reserve

The longer you spend admiring the exterior of the house, the more the subtle intertwining of nature and architecture becomes apparent. The buttress walls, constructed from sandstone quarried from the site itself, merge into the slope behind them. The terraces mirror the overhanging rock ledge below. The concrete slats of the extensive canopy over the main walkway are exquisitely shaped to bend around existing trees. Sunlight and shadow fall on surfaces with the chaotic beauty that is found in the woods of Bear Run Nature Reserve.

This meshing of nature and creative design continues inside Fallingwater. The fireplace is half cut-stone, half natural bedrock.

Main lounge, Fallingwater

Stairway leading to Bear Run stream

Canopy bends around a tree trunk

Countless framed panes of glass allow light to flood in through the windows, which reflect the surrounding trees and landscape in such a way that it is, at times, impossible to tell what is interior and what is exterior.

There are several trails around the property, the most striking of which leads to a lookout downstream where the valley widens. From here, the house is dwarfed by towering trees and rising slopes, and the multi-tiered drop of the waterfall is as mesmerizing as the house itself. Here it is the wonder of nature, not architecture, that is overwhelming – just as Frank Lloyd Wright intended.

ⓘ

Access to the interior of the house is strictly controlled by the Western Pennsylvania Conservancy, with limited numbers of visitors allowed in each day, except on Mondays when the house interior is closed. Tickets are usually booked up well in advance, but it is possible to get on to an interior tour on the day if the allocation is not already taken up. The tours range from 55 minutes to two hours in duration. The grounds are open daily and less restricted, and you can buy entry tickets on arrival. No tickets are necessary for the Bear Run Nature Reserve. Trail maps are available in the car park.

Sculpture on cantilevered deck

Interior and exterior become one at Fallingwater

Cantilevered decks span the river

Canals of Amsterdam

The Netherlands

One of Amsterdam's 'Seven Bridges'

The hubbub of café life spills a chorus of chattering voices beside them, clock towers peal their chimes above them, while bicycle wheels clink and rattle on the cobblestone bridges that cross them. Wandering along the waterways of Amsterdam is the perfect way to soak up the laid-back charm of a city carved by its canals.

The major ones are collectively known as the *grachtengordel* (girdle of canals) and ring the city centre. On the adjacent cobbled walkways, in a harmonious jumble of offices, houses, restaurants and bars, you will find the life and soul of Amsterdam – at work, rest and play.

Canal boats and townhouses both offer city centre living

The Amstel river, one of Amsterdam's busiest waterways

This radial network of waterways – a total of 165 wind neatly through the city – plots an intuitive pathway, so route-finding is easy: you simply choose a canal and follow it. Very quickly it will lead you to another and then another. While it might be tempting to join the 600,000 bikers speeding through the streets, or hop aboard one of the many boats that cruise the canals, this is a city perfectly suited for wandering, strolling and ambling. You never have to go far to find the next interesting stop-off.

From the Singel, Amsterdam's original medieval moat, three other canals, built during the Golden Era of the seventeenth century as part of the city's urban-regeneration scheme, spread concentrically outwards: Herengracht, named after the *heren* ('gentlemen' or, sometimes, 'lords') who were responsible for its construction; Keizersgracht, which commemorated Maximilian I – the Kaiser and Holy Roman Emperor – and Prinsengracht, named after Prince William of Orange. This area, where the rich once lived, is now the ideal starting point for walks. Interconnecting streets and canals offer further opportunities for exploring.

Gable-gazing is a must on canal streets lined with slender five-storey buildings. The most famous is the seventeenth-century

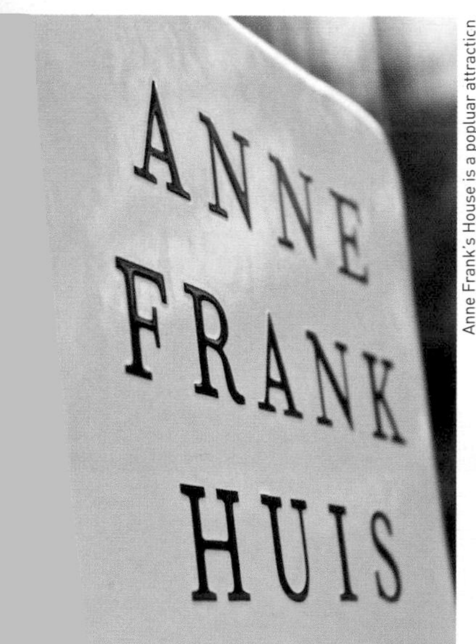

Anne Frank's House is a popluar attraction

Gable-topped townhouses line the city streets

residence at 263 Prinsengracht, where teenage diarist Anne Frank and her family hid for two years during the Second World War. Despite the house attracting almost a million visitors annually, it isn't difficult to get away from the crowds on Prinsengracht. As you walk along the canal you can soak up the atmosphere at some of the city's unique brown cafés. These hark back to the time when Amsterdam was the richest port in the world, with a steady stream of incoming traffic, people and goods. They offered up *gezelligheid*, a kind of Dutch cosiness or conviviality that was sorely missed by sailors on long sea journeys. Dotted throughout the city, they have barely changed, with their dark wood-panelled interiors, smoke-stained walls and often sand-covered floors.

At Bloemstraat, just off Prinsengracht's main thoroughfare, is Café Chris. A tap house since 1624, it is opposite the Western Church (Westerkerk) and is where its thirsty builders went to receive their wages. Heading north along the canal to Egelantiersgracht reveals Café 't Smalle. Beyond the pretty canalside patio with its line of fluttering sunshades, creaking wooden doors lead inside to reveal a moment caught in time. Orderly glass bottles line the shelves,

Leliegracht and Keizersgracht are lit at night

Moored houseboats on the *grachtengordel*

wooden seating carves shadows in the dim light and travellers wander in to pull up a stool at the panelled bar and catch up on news.

Much of the charm of Amsterdam is in what remains behind closed doors. The hidden courtyards and secret gardens of the *hofjes* (almshouses) are another telling find. Often the only clue to

Early morning on the Keizergracht, one of the main canals

their existence is a small nameplate hinting at the oasis that lies behind it. Some of the gardens are open to the public, and at 107 Egelantiersgracht a green door leads through a narrow, blue-tiled corridor to an inner courtyard. Here, among swaying foxgloves, the sounds of the city fade away.

Short cuts and stop-offs are all part of experiencing Amsterdam on foot, and almost every corner on Prinsengracht beckons you to a detour. If you dip into the Nine Streets (Negen Straatjes), where each boutique-filled lane looks like the next one, you will find almost anything you may want to buy. One store, the White Teeth Shop (De Witte TandenWinkel), is dedicated solely to toothbrushes and dental care.

Kloveniersburgwal, the outermost of the three eastern canals in the medieval part of Amsterdam

Modern buildings line the Ijhaven waterfront

Bridge leading to Scheepstimmermanstraat

The far eastern end of Prinsengracht leads to the wide reaches of the Amstel river and the seventeenth-century sluice gates that allow the city's canals to be flushed with fresh water. Just above these is one of Amsterdam's most famous sights: the Skinny Bridge (Magere Brug), a hand-operated wooden drawbridge.

In a city that can boast 1281 different bridges it's easy to find yourself lingering simply to take in how much they are a part of Amsterdam life. Boats glide gracefully beneath them and people lean on black metal railings or thick stone edges to catch a moment's sun, while the shrill peal of a bicycle bell warns walkers to move to the side. A deviation worth making is to Herengracht Bridge, from where the graceful stone arches of the famous seven canal bridges can be spied. At night they light up in a kaleidoscope of converging colours.

Every aspect of life can be seen around Amsterdam's canals and now, as the city expands, these waterways continue to define its urban spaces. In the waterfront area bordering the IJ, the waterway artery that allows access to the city, there are new developments and exciting architecture. On Java island you can find a modern twist of geometric lines and bolder vivid colours redefining the traditional canal house. And if you cross to Borneo island from Sporenburg, via either of two distinctive curving red bridges, you can wander along Scheepstimmermanstraat with its eccentric façades.

In the midst of this maze of modern glass-fronted buildings the brick Lloyd Hotel is an intriguing testament to change. This former youth prison, which still retains a host of original features including bars on some of the windows, has been carefully redesigned and now provides accommodation, a bar and restaurant. In front a broad walkway overlooks the water's edge and, as the sun dips over the water, Amsterdammers can be spotted taking their final canalside walk for the day.

ⓘ

Amsterdam is a year-round destination, but the summer months attract the biggest crowds to main attractions like Anne Frank's House. The city offers accommodation of all ranges and to meet all budgets. Well worth it for its sweeping panoramic views is the Amsterdam Movenpick, which sits between the old town and the newer waterfront developments on the IJ. The main canal areas are all within walking distance.

The Nemo Science Centre, Oosterdok

One of the planet's iconic features, Mount Kilimanjaro rises above the Tanzanian plains like an ice-crested stairway to the gods. It is the tallest free-standing mountain in the world and the highest peak on the African continent, and every year thousands of people are drawn to its slopes in the hope of standing atop its snow-clad summit.

Acclimatization hike from Barranco Hut

At 5895 metres above sea level, this solitary, inactive volcano is not in the Earth's upper league of lofty mountains, but with the plains that surround it languishing around 4600 metres below its summit, the first glimpse of it as you fly into Kilimanjaro airport, near the town of Moshi, is both daunting and breathtaking. It was first climbed in 1889 by a local guide, Yohanas Kinyala Lauwo, along with a German climber, Hans Meyer. But it wasn't until 1936, when Ernest Hemingway published his short story 'The Snows of Kilimanjaro' in *Esquire* magazine, that the mountain began to enter the wider public consciousness. Since then the numbers of people attempting the climb have increased dramatically, so you will not find yourself trekking alone.

Mount Kilimanjaro

Tanzania

Kilimanjaro peeks through afternoon cloud above Barranco Hut campsite

The giant endemic lobelia (Lobelia deckenii)

First views of Kilimanjaro on the Umbwe route

There are several recognized routes to choose from, the most popular of which is the Marangu, where you stay in basic mountain huts during the five- to six-day trek. The six- to seven-day Machame trail, via the Shira Plateau and Lava Tower, is the current favourite for those looking to avoid the Marangu crowds. However, the preferred choice of many of the local guides is the Umbwe route, which also takes six to seven days. Tagged as the most difficult of the climbs, the

Umbwe is also one of the most beautiful. For the first two days, before it merges with the Machame and Shira trails at the Barranco Hut campsite, it is far less trodden than the other main paths.

One of the most striking features of trekking up Mount Kilimanjaro is experiencing five distinct climatic zones, from the semi-arid lower slopes, through montane forest, moorland and highland desert to the arctic conditions around the summit. As you set out on the Umbwe route you are immediately encircled by lush forest, where colobus monkeys swing through the canopy. Occasionally,

Ascending through cloud forest on the Umbwe route

local villagers scuttle past you on the trail carrying plants and tree leaves used for everything from cooking to bedding.

On the first day, the six-hour trek starts gently before the trail steepens towards the overnight camp, set in a small clearing among a twist of trees at just below 3500 metres. Although altitude can suppress appetite, a substantial evening meal supplies essential energy for the next day's climb – the section that has earned the

Spectacular view of Mount Meru from the top of Barranco Wall

Umbwe its tag of being the most difficult route on Mount Kilimanjaro. Relentlessly steep, it takes around six or seven hours, but the upside is that you should be distracted from the effort by the stunning scenery en route.

The path climbs through a fairytale land of juniper trees dripping with wispy, pale mosses, which filter the sunlight into an ethereal glow. The ridgeline grows ever narrower until it seems you are almost walking in the air, with plunging, forest-clad valleys on both sides. Now and then, clearings give stunning views across the plains far below to the soaring bulk of 4566-metre Mount Meru, Kilimanjaro's only mountain neighbour, far off to the west. Eventually, the shining white glaciers on the summit of Kilimanjaro appear high above you. It is inspiring to see them, but they still seem distant even after the day's long climb, and this will bring home the challenge involved in getting to the top of Africa's highest peak.

After the 3900-metre-high Barranco Hut campsite, spectacularly set below the southwest flank of the mountain, the route gains

Cliffs above the Western Breach

relatively little altitude over the next couple of days. The Umbwe used to follow a more direct line up the Western Breach, but this was closed in 2006 after a serious rockfall that claimed the lives of three American trekkers. It now traverses from Barranco Hut to the Barafu Hut campsite, at 4600 metres on the southeast flank.

The imposing Barranco Wall is ascended on a precipitous path, and the trail then eases around the mountain before a sharp descent and subsequent ascent herald your arrival at Barafu Hut – the base camp for the summit attempt. This often starts at midnight, so nervousness increases as darkness descends and you wait for the late evening wake-up call. At this altitude it is very cold, no matter what the time of year and, when the sky is clear and the stars are twinkling in their millions, the temperature is likely to be well below freezing. Every available layer of clothing is needed for this part of the trek.

This last day is by far the most epic. It takes eight to ten hours through the night to climb the 1400 metres to the summit at Uhuru Peak, with its vast volcanic craters and harsh, black rock terrain.

Sunset on Kilimanjaro at Barranco Hut

Dawn above cloud-covered Moshi

Following your triumphant arrival there, and a brief appreciation of the breathtaking views over the plains below, there is a steep, three- to four-hour descent back to Barafu Hut for a snack break. The next four or seven hours are spent descending to one of the lower campsites on the Mweka route or all the way to the park gate. The steep and oversized steps pound your knees, but the sense of achievement at standing atop the roof of Africa makes such momentary suffering worth while.

Innovative tour operator High & Wild, based in the United Kingdom, offers guided trips on the Umbwe route. These include rest days, which significantly increases their success rate in getting clients to the summit. It is also pioneering the use of the latest Himalayan mountaineering-style oxygen systems, where oxygen fed through the nose is used for the final ascent. It is imperative to investigate your trek operator, to ensure they are not taking logistical short cuts, which can affect your chances of reaching the summit and may threaten your health, or offering low prices through not paying their porters properly. Five-day treks, offered by several companies, are often too short to allow most people to acclimatize properly. Many people suffer with some degree of altitude-related sickness. Acute Mountain Sickness is a very serious condition and can be fatal, so read up about the symptoms before going.

Dusk view of Mount Meru from Barafu Hut

Meteora
Greece

Great Meteoron Monastery

Agios Antonios Monastery

At Meteora, in central Greece, grand rock spires crowned with Byzantine monasteries glide skywards above the sweeping Thessaly plain. Amidst these lofty pinnacles, a place of spiritual retreat for monks of the Greek Orthodox church, smaller spiralling outcrops resembling whipped cream are topped with overhanging scrub. In between, a network of paths connects these religious sanctuaries, enabling walkers to make their own spiritual ascent.

Roussanou Monastery is surrouned by Meteora's towering pinnacles

The area first became the focus of religious attention in the eleventh century, when devout hermits seeking solitude built rudimentary wooden structures that clung to the rock faces. More ascetics followed them and made use of existing caves gouged in the weathered rocks.

The first monastery was founded in the fourteenth century by the monk Athanasios, on a rock he called Great Meteoron (Megalo Meteoron) – which later gave its name to the whole complex of monasteries: Meteora. The word means 'suspended in the air', and is

an apt description for these precariously sited buildings, whose wooden galleries and corniced roof tops crown the formidable rock towers that rise from the vast Thessaly flatland. In their heyday there were 24 working monasteries with ornate frescos and vast libraries containing rare handwritten manuscripts.

The target of German mortars during the Second World War and used by communists during the Greek civil war (1944–9) the mona-

Dawn over the Thessaly plains

Dramatic cliffs at Kalambaka

steries sustained heavy damage. But a period of revival followed and in 1988 Meteora was named a UNESCO World Heritage Site.

The mighty sandstone rocks on which the monasteries were built stand like sentries, weathered by the ravages of wind and rain. Given their scale as they rear up from the plains, it is almost impossible to believe that this area was once under water. It was a huge lake that eventually drained into the Aegean Sea, and a mass of stones, sand and mud that had previously formed a single cone was split by erosion. Seismic vibrations, strong winds and heavy rain further sculpted the twisting rock formations of today's Meteora.

With a busy road now connecting the six inhabited monasteries, which are open to visitors, and the bustling town of Kalambaka spread beneath the rocks, it may be difficult to comprehend that Meteora was once a spiritual outpost, reached only by the truly determined.

Wind and rain sculpted the rock spires of Meteora

However, the well-worn twisting paths that led the monks to their sanctuaries still lace through the pinnacles, gradually weaving upwards. As they have done for centuries, they continue to take travellers into the heart of this majestic geological garden.

The village of Kastraki, 2 km north of Kalambaka, nestles beneath a weighty outcrop, on which the uninhabited Holy Spirit Monastery (Agio Pneuma) stands, and is the starting point for a

Evening light on Roussanou Monastery

Stone carving, Great Meteoron Monastery

number of routes. A couple of cafés edge the central square where morning customers sit in the sun, sipping ice-cold frappés charged with strong Greek espresso coffee.

One of the most popular paths, a leisurely day-walk of approximately 10 km, heads north to the secluded church of Agios Georgios Mandelas where paved steps lead up from the road into beautiful woodland. Normally a peaceful section of the route, on St George's Day, 23 April, it is transformed as villagers line the path eagerly awaiting the young men of Kastraki, who climb the soaring rock wall above the wood to place cloths in a small cavern shrine. The fluttering scraps of fabric look almost like prayer flags.

The route winds through the woodland down to the main road and crosses it a few hundred metres from the monastery of Agios Nikolaos, set on an isolated column close to the tooth-like Doupiani rock. An initially cobbled pathway leads gently upwards through a steep-sided gorge where moss-laden branches almost obscure the track in places. It then passes the Varlaam and Great Meteoron monasteries, where stone stairways lead to bulky wooden doorways that provide a glimpse into a remote devotional way of life.

The trail continues roughly northwards and takes you through secluded woods past cairns that mark the way to the uninhabited Ipapanti Monastery. The austere Vlahava monument, an incongruous metal statue of a lone swordsman, overlooks rolling farmland below. Now a dirt track, the path winds back through this gentle countryside giving further views of Meteora. Here tall, yellow grasses frame the west-facing rocks and in the late afternoon, as the sun begins to dip, the scene is bathed in a golden glow. The route then leads southwards to the bulky mass of Doupiani and the road back to Kastraki.

The imposing nature of Meteora's jagged columns often makes the monasteries above them seem inaccessible – and for the most

Church window, Great Meteoron Monastery

Roussanou Monastery

Holy Trinity Monastery

The uninhabited Ipapanti Monastery clings precariously to the cliff face

Rock pinnacles at dawn

Roussanou Monastery is home to a community of nuns

Great Meteoron was Meteora's first monastery

A sunset walk above Kalambaka

part the rock faces themselves can only be explored by equipped climbers using ropes. But it is possible to walk to the Holy Spirit Monastery above Kastraki, a round trip of about two hours. A path round the base of the pinnacle on which it is built continues past the wooden-slatted platform of a cave hermitage, known as the monastic prison, and takes you into a narrow inner gorge. Halfway along this a pathway leads up to the monastery, a cave shrine gouged into the rock wall.

A scramble on to the rocks above the shrine will reward you with views across the Thessaly plain to the encircling Pindos and Antichasia mountain massifs and the Peneios river below; for a moment you may well feel that you are suspended in the air.

ⓘ

The monasteries of Meteora can be busy, particularly during the summer months when it is worth while arriving early to avoid the crowds. The best walking temperatures are in spring and autumn. The nearest airport is at Thessaloniki, about a four-hour drive away on good roads. It is also possible to take a train from Thessaloniki or Athens with a switch at Larissa. If you travel from Athens, take a morning train so that you can enjoy the spectacular scenery as you pass through the mountains between Livadia and Lamia.

Ennerdale Water, the most westerly lake in the Lake District National Park

Coast to Coast
England

Two coasts, three national parks and the chance to cross an entire country are just some of the features that make the Coast to Coast walk an enduring classic. This 307-km route links the Irish Sea and North Sea, and is a testament to the dedication and passion of perhaps Britain's most famous walker: Alfred Wainwright.

The climb up from Ullswater leads to Angle Tarn

Best known for his pictorial guides to the Lake District, Wainwright expanded his vision beyond the boundaries of the Cumbrian fells he loved so much. In 1973 *A Coast to Coast Walk*, his illustrated guidebook to the long-distance trail he created through the valleys, hills and moors of northern England, was published. The route is not, however, a nationally recognized footpath and does not carry any official status. It offers one way to cross the country – through the Lake District, Yorkshire Dales and North York Moors national parks – but there are many potential variants. It was this sense of possibility and the joy of route-finding that Wainwright championed so enthusiastically. He encouraged hikers to adopt their own approach and seek out alternatives to his suggestions.

As a result there is no fixed direction in which to tackle it. Wainwright's preferred route begins in the west at St Bees and takes you eastward to Robin Hood's Bay, just south of Whitby. This has become a popular choice for hikers, as the push of the prevailing winds is behind them. But many choose to start in the east and keep the Lake District as the dramatic climax to their walk. Whatever your choice, Wainwright conceived the Coast to Coast so that it can either be broken down into smaller sections that are completed individually over a period of time, or – as many favour – so that it can be done as one continuous walk over a two-week period.

Thousands of people embark on the route each year, the lure of the opposing coast spurring them onwards. If you start in the west,

The Lakeland frontier is reached at Ennerdale Bridge

Wainwright advises that you dip a booted toe in the Irish Sea at St Bees and a naked foot in the waters of Robin Hood's Bay. There will be times when this refreshing meeting with the North Sea can't come soon enough.

The walk gets under way by traversing the high cliffs of St Bees Head, where nodding rosebay willowherb sways in the wind and seagulls squawk and dive-bomb. It then meanders across easy countryside, passing Cleator Moor, leading ultimately to Ennerdale Bridge. Here, at the head of Ennerdale Water, you truly get the sense of being on a frontier, as the distinctive shapes of the Lakeland fells that Wainwright loved so dearly, and which he described as 'paradise on Earth', rear ahead.

Journey's end at Robin Hood's Bay

Farms near Reeth village, Yorkshire Dales National Park

Grosmont, a 1950s station on the North York Moors Railway

Previous pages: Fields overlooking St Bees Head

Twisting street in Robin Hood's Bay

If you don't have time to undertake the whole walk, and only want to select a single section, it would be hard to find a rival to the one that takes you through the Lake District. Spanning three to four days, it marches across the heart of this famous national park, often along passes and packhorse routes carved by quarrymen many years ago. In doing so it takes in such well-known highlights as Helm Crag, rising loftily above Grasmere, home to William Wordsworth, as well as a multitude of tumbling becks, isolated tarns and lakes such as Ullswater and Brothers Water.

A highlight of the route comes as you climb out of Patterdale and on to the Straits of Riggindale, a narrow pass that leads down from the summit of High Street and follows the Roman road that once linked Ambleside and Brougham. Just above this narrow spine the path eases upwards to Kidsty Pike, which, at 780 metres, is the highest point in the walk. Beneath its distinctive rocky pinnacle, Haweswater reservoir shimmers and far beyond, on a clear day, the softening slopes of the western Pennines beckon.

What lies between the Lakes and the Pennines is different again. After passing the ruins of Shap Abbey you reach the pretty market town of Kirby Stephen and then the distinctive Nine Standards – a collection of cairns used as county-boundary markers. Ahead, sheep farms and a patchwork of drystone walls and lush green rolling fields herald your entrance to the Yorkshire Dales.

Swaledale awaits, with its meandering river, tumbling waterfalls like Wain Wath Force and the sleepy settlement of Keld, an isolated outpost of farms that is the halfway point of the Coast to Coast walk. A path along the river and onwards to Reeth takes you through some of the prettiest landscapes in the Dales. Alternatively, Wainwright's traditional path follows higher ground through the intriguing ruins of Swaledale's lead industry.

Climbing towards Kidsty Pike above Brothers Water

Then follows the market town of Richmond, the most fortified and perhaps the most elegant settlement on the walk. It has many well-preserved Georgian houses as well as a Norman castle, dating from the eleventh century, that perches impressively on a rocky outcrop above the Swale river.

Hasty Bank, North York Moors National Park

Dusk at Ennerdale Bridge

The route continues eastwards through rich, flat farmlands – the heart of the Vale of Mowbray – and onwards to the Cleveland escarpment, which gives entrance into the North York Moors National Park. Here the landscape glows purple when the heather is in bloom.

The final stretch will have you hankering for a glimpse of that long-awaited sea. Impressive cliffs lead to shapely Robin Hood's Bay where a dinky town of narrow, twisting streets clusters at the bottom of a steep rise. There is only one thing left to do once you get there: it is time, as Wainwright instructed, to unlace your boots and dip your toes in the waters of the North Sea.

This walk can be undertaken at any time of the year although the spring months, when there are fewer people, are preferable; booking your accommodation in advance is always advisable. Various companies offer bag-transfer services, which will help to lighten the load, as you will only need to carry a daypack.

Early morning stroll on St Bees Head beach

Sunset views towards the Irish Sea from above Cleator Moor

Takesi Trail

Bolivia

Lake Titicaca is the world's highest navigable lake

Morning light on the Royal Mountain range (Cordi.lera Real)

Dramatic, brooding and laced with history, Bolivia is a living, breathing landscape of legend. Here you can literally step through time and walk to the origins of the Inca dynasty on Sun Island (Isla del Sol), and follow the Takesi Trail, an ancient, paved trading route that stretches 43 km from the high Andes to the gateway of the Amazon.

While Bolivia offers an abundance of walking opportunities you won't be going anywhere immediately if you fly directly into La Paz. Located at 4058 metres, it is the world's highest capital city. At such a height the rarefied air may well make your head spin, so it is essential to allow yourself time to acclimatize before you embark on the higher ground of the Takesi Trail. Part of this process will allow you to explore the extraordinary Inca culture and its remarkable history.

Less than a two-hour drive from the city, the huge expanse of Lake Titicaca, the highest navigable lake in the world, is an ideal place to

En route to Chincana ruins, Lake Titicaca

adjust to conditions with some easy walking trails. Equal in size to Corsica, its striking blue waters lick at the edge of the windswept Altiplano. An almost entirely straight road runs out of La Paz. It is speckled with smallholdings and simple low-slung brick houses and flanked by the awesome jutting bulk of the Cordillera Real range.

Lake Titicaca is actually two lakes joined by the Straits of Tiquina. To the north, in the larger lake, Lago Mayor (or Chucuito, which means

Rock sculptures, Sun Island

Terraces, San Baya Peninsula

Copacabana, a pilgrim town on the shores of Lake Titicaca

'fertility'), are Sun Island and Moon Island (Isla de la Luna), key locations in the Inca creation myth.

Sun Island is widely regarded as the place where it all began, the cradle of the formidable Inca nation, or *tiksi marka* (the place of origin). While there are a number of creation myths, the most popular suggests that Viracocha, the creator god, took a handful of land and a handful of water from the lake and created his children, Manco Kapac

Traditional Aymara life continues on Sun Island

Llamas are used as pack animals

and Mama Ocllo, who were charged with the task of finding somewhere to base Viracocha's people. They left the high plateau and discovered Cuzco – in Peru – the eventual capital of the Incas. At the northwest end of the island is a sacred rock, called the Puma Stone – 'Titi Kaka' in the Andean Aymara language – which is worshipped as the birthplace of the Incas and gave the lake its name.

The site became the ultimate destination for pilgrims, who forged a trail across the spine of Sun Island. Starting on the eastern edge from Pilcocaina, the once resplendent sun gate, it took them to the Puma Stone and the Chincana Temple, the ruins of which are believed to predate the Incas and extend back to the Tiwanaku (AD 600–1100). This sophisticated civilization was noted for remarkable developments in agriculture, including advanced irrigation systems.

Allow a full day for the Sun Island trail, which will take you vividly back through history. At Chincana, a sacrificial stone, where virgins were killed and offered to the gods, remains a brutal testament to the demands the Inca deities made on their worshippers. The route ends at the Sacred Fountain (Fuente Sagrada): traditionally pilgrims drank its waters to prevent them abusing the fundamental cosmic laws by lying, being lazy or stealing. Also known as the font of eternal youth, it is rumoured to knock ten years off your age, and drinking from it may well be the final, enlivening part of your acclimatization process.

The ancient trading routes of the Tiwanaku and the Incas are defining features of the landscape and have become popular with walkers. Four different Inca trails surround La Paz and link the majestic high Andes with the Yungas, a subtropical region where citrus trees, coffee and coca grow. The three-day Takesi Trail is perhaps the easiest of these.

The journey to the trailhead, roughly two hours by minibus, takes you along a twisting road below the strange, fluted formations of the

Reed boat, Lake Titicaca

Urus-Iruitos, a floating reed island village

Chojlla River, Takesi Trail

Valley of the Souls (Valle de las Ánimas), which widens to reveal awesome views of Illimani, the 6439-metre mountain that dominates the La Paz skyline. Snow-capped peaks tumble on either side, tumultuous clouds build overhead and below you llamas roam freely in tranquil, dusty fields.

The trail begins by steadily climbing a broad valley past Mina San Francisco, a former silver mine, to the Takesi Pass (Apacheta) at 4630 metres. This three-hour section takes you across some of the best examples of traditional Inca paving stones. As you gradually climb to the top of the pass it is common to find that the clouds you may have seen earlier are lingering. At a cairn amidst the swirling mist it is traditional to make an offering to Pachamama, the Inca earth mother and a goddess of fertility, by adding a stone and throwing a few drops of alcohol on the ground.

The uphill work is over and most of the walk is now downwards, snaking through the high mountains and past the waters of Lake Wara Warani. More Inca paving stones line a route to the tiny hamlet

Aymara woman and llama, Lake Titicaca

of Takesi, a remote outpost that once served as the main stopping point for traders passing through. Nowadays most travellers camp a little further down, next to the tumbling waters of the Takesi river.

The next section takes you from the rugged mountains of the high Andes into cloud forest, where temperatures soar and bamboo plants grow alongside rose bushes. Jukumarini (rare Andean bears) still roam wild through this thick vegetation.

The thin line of the trail flashes white against this veil of green, clinging to the steep-sided valley as it curls down to the village of Kakapi; seemingly precariously placed, the buildings look ready to slide down the slopes at almost any moment. Here a lush, trellised garden provides a potential campsite where hanging vines and sweeping clouds add to a distinctly jungle feel.

After Kakapi, the final day's walk brings you to the tumbling Chojlla river, a boulder garden of fast-flowing white water, which signals that you are nearing the end of the trail. There is one last climb up to the village of Chojlla, after which your final challenge is surviving the rough jungle road, with its cascading hairpin bends, that takes you back to La Paz.

Illimani summit can be seen from La Paz

ⓘ

The Bolivian trekking season is generally regarded as running from May to September, with the most stable weather from June to September. If you fly directly into La Paz, a period of acclimatization is essential before you attempt any form of trekking. London-based travel specialist Tim Best Travel provides full advice and organizes bespoke tours throughout Bolivia, including fully staffed treks on the Takesi Trail with English-speaking guides.

Entering Cardiac Canyon

The Wave, North Buttes

Not even Salvador Dali with his creative genius could have conjured up the surreal landscapes to be found around Coyote Buttes. Multilayered rock formations in countless shades of pink, purple, orange and yellow have been sculpted into unimaginable whorls by wind, rain and flash floods. One of the most extraordinary places on the planet, hiking through it is at times like making your way through a fanciful geological cake mix.

Coyote Buttes

Arizona, USA

Coyote Buttes lies in northern Arizona, near the Utah border, and is most easily accessed from Page, a small town set above the dramatic Glen Canyon dam. Surrounded by major national parks, such as Bryce Canyon to the north and the Grand Canyon to the south, Coyote Buttes and its environs are often bypassed, so exploring the canyons and outcrops there rarely involves dodging crowds. Just one word of warning: the landscape can be bewildering, so a local guide is virtually essential.

Access to Coyote Buttes, which lies within the Paria Canyon-Vermilion Cliffs Wilderness area to the west of the Paria River, is strictly controlled, partly via a permit lottery system, to help protect the fragile formations. While waiting for your number to come up, a fantastic adventure can be had near Page in Cardiac Canyon and Canyon X. Two of Arizona's numerous slot canyons (sheer-walled and very narrow sandstone chasms that can be hundreds of feet high), they can make an

Slots and rock waves in Cardiac Canyon

Juniper branch in North Buttes

excellent one-day hike. The adjoining Antelope Canyon is the most famous slot canyon, but it is often overrun with tour groups who are marched through on a feature-list-ticking time schedule. In contrast, Cardiac and X are so far off the beaten track, on Navajo reservation land, that they are almost a secret, even though they are every bit as mesmerizing as their more illustrious neighbour.

It is often hard to see slot canyons from ground level until you stumble right upon them. And when you stare into the deep chasm of

Cardiac Canyon, dark as a moonless night at the bottom, it seems like a gateway to the centre of the Earth. It is impossible to penetrate many slots without ropes, but here the route in is a fun-filled scree run down a steep gully. The searing desert temperatures of the surface drop noticeably as you descend into the shade of the canyon walls.

Craning your neck to glimpse the top of the cliffs soon becomes futile in the ever shrinking entrance to the slot itself. Barely wider

Colourful rocks in South Buttes

Life on the rocks, North Buttes

The Teepees at South Buttes

than a hotel corridor to start with, the trail is swallowed by the overbearing rose-coloured sandstone walls of the gorge, then narrows down to shoulder width or less. The sculpted rock melts and merges into waves, lips, scoops and twirls, like those made by a warm spoon run repeatedly through a tub of ice cream.

A short hike through a wider part, or wash, of the canyon system links into Canyon X. Rarely seen by outsiders, or even by the Navajo

Gnarled juniper branch at South Buttes

Morning light at South Buttes

themselves, for whom the great owls that reside in it are bad omens, it is very different to Cardiac. Halfway through, the slot becomes a tunnel with only dapples of light creeping through tiny rock windows above. The intensity of the colours rippling across the wavy sandstone reaches new depths before you emerge for the scramble back up to the blinding brightness and sapping heat of the surface world.

The Coyote Buttes area is split in two: the South Buttes and the North Buttes. The most popular attraction is the Wave, in the northern half. A 4.8-km hike from the Wire Pass trail head – off Highway 89 to

Crazy 'brain' paving at White Pockets

Kanab – across a trail-less area of dunes and rock outcrops, it is a riot of cross-bedded, multicoloured sandstone. The main formation is the bowl, where the perfectly smoothed rock sweeps up high on all sides like a petrified sea in a violent storm. Visitor numbers are severely restricted here – just 20 people a day are allowed into the North Buttes – but the small size of the Wave area, and the fragility of its surface, leave no doubt that such controls are essential.

A short drive east, before you arrive at the South Buttes, takes you to the unheralded White Pockets area, perhaps the most astonishing of all the rock formations. A thin sheet of white sandstone, formed into brain-like blocks and mounds, overlays the region's more predominant red sandstone and some layers of banana-yellow rock. Where the three mix, they create a visual feast of white, pink, cream and cappuccino-brown swirls that really do look good enough to eat.

The South Buttes are more difficult to access than the North Buttes (a 4WD vehicle is necessary), but it is generally easier to secure permits for them. One of their most beautiful features is the Teepees, an

Dusk light at White Pockets

Sunrise at White Pockets

Coffee-coloured rock swirls dominate at White Pockets

isolated huddle of conical hills that glow golden in the early morning and late afternoon sun. Exploring further, behind the Teepees, reveals precariously balanced sandstone spires, delicate rock fins and ancient, gnarled juniper trees. With extensive views over the entire Paria Canyon-Vermilion Cliffs Wilderness area and Bryce Canyon far to the north, this is a perfect place to sit and contemplate an extraordinary landscape that has been 200 million years in the making.

ⓘ

Hiking takes place year-round, but the summer months can be searingly hot. Flash floods are most likely in July, August and September. Overland Canyon Tours, based in Page, is the only company with Navajo permission to enter Cardiac Canyon and Canyon X. It arranges tailor-made trips to all the main formations. Half the permits for Coyote Buttes are available at the Arizona Bureau of Land Management website, but are snapped up quickly. The remainder are allocated at the daily permit lottery at the Paria Ranger Station. Lotteries for the Wave are heavily oversubscribed, so plan well ahead. Arizona Tourism can advise on travel arrangements, and the Page Boy Hotel is an affordable base.

Canal du Midi
France

Trees enclose many parts of the canal, such as at Trebes

Poppies line the canal

Flying the tricolore at Le Somail

Stretching halfway across southern France from Toulouse to Agde, and part of the link between the Atlantic Ocean and the Mediterranean Sea, the Canal du Midi is one of Europe's greatest engineering feats. Navigating its tree-lined, gentle waters takes you through landscapes, villages and towns that are quintessentially French.

Masterminded by Pierre Paul-Riquet, more than twelve thousand men were employed in its construction, which began in 1666. It was inaugurated in 1681. So impressive was the achievement, and so important is the canal to the heartbeat of the region, that it has recently been given UNESCO World Heritage status. Starting from Toulouse, where it joins the Canal Latéral à la Garonne, which comes from the Atlantic Ocean, it twists and turns for 240 km through the beautiful rolling countryside of Languedoc-Rousillon to Bassin de

Thau, near Agde, on the Mediterranean coast. Once an important trading route, which replaced a 3000-km voyage around the south of Spain, the canal is now the preserve of travellers aboard barges and pleasure cruisers. Some people have made it their home, but most come on holiday to spend a week or so plying its waters.

Winding through the country near Capestang

From Toulouse, it passes through the delightful town of Castelnaudary, where houses roofed with terracotta tiles rise majestically out of the water to the crowning glory of the cathedral with its tall spire. This is the heart of Cathar country, where the heretical sect spread its religion in opposition to the Church of Rome at the end of the 11th century. It was crushed in a series of brutal massacres during the 20-year Albigensian Crusade led by Simon de Montfort, and later persecuted by the Inquisition. Cathar castles dot the ridges and hilltops in several towns of the region and are well worth visiting.

Heading further east, the canal gently winds its way through open country and a series of locks, including a picturesque, tree-lined one at Bram. Most of them offer a chance to take a coffee break and the

Passing under a Roman bridge near Portiragnes

Café at Le Somail

larger ones are good overnight mooring spots. After Bram, in the broad reaches of the Aude valley, lies one of the gems of the entire journey: the spectacular medieval walled city of Carcassonne with its fairy-tale ramparts. The canal runs into its adjacent modern area – an ideal place to stop for a couple of days at least. La Cité, the old part of the city, is protected by an imposing double ring of walls that features 52 towers and is deservedly on UNESCO's World Heritage list.

From Carcassonne, the canal follows the path of the Aude River, taking you through quintessential French terrain where vineyards stretch to the horizon and long, regimented stretches of plane, poplar and cypress trees line its banks. Apart from looking pretty, the trees provide shade, which in turn significantly reduces evaporation, and

Classic French country house at La Croisade

A houseboat at Villeneuve-lès-Béziers

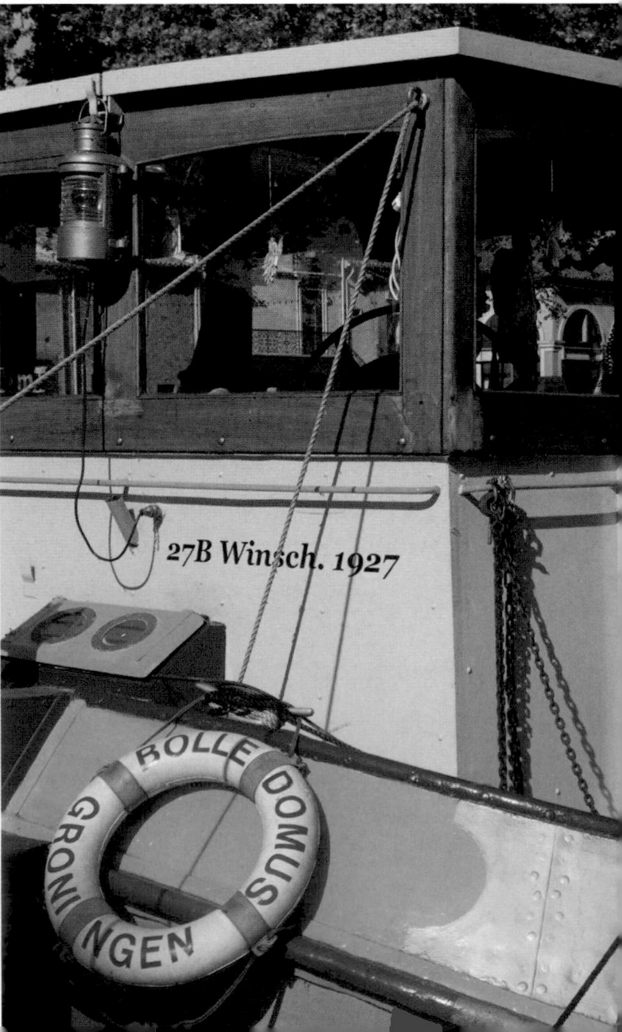

PORT DU SOMAIL
À 12096 MÈT.
DU PONT
DE PICASSE.
À 13343 MÈT.
DE L'ÉCLUSE
D'ARGENS.

AUX MILLE PAINS

BRAM.
CONTRÔLE INTERMÉDIAIRE
DES DROITS DE NAVIGATION.
DISTANCES:
DE L'ÉCLUSE
DE BETEILLE.
4962 MÈTRES.
DE L'ÉCLUSE
DE BRAM.
630 MÈTRES.

ÉCLUSE DE FONFILE
DISTANCES:
DE L'ÉCLUSE
DE MARSEILLETTE
3308 MÈTRES.
DE L'ÉCLUSE
DE St MARTI
1242 MÈTRES

Canal west of Capestang

Radiating fields at Etang de Montady

also strengthen the banks. After negotiating the locks at Trebes, around 8 km out of Carcassonne, the canal returns to open country and you may make it to the village of Puicheric by the end of day.

You will probably enjoy the most memorable moments of your journey in one of the many tiny villages you pass through. Once the canal has left the Aude River and ventured further north, the village of Le Somail awaits with its enchanting ivy-covered lock-keeper's cottage, old medieval church and a couple of excellent waterside restaurants. A glass of fine Languedoc red wine is a perfect dinner companion as you enjoy the tranquillity and watch ducks waddling on the cobbled towpath.

From Le Somail, the canal snakes effortlessly towards La Croisade then on to Capestang – prosperous during the Middle Ages, the town still retains a vestige of its former glory in the commanding collegiate church that dominates the landscape for miles around. Soon after passing Poilhes, you will skirt the southern edges of the Etang de Montady, a plain famed for its radiating fields. From the sleepy village of Montady, high on a nearby hill, they look like slices of

La Cité at Carcassonne

a large pie. The last big population centre on the canal is the lively city of Béziers, about 5 km further east, where the cathedral of Saint-Nazaire is the highlight.

The Mediterranean Sea beckons, and for the last day or so the canal takes you across a flat coastal plain – at times running arrow-straight to the horizon – to the old port of Agde. With its fleet of colourful fishing boats, it is known as the 'black pearl of the Mediterranean' and is a fitting end to a voyage along the Canal du Midi.

Old men chatting at Castelnaudary

ⓘ

Several international airlines fly directly to Toulouse. Numerous companies, based in Toulouse and other villages and towns along the canal, hire out boats ranging from modern motor cruisers to traditional old barges, for periods that can last from as little as one day to several weeks. Traffic levels on the canal can be a little intimidating for novice boat-handlers during the peak summer months of July and August, so try to travel at some other time if possible – the canal is open year round. You don't need a licence to hire a boat, and the hire company will give you lessons in vessel control. If you prefer to leave the stress of driving to someone else, larger barges with professional pilots are available. Most boats are hired out on a self-catering basis.

Yukon river journey
Canada

Stocked up with provisions and paddling onto Lake Laberge

The Yukon River runs through wild, unpopulated country

One of the most famous gold rushes took place in 1897, when the precious metal was discovered in the Klondike. Yet it was far more than just a story of gold and glory. To get to their destination, aspiring miners had to endure a daunting and perilous river journey from Whitehorse to what rapidly became Dawson City. These days, with modern canoe equipment, paddling the same route is one of the best ways to see the raw wilderness of the magnificent Yukon while getting a little taste of what life was like for a Klondike gold rusher.

With 742 km and a week or so of paddling separating Whitehorse from Dawson City, and very limited encounters with civilization en route, this is a trip that must be planned. You need to carry enough food for the entire journey, a barbecue and, of course, seats and a table for dinner in the evening. With expert help from a Whitehorse canoe-outfitter all this, and more, will fit into a standard Canadian canoe – you can even take a cheeseboard.

By the time the original gold rushers reached Whitehorse they had already made an arduous 53-km trek across the mountains on the Chilkoot Trail from Dyea, near Skagway on the Alaskan coast. In the tough winter conditions many people froze to death and others succumbed to exhaustion brought on by transporting huge loads of equipment and belongings. Those who survived the trail were faced with having to build boats at Lake Bennett, to tackle the Yukon River and its notorious rapids. Thankfully, the most dangerous of these, at Miles Canyon, are above the starting point for the modern paddling journey.

The 3700-km-long Yukon flows into the Bering Sea and, along with the Missouri, is the second-longest river in North America – the longest is the Mississippi. In Whitehorse it looks wide and lazy from afar, but up close you'll see that the flow is relentless and rapid. Packed to the gunnels with food and camping gear, the canoe feels heavy and listless when it is first turned into the river. The current carries you swiftly along, then goes slack when the Yukon enters the vast expanse of Lake Laberge.

Rainbow over the river near Camacks

Paddling along the 52-km east shore – preferred by many canoeists as it is 3 km shorter than the opposite one – is a challenge. Catch the lake on a calm day and it is a mirror of tranquillity, especially in the golden evening light. However, when the wind gets up, which may happen without warning, it can turn into a raging sea of white horses with substantial waves. Whatever the weather, it is at least a six-hour paddle to the other end of the lake, more than enough for the first day of the journey.

Before setting up camp alongside the river it is wise to check for bear tracks. There are both black and grizzly bears in the Yukon, and blocking their habitual trails with your tent would not be a good start to your stay in their territory. It is also wise to heed advice about cooking away from your living quarters and storing food either high up in a tree or in airtight barrels. Luckily, your only encounters with these magnificent creatures are likely to be while you are paddling and they are foraging on the river bank.

Loading the canoe at Lake Laberge

The most dramatic section of the Yukon, with a swift flow and sharp bends, is known as the Thirty Mile, and is where you will begin to see evidence of the gold-rush heydays: old woodyards and huts that stored the fuel for the paddle steamers that negotiated the rapids to Dawson City once the rush was well under way. It was a journey fraught with danger, and you soon pass the SS *Klondike*, now engulfed by silt, before reaching Hootalinqua island, final resting place of the SS *Evelyn*. This huge disintegrating ship, built in 1908, was abandoned after only one season. Wandering around the hulking wreck, set back from the river at the top of a ramp, gives a striking insight into the expectations – ultimately unfulfilled – that the gold rush must have generated in many of the people who took part in it. Of the hundred thousand people who came seeking their fortunes, only around thirty thousand made it as far as the goldfields. Far fewer struck it lucky.

SS *Klondike* shipwreck

After Hootalinqua the current becomes more gentle, and you may be fortunate enough to see moose crossing the river, elusive dall sheep with fancy curved horns or bald eagles swooping from their

Shipwreck of the SS *Klondike*, victim of the treacherous rapids

Fort Selkirk is an old trading post

perches high in the trees to take fish from the water. At times the flow is so gentle that you can up your paddles and lie back, enjoying the peace of wilderness life as the canoe drifts downriver. It may come as a rude shock to arrive at Camacks, a small village with one of only four bridges along the Yukon.

The most difficult rapids of the journey await you beyond Camacks, at Five Fingers. The ride through them is bumpy, but once you bob out on the other side you'll soon be back to the gentle, relaxing waters you're used to. From Minto, a good place to stay overnight – one of the campsites is owned by an ex-trapper called Heinz – it is a short paddle to Fort Selkirk. The best-preserved settlers' community on the river, it was established as a trading post in 1848 by Robert Campbell, of the Hudson's Bay Company. It became a major stopping point during the gold rush and even housed a police force. Wandering around its fascinating wooden houses and other buildings gives you a real feel for what life was like at the time.

The final stretch of the journey seems to take a long time, as the river widens and the current becomes even slower, but the wait is well worth it. Dawson City is unique, with its dirt streets, wooden boardwalks and brightly painted, yet slightly dilapidated, wooden houses. You could be excused for thinking you have walked on to the set of a cowboy movie. It was here that many gold rushers ended up, and it still evokes their lawless, hard and fast lifestyle. You can pan for gold, even today, so strike it lucky and you may not want to leave.

Abandoned gold-mining tools at Fort Selkirk

ⓘ

You can fly to Whitehorse via Vancouver with, among a few other airlines, Air Canada. It is a spectacular flight. Several operators in Whitehorse offer canoe trips on the Yukon, including Kanoe People, who have excellent knowledge of the entire river. You need to take the bear threat seriously and carry pepper spray and bear bangers – small fireworks that create a loud bang – just in case you have an encounter. The best time for paddling is during the summer months, June to September, when there is plenty of daylight and it is warm.

Gold-panning competition in Dawson City

The bench in Parque Güell

Tracing the life of Gaudí

Barcelona, Spain

Few geniuses have had the impact on a major city that architect Antonio Gaudí had on Barcelona. His stirring use of colour, shape and form, often inspired by his admiration for nature, are reason enough to visit the great Catalan capital. However, venture just a little further and you can follow the trail of Gaudí's life from Reus, where he was born and went to school, and across the sweeping landscapes of Catalonia, which gave him so much inspiration.

Ceiling roses beneath the square at Parque Güell

Bronze statue of the young Antonio Gaudí in Reus

Born in 1852 in rural Reus, 110 km south-west of Barcelona, Gaudí was the youngest son of an ironmonger and boilermaker. His early life was sculpted by difficulties brought on by rheumatism. Unable to walk far, he was often forced to stay at home, leaving him plenty of time to absorb the elements of nature that surrounded his parents' house.

Today Reus is a busy provincial town, but Gaudí's influence is still felt and honoured there. A short stroll around its pleasant streets takes you to the touching, bronze sculpture of the young Antonio sitting on a bench playing marbles, then past the Iglesia de San Pedro where he was christened and on to the interactive Gaudí museum.

Spiral stairway in La Sagrada Familia

Façade de Passion, La Sagrada Familia

La Sagrada Familia's towers

Tree-like forms inside La Sagrada Familia

Driving through the countryside around Reus you see the natural forms that shaped his thinking. In the rugged and beautiful Pradell mountains to the west, accessed via steep and snaking back roads, tree trunks in open forests echo the support structures that Gaudí used so effectively in his buildings. Indeed, while designing La Sagrada Familia, his iconic cathedral in Barcelona, he said the interior would resemble 'a forest of trees'. Wonky towers of limestone

stand sentinel over the Mediterranean coastal plain and shimmering sea far below, while palm fronds, one of Gaudí's favourite design motifs, fan out from the dry, sun-scorched ground.

As you head back into Barcelona, it is worth making a short detour from the main coast road to see Gaudí's unusual work in the tiny village of Garraf, between Sitges and Castelldefels. Built between 1895 and 1901, the angular Güell Bodegas was used by Eusebi Güell

Curves in the attic at Casa Batlló

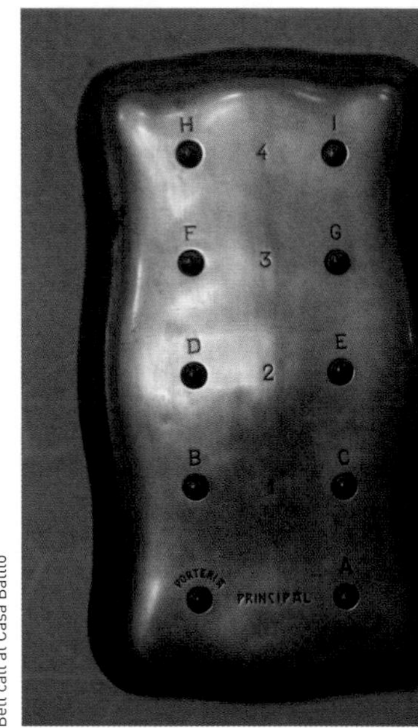

Bell call at Casa Batlló

Sensuous curves in Casa Batlló

to store wine for his export business and features an imposing, iron chain-mail gateway. Another Gaudí masterpiece within easy reach on your return to the city is the remarkable crypt of the church of Colonia Güell at Santa Coloma de Cervelló, which is often regarded as the architect's most pure work.

Deep in the heart of Barcelona, on the Passeig de Grácia, its main thoroughfare, Casa Batlló looks as if it has melted in the intense Spanish sun. Its curvaceous exterior is brought to life by thousands of coloured ceramic tiles and stained-glass windows, balconies shaped like theatrical eye-masks and a roof that looks like an iguana's scaly skin. Inside a seamless flow of curves on swishing staircases and sensuous doors leads you up, around a sky-blue atrium, into the attic area. Here, simple white roof arches tempt you onwards and up, on to that scaly roof where a whimsical collection of chimneys topped with colourful, ceramic balls awaits you.

Not far from Casa Batlló is La Pedrera, also known as Casa Milá, one of Gaudí's final private works in the city. Also built for the Güell family, it is most noted for the unique wave-like forms of its exterior walls and the fantastical Expressionist chimneys and vent structures on its roof.

Of course, no visit to Barcelona or journey into Gaudí's life can ignore La Sagrada Familia, the towering spires of which dominate the skyline and have become the symbol of the city. This was his greatest work, but sadly it wasn't finished in his lifetime – in fact, it has still not been completed and is almost always surrounded by scaffolding. The Façade of the Nativity and the more modern Façade of the Passion alone warrant a few hours of inspection. Inside, among Gaudí's promised forest of trees, a seemingly endless coil of spiral steps takes you to the towers, which afford stunning views of Barcelona.

A window inside Casa Batlló

A perfect place to finish your journey through Gaudí's life is the Parque Güell, on a hill in the suburb of Gracia. This beguiling public park boasts an array of his most vibrant work, including the sinuous, mosaic-tiled bench seat on the raised, colonnaded square and candy-coloured, gingerbread-shaped pavilions. This is where the people of Barcelona come to relax and enjoy the sunset, so you might as well join them and bask in the genius that was Antonio Gaudí.

The roof of Casa Batlló

If you intend to visit several of Gaudí's buildings buy a Gaudí Route Ticket, which entitles you to discounts off the entry fees. There is no entry fee for the Parque Güell. The main Gaudí attractions get very busy, so be prepared to queue. As usual, it helps to get there as early as possible. You can take a train to Reus from Barcelona, but you will need to hire a car if you want to explore the surrounding countryside.

Central courtyard at La Pedrera

Casa Batlló's wavy façade

Horse-drawn caravan

Wicklow, Ireland

Beautiful upper lake at Glendalough

If you fancy life in the slow lane, jump aboard a horse-drawn caravan and explore the sleepy country byways and highways of Wicklow in Ireland. It will be just you, an Irish carthorse and the lure of the open road.

This delightfully simple, back-to-basics journey takes you through idyllic pastoral scenes where the barking of farm dogs and the cries of shinty players mid-match mingle with the hum of tractors at work. With your home for the week towed behind you, courtesy of your sturdy horse, you will have the flexibility to go wherever you wish.

Head west and you will discover heather-clad rolling mountains and sharply hewn valleys, including the dramatic Glenmalure, the

longest glacial valley in the British Isles, and Glendalough, with its stunning lakes. To the east you can find a very different landscape of broad, empty beaches backed by tumbling dunes. The road ahead is yours to explore, with the freedom to make up your own itinerary and schedule as you go along.

One of the advantages of this area is that an intricate network of quiet country lanes is immediately open to you, which makes it easy to plan your route. On a few occasions you may need to stray on to busier roads, but these are well marked on the maps you will be given and are not difficult to negotiate.

There are no fixed itineraries as such, but there are a number of

On the trail at Glendalough

recognized overnight spots that have facilities such as showers as well as grazing and water for horses. Most caravanners simply decide on a route that takes them to these spots along the quietest roads.

Caravan country is less than a two-hour drive south of Dublin in the county of Wicklow, also known as the 'garden of Ireland' for its green lushness. But the joys of the open road can be savoured only after a crash course in carthorse management. You will find that having a horse of your own for a week is rather like suddenly gaining a child – an unusually big and hungry one. It becomes the centre of attention and the focus for the start of the day.

At the base at Carrigmore, where you collect the caravan and horse, you will learn all you need to know about your equine friend, including the art of enticing it from its paddock – something you have to do each morning. The secret is to carry a large bucket of oats, which horses are very quick to sniff out and remarkably deft at getting their noses very firmly and quickly planted inside. They then become much more obliging. After the feed you will need to have your hoof pick at the ready to clear the horse's feet of any stones that could make it lame, and will have to brush down its coat and mane.

The job isn't finished when you have caught and cleaned your steed. Next comes fixing the bridle, saddling up and attaching the shafts from the brightly coloured Romany-style caravan so that the horse can pull it. Controlling a half-ton animal can seem daunting to start with, but everything is geared towards helping people who have no previous experience of horses.

Before you know it you are swinging out from the farm gates and on to your first stretch of road, listening to the steady rumble and creak of the wooden caravan and the clipped rise and fall of hoof beats.

Perched on the wooden seat in front of your caravan, reins in hand and with seven days stretching ahead, you can explore the

Forest trail near Glendalough

hedgerow lanes leading from Carrigmore, and slowly go north through the lush green fields surrounding Glenealy and around the foot of Carrick Mountain, to Garryduff and O'Byrne's farm. Here home-made scones and traditional brown bread provide a delicious end to the day.

As you move westwards the landscape steadily begins to change, from leafy hedgerows that in places have grown almost into full arches to more open and mountainous scenery. Glenmalure – a dramatic glacial valley with jagged cliffs at its upper reaches, tumbling waterfalls and dense, fern-covered slopes – offers the very best of this. It's not hard to see why Michael Dwyer, rebel and local folk hero, made this glen a hideout when he was attempting to escape capture by the English army following the rebellion of 1798. Its steep sides, rocky outcrops and thick forests would have provided the perfect cover.

When you head towards the bustling seaside town of Arklow, nestled on the edge of St George's Channel, the scenery is different again: quiet coastal roads provide open views out to sea and lead to the stunning, uncluttered beaches of Brittas Bay to the north.

Fitzgerald's pub in Avoca, which appeared in the BBC TV series *Ballykissangel*

Arriving at Glenmalure

On the road to Garryduff

The slowed-down pace of the caravan, with its steady rhythm, allows you to sit back and take in each new view that comes with every twist in the road. With speed limited to about 6 km an hour you won't be going anywhere fast, so there's plenty of time to soak in the scenery. It's an altogether relaxed, unfussy way of life.

At the end of your journey you will feel that you have covered a lot of ground in only seven days; and find it hard to believe that you have seen so much of the landscape – given just how slowly the horse plods along. You may even feel that a week is not long enough – that the Romany in you has been stirred and the open road ahead is calling.

Dawn near Glenmalure

Clissmann Horse Caravans have been providing self-drive tours since the 1960s and rent four-berth horse-drawn caravans with cooking and sleeping facilities for a week or more. They give full tuition in horse handling and have an established network of farms, hotels and pubs with fields for grazing and overnight parking for caravans. Several international airlines fly to Dublin, and Irish Ferries provide a regular daily service to the city from Holyhead, Wales.

By rail through Copper Canyon
Chihuahua, Mexico

Slicing its way through the steep, ragged mountains of the Sierra Madre range in north-west Mexico, Copper Canyon is home to one of the world's most dramatic rail journeys. Within 653 km, the Chepe train takes you on a breathtaking ride to a height of over 4000 metres and back to sea level – across the great plains of Chihuahua, through the mountains and across the Pacific coastal plain to Los Mochis.

Chepe train engine

Opposite: Winding into the foothills of the Sierra Madre from Chihuahua

This is not a trip where you simply sit and gawp out of the window. There is plenty to see and do en route, from visiting traditional Mexican towns and Tarahumara Indian villages to hiking through a canyon, so most travellers break up the 15-hour journey by spending a night or two at stops along the line. With only one first class, or 'tourist', train a day – the Chepe Primera Express – running in each direction any break entails an overnight stay. The first class train benefits from smartly uniformed guards, air-conditioned carriages and seat space to rival flying business class, so you really can relax.

The Chepe leaves the town of Chihuahua in the murky light of dawn, and doesn't take long to exit it and enter the open grassy plains – an opportunity for majestic sunrise watching. As the heat of the day rapidly vanquishes the night chill the train speeds along the often arrow-straight line. From it you get a snapshot of daily Mexican life unaffected by your presence. Alongside the track young and old men, most of them wearing cream-coloured panama hats, head off to work on foot or by bicycle. A little later, passing through small towns like Santa Isabel and San Andrés, scores of children in neat crisp uniforms can be seen walking eagerly to school.

Open country near Chihuahua

Beyond the first main stop, the town of Cuauhtémoc, the line passes through thousands of hectares of apple orchards grown by the large population of Mennonites who came to the region in the early 1920s. Their beliefs are based on 16th-century Anabaptist teachings with an emphasis on community, and some of the older order still lead a traditional existence, rather like the Amish, without electricity or cars. Some 50 km further on, at La Junta, the train begins its inexorable journey up into the Sierra Madre mountains, travelling alongside small rivers and traversing beautiful, lush valleys. The windows in the doors between the carriages are the only ones that open, and offer the best views of the dramatic landscape. The temperature will begin to cool noticeably, though, as the train gains height.

Even now, with the most spectacular parts of the journey still to come, what has been achieved by building the railway line in such a wild and unforgiving environment is something to marvel at. The track bends and twists upwards like a serpent, passing through cuttings hewn from the rock and, in its entire length, crossing no fewer than 36 bridges and going through 87 tunnels. Completed in 1961, after

Divisadero is perched on the edge of Copper Canyon

Copper Canyon, the world's largest canyon system

Bridge at Témoris

almost 90 years of on-and-off construction, it is widely recognized as one of the world's greatest feats of engineering.

Many travellers opt to spend a night at the next stop, the sawmill town of Creel, which is a good base for tours into Copper Canyon and out to surrounding Tarahumara villages. However, if you want to stay somewhere very special it is worth remaining on board for the next 50 km until the train reaches Divisadero, a tiny, one-hotel village perched on the very edge of the canyon. The Chepe routinely stops here for 15 minutes so that passengers can take photographs. It is a pity to rush through, though, especially as you arrive in Divisadero around midday when the light bleaches the canyon, making it look less impressive. An overnight stop also means that you get to stay in one of the world's most spectacularly located hotels, where the best rooms have balconies literally on the canyon edge, giving spectacular views of the sunset and sunrise.

Divisadero is a good spot for a guided hike along the rim of the canyon or, for those with a few days to spare, an extended hike to the bottom, which involves camping en route. There, the alpine terrain of the upper canyon is replaced with a tropical landscape where mango and orange trees grow. Copper Canyon is in fact a commonly used term that refers to an interconnecting network of six canyons. Together they cover an area four times larger than the USA's Grand Canyon. They go much deeper too, with the deepest – Urique Canyon – plunging 1879 metres from the rim.

Another good reason to stop overnight in Divisadero is that you can board the train again refreshed for the most spectacular part of the journey. The line plummets through incredible tunnels and switchbacks as the steep canyon walls and rugged peaks soar high above. At times it seems to defy gravity as it clings to a cliff face on one side with, on the other, a sheer drop to a turbulent river. At Témoris

Crossing the plains near Creel

Narrow tunnel above Témoris

it performs a virtuoso triple switchback, during which you can see all three levels, that will leave you amazed at how far the line has dropped towards the valley floor. With a waterfall cascading into the Septentrión River and monolithic rock pinnacles thrusting from the river bed, Témoris is one of the jewels in the Copper Canyon crown.

The landscape continues to enthral as the line winds its way towards El Descanso and Loreto, crossing tall river bridges and skirting beautiful lakes. Eventually, the terrain relents, the temperature increases and the train returns to its higher speeds as it heads west over the coastal plain to El Fuerte. A few hours further on, Los Mochis is the official end of the line. However, as this town is rather characterless,

Previous pages: Hiking trails from Divisadero offer great views of Copper Canyon

Lake scenery near Loreto

many people choose to end their journey at colonial El Fuerte. Sitting in its resplendent plaza lined with palm trees, enjoying the warm evening air, you will be able to reflect on the train ride of a lifetime.

ⓘ

The Chepe first class train runs once a day in each direction all year round. The second class train, used mainly by locals, also operates once a day but is slower and offers none of the comforts of the first class one. Tickets can be bought with as many stopovers as you require, and the journey is very reasonably priced. Although you can buy tickets on the day it is better to reserve them in advance, especially during the busier period of May to October. There are excellent hotels in Chihuahua, Divisadero, Posada de Barrancas and El Fuerte. Other stops may not offer accommodation in the higher range. Both Chihuahua and Los Mochis have airports; flights to the former are usually more competitively priced.

Cutting through the Sierra Madre at Divisadero

Sunset on the plains near Creel

Into the ice bear kingdom

Churchill, Canada

Hudson Bay begins to freeze around November

Every winter in the far northern reaches of Manitoba, at Churchill on the shores of Hudson Bay, polar bears gather to wait for the water to freeze over so that they can hunt seals. Exploring their kingdom aboard an oversized buggy is a remarkable journey into the wild and beautiful tundra at the edge of the Arctic. The reward can be moving, and at times hilarious, encounters with these playful yet deadly bundles of white fur.

Many places in the world are deemed remote, but then you find towns like Churchill. No road has ever made it there, so the only ways in are either to fly – a 2½-hour flight on an old twin-propeller plane – or to go by rail, which takes at least 36 hours. Both plane and train depart from Winnipeg. Whichever way you travel, arriving in the town will

Churchill's main street

initially shock your system. The window of opportunity to see the bears gathering opens in early October and closes in mid-November, lasting around six weeks, which means it is cold, very cold. Not as cold as it gets in January, but chilly enough to make chunky jackets and windproof clothing essential.

At first glance, the simple and unpretentious town – first established in 1717 as a trading post by the Hudson's Bay Company – seems windswept and forsaken. But a short exploration of your surroundings takes you past the ice-covered roads, snow-laden houses and endless surrounding tundra to its Inuit culture, and the warm and hardy people who have made it their home. There are three things that Churchill has in abundance: polar bears – it is tagged the 'polar bear capital of the world' – unrestricted views, and people with

Sunset over the tundra

Sunrise drive to the bear station

Sunset on log house, Churchill

characters big enough to fill a stadium. It seems everyone from your bus driver to restaurant staff has a fully loaded clip of quips ready to fire off on the briefest of encounters. The longer you stay, the more the town, the people and its remarkable landscape get under your skin, and its isolation soon becomes its real appeal.

With only a few other distractions, namely a bar, a sprinkling of restaurants and, if you are lucky, the spectacular aerial shows of the ethereal Northern Lights, the quest to see the polar bears is the main attraction. In the sharp air of early morning, as the sun rises along Kelsey Boulevard, Churchill's main drag, you board a classic old school bus. About half an hour out of town, along the edge of Hudson Bay, you reach the station for the unique tundra buggies. These monster machines are the brainchild of a local guide – they are manufactured in Churchill – and feature tyres big enough to 'float' on top of the soft tundra soil. They may seem over-the-top in the natural wilderness that surrounds you, but as you plunge into the first icy puddle you soon realize that they are the only way to get around such inhospitable terrain. Their impact is limited to an established network of tracks, most of which were made by American tanks: Churchill was a strategic armed forces base from the Second World War to the mid-1980s.

As with most wildlife-focused journeys patience is a prerequisite, but scanning the brown-and-white landscape for any signs of life keeps boredom at bay as the tundra buggy slowly winds its way out towards Gordon Point and further east to Watson Point. In addition to polar bears, you may see other unique northern inhabitants, including caribou, Arctic hares, Arctic foxes, snowy owls and ptarmigans. It is a thrill to see any kind of wildlife, but the first sighting of a polar bear always has the buggy's passengers in raptures. The expert eyes of a naturalist like David Hatch will be a help, as resting bears do excellent imitations of boulders and shrubby mounds when the ground is not entirely covered with snow.

They rarely seem to rest for long, though. They love to play-fight, and if you stop and wait a while you will see them sizing each other up, wrestling and even standing on their back legs – tall and proud like world championship boxers – trading blows and slaps. With male bears weighing in at around 500–600 kg, they are definitely in the heavyweight division, but it is rare for them to inflict any serious injury on each other during these sparring sessions. Females can sometimes be seen escorting their cubs as they pad across one of the

thousands of small, shallow lakes that cover the tundra. The bears' extremely large paws, with exposed black pads and lengthy claws, help to spread their load on thin ice.

As Hudson Bay starts to freeze, which can happen in a matter of days with temperatures of –20°C or below, the bears begin to edge their way out on to the vast expanse of ice in search of seals, their favourite meal. They travel long distances alone and move with the seasonal ebb and flow of the ice looking for tell-tale breathing holes where seals intermittently surface. There they lie, waiting in ambush.

Young males play-fighting

Bears wait patiently for the bay to freeze

Male bears often stand to fight

After driving around the tundra over the course of a few days – the hardy can even stay in special tundra 'motels' made of buggy trailers – you will realize that what at first appeared to be a relatively lifeless, uninhabitable wasteland is in fact awash with life and beauty.

ⓘ

Several companies, including Discover the World, organize trips to Churchill to explore the land of the polar bears. Demand is high, and the short season and limited buggy permits mean that booking well in advance is recommended. Hudson Bay Helicopters is one of the companies that offers thrilling flights over the bay area that give wonderful overviews of the tundra and a different way to see the bears and other wildlife. Accommodation options in Churchill are limited, with the Churchill Motel being one of the best. Temperatures can drop severely at any time, and the wind chill can make it feel even colder, so take plenty of warm clothing.

Driving the Uyuni Salt Flat
Altiplano, Bolivia

Few places on the planet are as wild and difficult to access as the awe-inspiring salt flat around Uyuni in the south-western deserts of Bolivia's Altiplano. With few surfaced roads, exploring the world's largest expanse of salt requires a four-wheel-drive vehicle and a sense of adventure. The rewards are startling, as you see volcanoes in the majestic Sajama National Park, encounter unspoilt Aymara Indian villages and experience the unique thrill of driving across endless salt with virtually nothing to be seen on the entire horizon.

The starting point for any journey in Bolivia is La Paz, which, stunningly located at 3600 metres, is the world's highest capital. It won't take you long to be aware of the altitude – you begin breathing heavily on arrival at the airport – and it is worth planning a day or two

Sajama volcano, Bolivia's highest peak at 6549 metres

Driving into Sajama National Park

Llamas in Sajama National Park

in the city to acclimatize before heading elsewhere. Built in a huge bowl surrounded by 6000-metre-high, snow-capped Andean peaks, La Paz is a constant buzz of activity, with plenty of markets, cultural sights and fiestas to keep you entertained. It is claimed that there are three fiestas for every day of the year.

There are several routes for getting to the Salar de Uyuni (Uyuni Salt Flat) but a good option is to go via the less-frequented gem: the Sajama National Park, south-west of La Paz and right on the Chilean border. Even with an asphalt road going all the way to the park entrance the drive takes four or five hours. With only occasional small villages along the way, often overlooked by ancient, mud-brick Indian

Indian women herding donkeys to Sajama village

tombs, it gives you a sense of Bolivia's vastness and the awesomeness of its wilderness. It is a country ripe for exploring.

The national park is named after Bolivia's highest peak, the 6549-metre Sajama volcano, which, thanks to its isolation, dominates the landscape for miles around. A thick, glacial cap drapes across its summit and its blackened slopes plunge steeply to the Altiplano desert. Those with a head for heights and a guide can spend a couple of days hiking and climbing to its top. For the hardy Aymara and Quechua Indians, Sajama is a sacred mountain representing the head of Muruata, who was beheaded by the god Wiracocha as a punishment for being too arrogant.

Sajama village itself, tucked below the volcano, is a hotchpotch of mud-brick houses, many of which are painted in bright greens, whites and yellows, possibly to add life to the dusty desert landscape. From the village you can drive across the river to a nearby geothermal valley where hot geysers bubble and mud pools boil. With steam rising from the pools and various streams, the scene resembles a battlefield; but the only thing likely to attack you here is the sulphur fumes. If you are lucky, a full moon will rise behind Sajama at dusk, bathing the landscape in an ethereal silver glow.

Reaching the next village, Sabaya, calls for an early start and a drive along a little-used track that skirts the Chilean border, via Macoya and Tunupa. The ride is rough at times but spotting wildlife will be a distraction. Small groups of nervous and flighty vicuna

Driving on to Salar de Coipasa

Vast expanse of Salar de Uyuni

wander the plain. By the 1970s these small members of the camel family had been hunted almost to extinction for their valuable fur. The population has recovered now, thanks to major conservation efforts across the Andes.

From Sabaya, a one-street village way off the beaten tourist track, it is a few kilometres to the Salar de Coipasa, the second-largest salt flat after Uyuni, which boasts a host of small islands near the shore. Leaving the green and brown behind, and driving out along a causeway on to white salt for the first time is quite unnerving. Ahead there is nothing except distant mountains – this is definitely not a place for agoraphobics. The vehicle's wheels crack and crunch across the widespread hexagonal patterns, formed by the salt, that at times make the surface seem like crazy paving. The surface of Coipasa is less stable than that of Uyuni and so the temptation to drive off the main tracks should be resisted. Speeding across the flat is great fun and the route eventually takes you off the salt to Llica, close to the north-western edge of the Uyuni salt flat. Fuelled partly

Cacti grow on rocks above Salar de Uyuni

Sunset trek overlooking Salar de Uyuni

by illicit trade across the Chilean frontier, Llica is a 'happening' town in Altiplano terms, with a rapidly growing population. It is also among the best options outside Uyuni for finding a bed for the night.

The following morning, after checking out at the slightly bizarre military checkpoint at the entrance to the salt flat, it is time to head out into the big white yonder. Salar de Uyuni was part of a giant, prehistoric lake – Minchin – which dried up and deposited a thick layer of salt, covering about 12,000 sq. km and measuring over 130 km across. Near the centre it is possible to find places with an almost perfect 360-degree view of flatness, where you can hear the true meaning of a deafening silence. Occasionally you happen upon a cactus-covered island, shimmering like the mirage of a spaceship. Hike to the top of any of them for a literally breathtaking view.

Sunset over Lake Poopó, near Oruro

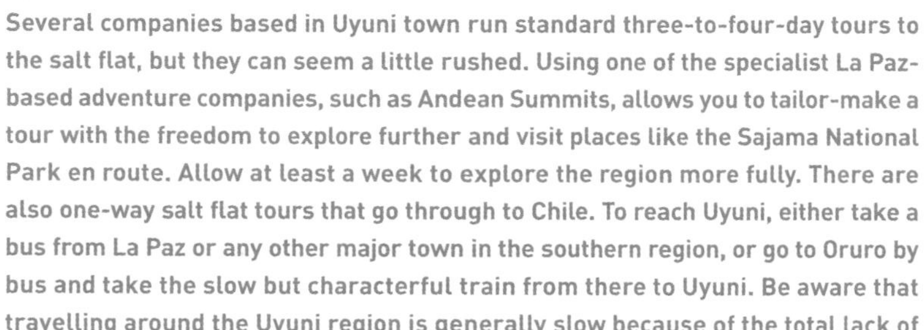

Several companies based in Uyuni town run standard three-to-four-day tours to the salt flat, but they can seem a little rushed. Using one of the specialist La Paz-based adventure companies, such as Andean Summits, allows you to tailor-make a tour with the freedom to explore further and visit places like the Sajama National Park en route. Allow at least a week to explore the region more fully. There are also one-way salt flat tours that go through to Chile. To reach Uyuni, either take a bus from La Paz or any other major town in the southern region, or go to Oruro by bus and take the slow but characterful train from there to Uyuni. Be aware that travelling around the Uyuni region is generally slow because of the total lack of surfaced roads. Accommodation is also very basic.

In one of Mother Nature's most impressive extravaganzas, the arrival of fall in New England sends an extraordinary swathe of amber, yellow and red sweeping across the tree tops. Although autumn colours can be seen around the world, here a unique combination of climate, tree species and terrain makes the display possibly the most spectacular on the planet – and a week or so driving around the region an unforgettable experience.

Driving into the White Mountains

Because it is an all-natural show, it is impossible to predict accurately from year to year where the best colours will be and, more importantly, when they will appear, so it helps to have a flexible holiday plan. October is usually the prime month in New England – a region that borders Canada and includes the states of New Hampshire, Vermont and Maine – and the blanket of colour spreads from north to south. There is no need to travel blind, though, as there are several websites that track the colours as they peak.

Driving through fall colours

New England, USA

Reflections in Lake Winnipesaukee

Sunset on Lake Champlain

Changes in colour are often localized and it can come down to particular roads being better than others if you want to catch them at their best. Displays can also alter fairly dramatically from day to day, and from one valley or mountain top to the next. Altitude plays a big part in how the colours spread, with trees at high levels tending to turn before ones in valleys. So, get yourself a good map, stock up on the latest information and tracking the changes will turn out to be part of the fun, like a relaxing form of tornado chasing. The lure of the leaf – enthusiasts are deemed 'leaf peepers' by locals – will take you to parts of New England no ordinary tour will reach.

A classic circuit from the city of Boston takes you north-west into Vermont, back east to catch the display in the dramatic White Mountains of northern New Hampshire and then south again to the beautiful lakes region near Laconia. It takes in most of the best areas and is loosely threaded by the mighty Connecticut River. Although the interstate highways are tempting for their directness and speed, the old roads, which often run parallel, offer the most absorbing drives.

Highway 12 takes you north along the river, past a series of New England's trademark covered wooden bridges, to Lebanon. From here, there is a stunning drive on Highway 4 through mountains and Woodstock to Rutland. Sweeping views southwards to the golden hills of the Green Mountain National Forest make stopping a necessity – your only problem will be to choose between several spectacularly located restaurants.

From Rutland, you wind across rolling hills to impressive Lake Champlain on the New York State border. With its shoreline dotted with idyllic retreats, it is a lovely place to watch the gentle warm rays of sunset wash across the water. Heading back eastwards, Highway 302 takes you across the Connecticut River and into the most beautiful part of New Hampshire: the White Mountain National

Hiking in the woods near Holderness

Rapids in the White Mountains

Holderness School

Forest. With 1916-metre Mount Washington topping the rugged peaks that pierce the skyline, the park is one of the prime places to see the autumn colours. A good way to access the area is along the twisting Highway 112, or Kancamagus Highway, from Woodsville to yet another Woodstock – rather confusingly, several village and town names are repeated throughout New England.

Long, warm summers lead to brighter red leaves

If you are there at the right time the vista is breathtaking, with towering mountains swathed in a forest of red, gold, bronze, yellow and green. Most of the leaves change colour because of the reduction in chlorophyll created by the cooler temperatures of the approaching winter. The brilliant reds of the maples, however, have their origins in the warmth of summer when the sunlight produces sugar in the leaves. The warmer the summer, the bigger the explosion of autumn reds.

One not-to-be-missed sight in the White Mountains is the Flume Gorge just off Highway 3, north of Lincoln. A short hiking trail leads through forest and past a tumultuous waterfall to a stunning, red, covered bridge, built in 1886, over the Pemigewasset River, and continues into the dramatic narrow gorge. There are numerous other trails, and walking any one of them provides a perspective to experiencing the colours that is different from a car. Back behind the wheel, other roads in the park lead over rocky mountain passes at Franconia Notch and Crawford Notch, both of which are worth exploring.

Trees alongside Route 109

Maple tree in White Mountains

Maple leaf on Squam Lake

Forest over Squam Lake, Holderness

In contrast, the land to the south of the White Mountains is more gentle and is dominated by a sprawl of lakes, including vast Lake Winnipesaukee. The small village of Holderness on the edge of Squam Lake, where the quaint general store sells a mouth-watering selection of home-made fudge, is a good place to begin a half-day circumnavigation of the lakes. A short drive along Highway 25 takes you to the tranquil fishing village of Center Harbor and on to Route 109, which follows a mazy path down the east shore of Winnipesaukee lake. Here the trees are mainly golden and bronze, bathing the road in a warm glow when the sun shines through them. From Alton Bay you can make your way up the western shore and

Heavy autumn rain swells the rivers

Covered bridge over the Pemigewasset River

back to Holderness, where watching the moon rise over the lake from your motel balcony is the perfect end to your journey through Mother Nature's autumn colour festival.

ⓘ

Although many companies offer guided tours of the New England fall colours, it is easy enough to rent a car in Boston and devise your own tour. The relevant state tourist offices can offer extensive advice on choosing routes. Accommodation in the region's smaller towns and villages can be fully booked during the peak weeks of October, but may be available in major towns on the interstate highways. One of the best websites for tracking the colour changes is www.foliagenetwork.com, where volunteers report regularly on conditions across the region. They also suggest drives that will catch the best colours.

On the Road to Mandalay

Ayeyarwady River, Myanmar

Ananda Pagoda in Bagan

With thousands of dramatic pagodas, a strong Buddhist culture and ancient rural landscapes, Myanmar is a unique travel gem. There is no better way to see what inspired Rudyard Kipling's poem 'Mandalay' than a luxurious voyage along the Ayeyarwady River from Bagan to Mandalay.

Once part of the British Empire, when the country was known as Burma, Myanmar gained its independence in 1948 and, after 1962, became relatively isolated under the socialist military regime of Ne Win. Frozen in time by decades of limited access for outsiders, in recent years it has started to open itself to visitors. Its cultural treasures and peaceful charm are, as Kipling noticed on his first visit, '... quite unlike any other land you know about'. And perhaps the most

Sunset over pagodas in Bagan

spectacular of Myanmar's treasures is the extensive, golden-topped Swedagon Pagoda in the capital Yangon (the city formerly called Rangoon) – a must-see before you head further north to travel the river.

If the Swedagon Pagoda is breathtaking in its size, the sight of the more than three thousand pagodas that await you in the beautiful old capital city of Bagan (Pagan), a 1½-hour flight north, is awe-inspiring. The starting point for your four-day voyage up the Ayeyarwady (Irrawaddy) to Mandalay, Bagan lies on the river's vast plain and its sensuous, pointed-topped pagodas spike the skyline from wherever you view them. The city became the capital of a powerful Burmese dynasty in the 11th century and flourished over the next 200 years;

Dawn balloon ride, Bagan

Hot-air balloon rides are a great way to see Bagan's temples

at its peak it boasted over 40,000 pagodas. Most of them are now completely ruined, but visitors are still spoilt for choice – you will feel like a Victorian explorer as you come across rarely visited 800-year-old, red-brick pagodas, crumbling and half-overgrown. More obvious highlights are the golden Buddha statues of the Ananda Pagoda and the fragile, ancient mural of the Buddha's life that fills the walls of the Gubyaukgyi Temple.

Bagan is also famous for its arts and crafts and is the production centre for the country's impressive lacquerware. You could spend all day shopping in Nyaung-Oo market but the real beauty of the city comes with sunset. The sun's rays wash the pagodas in a golden light and if you climb to the top of one of them you'll get a grandstand view. With ox carts working the patchwork of fields, people cycling and mauve-robed monks walking back to their monasteries, it is a scene of pure serenity; it is barely believable that such a way of life still exists in our modern world.

Dusk over Bagan and the Ayeyarwady River

You will probably be thankful, though, that the best aspects of this modern world can be found on board the exquisite *Road to Mandalay*. The ship offers luxury accommodation and fine dining, and as you sail up the Ayeyarwady you can relax on deck and watch age-old scenes of everyday living unfold on its banks. The river is the backbone of Myanmar and, as the roads are poor at best, it is still the main way of getting people and goods around the country. Timber

Novice monks at Shwe Kyet Yet

Carving bamboo at Bagan lacquerware shop

Zayar Theingi Nunnery, Mandalay

Fish stall at Nyaung-Oo market, Bagan

Door carving at Shwenandaw Monastery, Mandalay

Nuns collecting alms in Bagan

Lacquerware store, Bagan

Marble buddhas, Bagan

Rowing on Taungthaman Lake

barges mix it with fishermen in dugout canoes, even though the Ayeyarwady is so wide that there is plenty of space for everyone. The pace of travel is sublime and at dusk, as the stars become bright pinpoints in the inky sky, the ship seems to glide through the water with effortless ease.

By day three you pull into the small village of Shwe Kyet Yet, the main mooring port for the *Road to Mandalay* and just a 15-minute drive from Mandalay itself. Deliberately chosen to avoid the hustle of this large city, the mainly bamboo village is a lovely place for wandering. In the early morning the monks from its monastery queue up to collect alms from the villagers, while schoolgirls play skipping games, old men mend bicycles and old women cook food in clay ovens.

In Mandalay ancient wooden monasteries, like the ornately carved Shwenandaw Monastery, stand close to huge temple complexes, the most revered of which is the one in honour of Mahamuni. Inside, worshippers constantly cover his statue with fresh gold leaf. This is

Monk on U Bein bridge, Taungthaman Lake

Monks collecting alms in Shwe Kyet Yet

Nun praying, Yangon

made locally and it is an eye-opening experience to visit one of the factories and see just how much bashing it takes to make gold so thin. At sunset make your way to the long wooden U Bein bridge over Taungthaman Lake. Monks, nuns, fishermen and cyclists make their way across its stilted wooden beams, forming perfect silhouettes against the dusk sky.

Further upriver, reached by a smaller ferry boat, is the impressive Mingun Pagoda, an unfinished project built in about 1790 to house one of the Buddha's teeth. Its massive base is bigger than those of the other pagodas in the region and it would have been three times higher than any of them. The views from the top are worth the testing climb up steep steps. Mingun is also home to the world's largest working bell – the biggest is in Russia but it no longer functions.

There can be no more fitting place to bid farewell to Myanmar than from atop the Sagaing Hills, overlooking Mandalay and Shwe Kyet Yet where the *Road to Mandalay* is moored. With temples on either side and stretching out to the horizon, and the glinting lights of the ship piercing the twilight sky, it is easy to see what inspired Rudyard Kipling's famous poem about this beautiful, unspoilt place, and its refrain 'Come you back to Mandalay ...'

The *Road to Mandalay* takes four days to sail from Bagan to Mandalay and three days to travel the opposite way, downriver. A longer 12-day tour to Bhamo in the north of the country is available in August. The ship is owned by the Orient Express group so food, service and accommodation are of the highest standard. You can fly to Yangon from Bangkok or Singapore and there are good flights from Yangon to Bagan and Mandalay. Mandalay airport is new, while Yangon was having a new international terminal built at the time of writing. Excellent accommodation in Yangon can be found at The Governor's Residence, which is now a hotel. US dollars are the best currency and credit cards are not widely accepted, even in Yangon.

The *Road to Mandalay*

Buddhas in Sagaing Hills

Shackleton's voyage
Antarctica

The white continent, encased in eternal ice that reaches a thickness of 4000 metres; the greatest desert and last true wilderness on the planet, where the sun doesn't shine for three months in winter and doesn't set for three months in summer, where storms rage and silence reigns. A voyage to Antarctica is perhaps the ultimate adventure journey.

The region is confusingly tagged with many names, including the South Pole, the Antarctic Circle, the Antarctic Continent and the Antarctic Peninsula. While strictly speaking they are different geographical

Penguin colony at Salisbury Plain, South Georgia

Explorer II anchored among the icebergs at Cuverville Island

Sailing into Salisbury Plain, South Georgia

boundaries and locations, it is commonly understood that they refer to the vast expanse of ice-covered land at the Earth's southern extremity. Although it is possible to go there from several countries, the most popular departure port is Ushaia, the southernmost city in the world, which teeters on the very edge of Argentine Patagonia.

An increasing number of ships sail to Antarctica, and the options available range from a direct there-and-back trip to a more in-depth itinerary that takes you east to the Falkland Islands and then on to South Georgia before cruising south-west to the Antarctic Peninsula.

King penguins on early morning guard at Gold Harbour, South Georgia

King penguin sleeping

The latter, which is spectacular in its variety, is around 3400 nautical miles and takes two weeks given reasonable weather conditions. The seas can be the wildest on the planet and, while you would be unfortunate if they were very rough for the entire voyage, you need to expect some tossing and pitching en route.

After leaving Ushaia the ship, the *Explorer II*, sails via the dramatic Beagle Channel, which threads between the mountainous Patagonian mainland and a string of islands, into the Drake Passage – which is notorious for providing the roughest parts of the voyage. However, at these latitudes it is the luck of the draw and you may escape with just a gentle rolling. After a day and a half at sea, you arrive at Port Stanley on the Falkland Islands. A colourful array of houses and the notable Christ Church Cathedral, with its whalebone archway, line the shoreline and a short ride on one of the ship's Zodiac boats takes you to the jetty. The Falkland Islands came to international attention in 1982 when the United Kingdom and Argentina fought over their sovereignty, and the legacies of that conflict are visible around the many battlefield sites. This is also the first opportunity to see penguins, which are reached via an exciting trip in a four-wheel-drive vehicle across exposed hillsides.

In the evening you depart for South Georgia, a two-day sail across the Scotia Sea. Although not as infamous as the Drake Passage, the waters here can be equally wild, and most passengers will feel the effects to some degree if huge swells roll under the *Explorer II*. When the seas calm down, it is fascinating to stand at the stern and watch the spectacular flying displays of the numerous seabirds, including albatrosses, that follow the ship. And it is a thrilling moment when the first iceberg is spotted – an excitement surpassed only by the sighting of the first whales. With clear skies, and providing you can get yourself out of bed at 4 a.m., you may be treated to a glorious sunrise upon arrival at the mountainous island of South Georgia.

Before the voyage, most people expect that Antarctica will be the highlight of the journey, but South Georgia often ends up being their

King penguins on the beach at Salisbury Plain, South Georgia

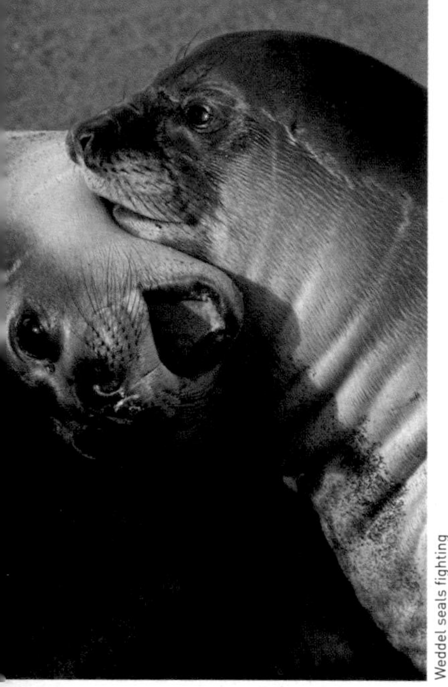
Weddel seals fighting

favourite place. It is one of the world's truly magical locations, isolated and yet crammed full of incredible wildlife and rugged scenery. Over two days the ship calls into bays such as Salisbury Plain, Gold Harbour and Larsen Harbour, and takes you to the historic Grytviken settlement. A whaling station from 1904 to the mid-1960s, Grytviken is the final resting place of Sir Ernest Shackleton. With five of his men he rowed the lifeboat *James Caird* 1300 km to South Georgia from Elephant Island where the rest of his crew were stranded – they had rowed there after HMS *Endurance* was crushed by the ice further south.

In magnificent Gold Harbour, backdropped by the blue ice of the high, hanging Bertrab glacier, the beach is alive with thousands of king penguins and their fluffy brown chicks, and with many species of seal, including the monstrous elephant and fur seals. Disembarking from the Zodiacs is like walking into your very own wildlife documentary, especially when the dominant male elephant seals, known as the beach masters, decide to warn off rival males with dramatic, lumbering charges. In the afternoon, the ship sails past the Heaney glacier and pulls into Drygalski Fjord for a Zodiac tour up the adjoining Larsen Harbour, edged by towering cliffs.

Seals, like this one in Gold Harbour, spend most of the day lazing

Glacier at the head of the Drygalski Fjord, South Georgia

Fur seals can be very aggressive defending their territory

Albatross taking off in the Beagle Channel

Geothermal hot springs at Whaler's Bay, Deception Island

Sunrise at Gold Harbour, South Georgia

Curious king penguin chicks

Space is limited on the beach at Gold Harbour

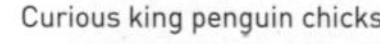

Point Wild on Elephant Island

Afternoon light in the Gerlache Strait

A further two days' sailing, over very rough seas, leads to Elephant Island and a call into Point Wild. The windswept spit, surrounded by soaring rock islands, is a daunting place even for a few hours. It is beyond comprehension that Frank Wild, who was left in charge by Shackleton, and after whom Point Wild is named, managed to maintain morale among the men who made camp there for four months, and ensured they all survived.

The next stop is Deception Island, where the ship passes through the narrow Neptune's Bellows into the flooded crater of a volcano. At the old Hektor whaling station geothermal springs beneath the beach, which is made of volcanic ash, create a series of steaming pools of hot water in which hardy travellers can swim.

Overnight, *Explorer II* sails into and through the beautiful, iceberg-strewn Gerlache Strait, heading for Cuverville Island, home to thousands of gentoo penguins, and then for Neko Harbour on the Antarctic Peninsula itself. The moment you step on to land will be a memorable one. And the stunning, ice-laden bay, its calm waters

Dusk over the harbour at Grytviken, South Georgia

Sunrise over South Georgia

reflecting the enormous, crevasse-ridden, ice-blue glaciers above, is a fitting place to end your visit to what is, without doubt, the most spectacular and pristine continent on the planet. A final two days' sailing takes you back across the Drake Passage to Ushaia – where you will probably yearn for the world of ice you've left behind.

ⓘ

Explorer II, which can be booked through Abercrombie & Kent, is one of about 30 ships that sail to Antarctica. Ushaia is reached via flights from Buenos Aires in Argentina, or Santiago in Chile. British Airways flies to Buenos Aires, and Aerolineas Argentina flies to Ushaia from there. Abercrombie & Kent will arrange flights if required. It is essential to take plenty of warm clothing; several thin layers are better than one or two thick ones. Passengers on *Explorer II* are given warm waterproof jackets as part of the package. Wellington boots are also essential as you will get wet during the Zodiac landings. Full briefings are given on board about how to behave around the wildlife. It is totally forbidden to remove anything from any of the places where you land. Daily lectures add significantly to the Antarctic experience. The itinerary and ports of call are all subject to change, depending on weather conditions. Take a flexible mindset.

Riding the Okavango Delta

Botswana

Evening ride on the flood plain

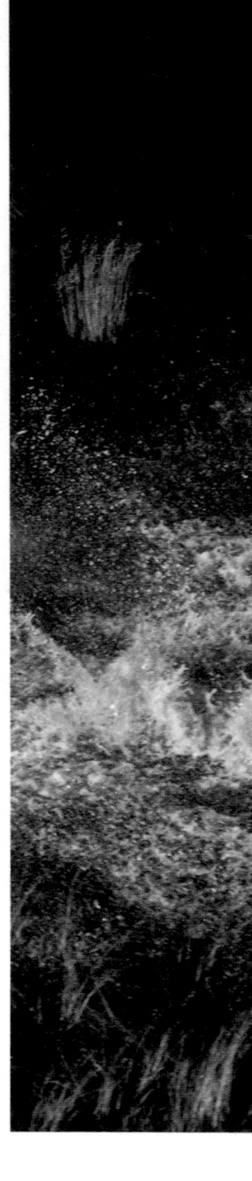

Riding a horse through the flood waters of Botswana's immense Okavango Delta, close to elephants, giraffes and the odd lion or two, must rank as one of the world's most exhilarating wildlife journeys.

The difference between being on horseback and in a safari vehicle may seem minor compared to the awe that seeing animals in their natural habitat inspires, but in the saddle you are most certainly part of the scene and not just a spectator. This extra edge of excitement may well re-awaken in you something of our primal past, taking you back for an instant to the time of our hunter-gatherer ancestors.

An exhilarating canter through the delta's shallow water

There are many places to go on safari in Africa, but the Okavango Delta in Botswana is held in particularly high regard because it is relatively untouched by humans and is, as a result, teeming with big game. Hundreds of elephants are thought to roam the area, as well as lions, cheetahs, panthers, wild dogs, giraffes, hippos and a raft of other supporting wildlife stars.

The delta, to the west of Maun in the north of landlocked Botswana, is formed by the Cubango and Cuito rivers, which flow out of the Angolan highlands before merging to create the Okavango river. When it reaches flat land it slows to a creep and fans out into myriad shallow channels, bringing an explosion of green life to the

semi-desert. Thousands of low-lying islands are created, providing dry ground for wildlife and a pitching spot for several luxury safari camps, including Macatoo, the base for this adventure into the delta.

A 30-minute flight from Maun airport in a small Cessna, Macatoo Camp is perched on the edge of one of the main channels, and offers spectacular sunset-watching from its sun deck – plus, if you are lucky, some very up-close-and-personal visits from big game. With a large stable of excellent horses, professional guides to lead the rides

Giraffes can be surprisingly well camouflaged

Flocks of cranes arrive with the flood water

Nervous impala

Riding allows very close wildlife encounters

and a host of support workers, the camp rightly has an enviable reputation for providing a great riding experience. It's not all about the horses either – good food, served in the open air, and large luxury tents that could easily be considered suites, also help to make this a truly memorable three- or four-day safari.

Rides twice a day mean it is easy to explore deep into the delta. The morning one, when the guides take you to beautiful, shallow lakes full of water lilies where you can canter your horse, tends to be

Long grasses cover the delta

the more active of the two. It is unlike any other riding experience. With rainbows forming in the splashing water around you and the thud of huge drops of water bouncing off your body and face, it is truly exhilarating. The horses love it, too, and have to be held back a little to stop them galloping off to the horizon. You will get wet – very wet – but the warm Botswana sun will quickly have you dry again.

Expect to get wet during the rides

In between canters you are very likely to encounter big game. On horseback it is possible to get quite close to elephants, giraffes and many other animals, as they do not perceive the horses as a threat. The sense of drama, and tension levels, rise immeasurably though, as does your heart rate, as you edge closer to them, your guide ever aware of the need to maintain a respectful distance. It is as different to being in a safari vehicle as riding a motorbike is to being in a car.

Flood waters creep across the delta

The evening rides are even more spectacular than the morning ones, though usually more sedate, with golden light streaming across the grassy delta and the animals coming out to eat and drink. It is a magical time, and as the sun's rays filter through the dust kicked up by the horses the romance of Africa comes to life. Back at the camp you can kick off your boots, sip a gin and tonic on the sun deck and watch the occasional giraffe or elephant wander by. The more active might like to take a boat trip down the channel – a refreshing way to see the sun go down.

As you sit round the lamp-lit dinner table, feasting on excellent food and wine, listening for any tell-tale sounds of animals roaming

Tranquil waters at Macatoo Camp

Fine outdoor dining at Macatoo

Riding the delta at end of day

into the camp and looking back on your day, you will find it hard to deny that a horseback safari is as close as you will ever come to answering the call of the wild.

ⓘ

Several operators, including African Horseback Safaris, owners of Macatoo Camp, run horse-riding safaris in the Okavango Delta. You need to be a fairly experienced rider, primarily because the horses may bolt when surprised by animals in the bush. You can stay at the camp for three or four nights, or longer. Several agents, including Tim Best Travel, will arrange flights to Botswana with British Airways or other airlines, and help to organize domestic transfers to Maun. Flights to Macatoo Camp from Maun will be arranged by African Horseback Safaris.

Sunrise at Castle Cove

Castle Cove

Campbell National Park. Winding through dunes, it ends near the unmarked track to Glenample Homestead. It is a short road walk on to Gibson Steps and the Twelve Apostles. Four of the sea stacks have collapsed, the latest one in 2005, but the eight that remain are still breathtaking, especially around sunset and sunrise when the light fires up their orange cliffs. You can easily spend a couple of hours exploring here before heading on to Loch Ard Gorge along quiet backcountry tracks.

The gorge is a series of inlets with impressive sea stacks, caves, islands and coves. It is named after the *Loch Ard*, which ran aground here in 1878, and you can enjoy your final lunch on this magnificent walk near the cave where the only two survivors, Tom Pearce and Eva Carmichael, huddled together awaiting rescue.

Johanna Beach

Loch Ard Gorge

ⓘ

Victoria-based walking-holiday operator Auswalk offers a range of supported tours for the Great Ocean Walk, either self-guided or guided. Covering the entire trail or shorter sections, they organize your pick-up and drop-off each day, overnight stays and daily luggage transfers. Carrying just a daypack is a major advantage on sandy beaches and the longer climbs. The trail is well set up, with numerous access points that give options on how much of it to walk, and campsites for those who want to carry their own gear. It is essential to know the times of the high and low tides – tables are available in local stores. There are points on the walk where the tide dictates your route; the low-tide routes, when safe, are often the best. There are poisonous snakes along the trail, so be aware of them and read up on how to deal with any encounter and the necessary first aid if bitten – a thankfully rare event.

77
81
20
12
62
59
68
25
45
57
27
35
82
53
65
61
67
52
85
36
56
23
40
11
6
7
34
47
44
9
33
49
51
54
83
86
13
37
16
73
17
29
24
41
21
4
78
48
60
1
75
19
14
80
84
46
42
87
5

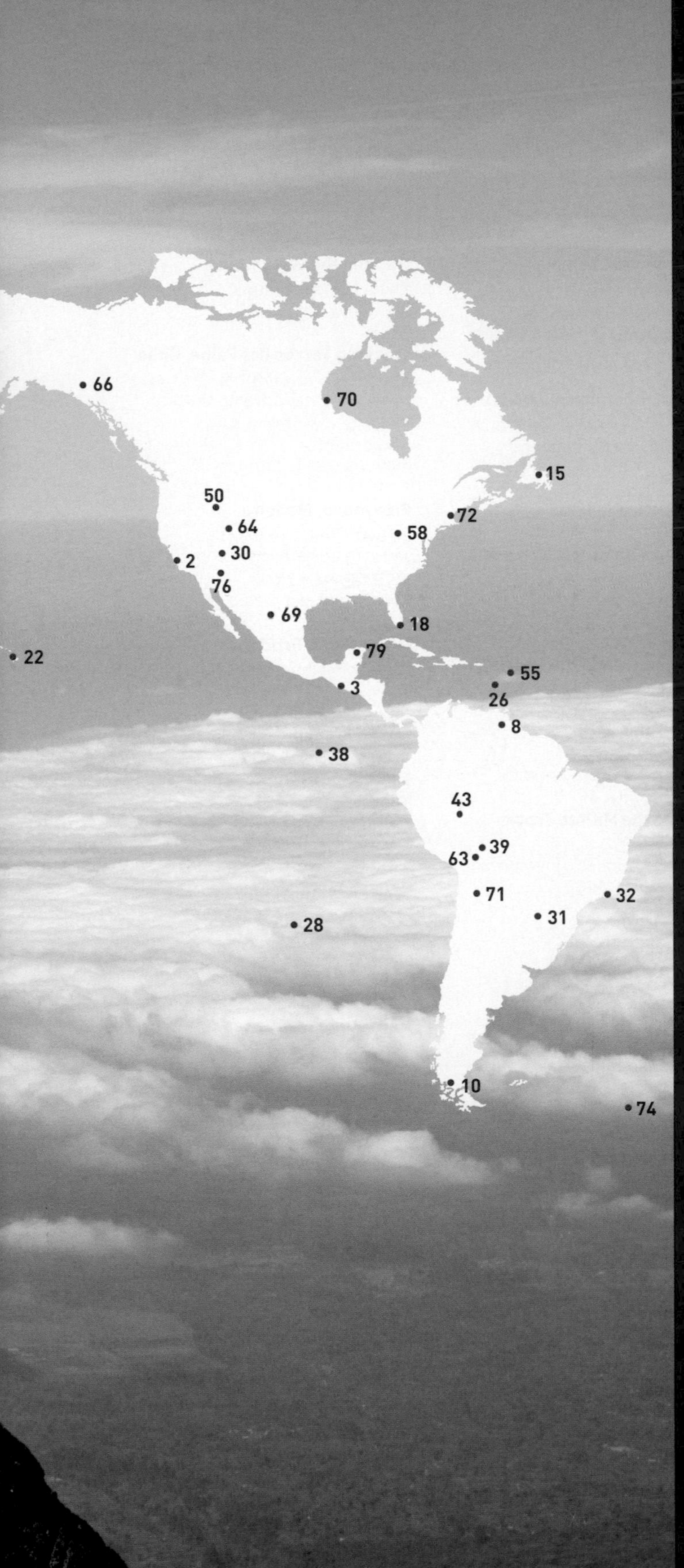

1 RIVER-RUNNING, ZAMBIA
2 DRIVING CALIFORNIAN SURF, USA
3 CLIMBING A VOLCANO, GUATEMALA
4 FINDING PARADISE, THE MALDIVES
5 TREKKING THE MILFORD TRACK, NEW ZEALAND
6 FESTIVAL OF THE SAHARA, TUNISIA
7 SOUK SHOPPING, MOROCCO
8 'LOST WORLD' RIVER JOURNEY, VENEZUELA
9 WALKING THE WALL, CHINA
10 TREKKING TORRES DEL PAINE, CHILE
11 PICO RUIVO, MADEIRA, PORTUGAL
12 ISLE OF SKYE, SCOTLAND
13 THE GOLDEN TEMPLE, AMRITSAR, INDIA
14 YASAWA ISLANDS, FIJI
15 NEWFOUNDLAND, CANADA
16 SAGAR, INDIA
17 HONG KONG ISLAND, CHINA
18 THE FLORIDA KEYS, USA
19 MADAGASCAR
20 STOCKHOLM, SWEDEN
21 SRI LANKA
22 BIG ISLAND, HAWAII, USA
23 SICILY, ITALY
24 SOCOTRA, YEMEN
25 SARK, UNITED KINGDOM
26 ST LUCIA, WINDWARD ISLANDS
27 MONT SAINT-MICHEL, FRANCE
28 RAPA NUI, CHILE
29 ANGKOR WAT, CAMBODIA
30 GRAND CANYON, ARIZONA, USA
31 IGUASSU FALLS, BRAZIL AND ARGENTINA
32 RIO DE JANEIRO, BRAZIL
33 TAJ MAHAL, AGRA, INDIA
34 PETRA, JORDAN
35 VENICE, ITALY
36 THE ALHAMBRA, GRANADA, SPAIN
37 KARNAK TEMPLE, LUXOR, EGYPT
38 GALAPAGOS ISLANDS, ECUADOR
39 LAKE TITICACA, BOLIVIA AND PERU
40 SANTORINI, GREECE
41 LALIBELA, ETHIOPIA
42 DRAKENSBERG, SOUTH AFRICA
43 MACHU PICCHU, PERU
44 LHASA, TIBET
45 MONET'S GARDEN, GIVERNY, FRANCE
46 ULURU, AUSTRALIA
47 SAMARKAND, UZBEKISTAN
48 NGORONGORO CRATER, TANZANIA
49 MAKALU, HIMALAYAS, NEPAL
50 YELLOWSTONE NATIONAL PARK, USA
51 TEMPLES OF KYOTO, JAPAN
52 AMALFI COAST, ITALY
53 TOUR DU MONT BLANC, EUROPE
54 TIGER LEAPING GORGE, CHINA
55 MORNE TROIS PITONS, DOMINICA
56 DROVERS' ROADS, SPAIN
57 KING LUDWIG'S WAY, GERMANY
58 FALLINGWATER, USA
59 CANALS OF AMSTERDAM, THE NETHERLANDS
60 MOUNT KILIMANJARO, TANZANIA
61 METEORA, GREECE
62 COAST TO COAST, ENGLAND
63 TAKESI TRAIL, BOLIVIA
64 COYOTE BUTTES, USA
65 CANAL DU MIDI, FRANCE
66 YUKON RIVER JOURNEY, CANADA
67 TRACING THE LIFE OF GAUDÍ, SPAIN
68 HORSE-DRAWN CARAVAN, IRELAND
69 BY RAIL THROUGH COPPER CANYON, MEXICO
70 INTO THE ICE BEAR KINGDOM, CANADA
71 DRIVING THE UYUNI SALT FLAT, BOLIVIA
72 DRIVING THROUGH FALL COLOURS, USA
73 ON THE ROAD TO MANDALAY MYANMAR
74 SHACKLETON'S VOYAGE, ANTARCTICA
75 RIDING THE OKAVANGO DELTA, BOTSWANA
76 DRIVING ALONG ROUTE 66, USA
77 FOLLOWING REINDEER, SWEDEN
78 TRACKING MOUNTAIN GORILLAS, RWANDA
79 PYRAMID OF KUKULKÁN, MEXICO
80 DEAD VLEI, NAMIBIA
81 ST PETERSBURG, RUSSIA
82 DUBROVNIK, CROATIA
83 THE BUND, SHANGHAI CHINA
84 GREAT BARRIER REEF, AUSTRALIA
85 EPHESUS, TURKEY
86 JAISALMER FORT, INDIA
87 GREAT OCEAN WALK, AUSTRALIA

Useful web addresses

There is a wealth of travel information available on the web, including general sites such as www.expedia.com, www. travelocity.com and www.travel.yahoo.com (Canadian travellers should visit www.expedia.ca, www.travelocity.ca and ca.travel.yahoo.com). You may also want to check government issued travel warnings by visiting www.travel.state.gov/travel warnings (Canadians should visit www.voyage.gc.ca/consular_home-en.asp).

Many countries require tourist visas, even for short stays, and you may need vaccinations, so contact a local travel agent as early as possible for specific information.

International airlines

Air Canada
www.aircanada.com

Air China
www.airchina.com.cn/en

Air Fiordland
www.airfiordland.com

Air Namibia
www.airnamibia.com.na

Air New Zealand
www.airnewzealand.com

Alitalia
www.alitalia.com

American Airlines
www.aa.com

British Airways
www.ba.com

Cathay Pacific
www.cathaypacific.com

Delta Airlines
www.delta.com

Egypt Air
www.egyptair.com.eg

Emirates
www.emirates.com

Estonian Air
www.estonianair.com

Ethiopian Airways
www.flyethiopian.com

Iceland Air
www.icelandair.com

Jet Airways
www.jetairways.com

Pacific Coastal Airlines
www.pacific-coastal.com

Qantas
www.qantas.com

Royal Air Maroc
www.royalairmaroc.com

Royal Jordanian Airlines
www.rja.com.jo

Scandinavian Airlines
www.flysas.com

Turkish Airlines
www.turkishairlines.com

United Airlines
www.united.com

River-running, Zambia

Sun International
www.suninternational.com

Zambia National Tourist Board
www.zambiatourism.com

Driving Californian surf, USA

Big Sur Chamber of Commerce
www.bigsurcalifornia.org

California Travel and Tourism Commission
www.visitcalifornia.com

Climbing a volcano, Guatemala

Guatemala Tourist Commission
www.visitguatamala.com/nuevo/mainE.asp

Finding paradise, the Maldives

Dhoni Mighili
www.maldives-resorts.net/dhoni-mighiili

Ministry of Tourism
www.visitmaldives.com.mv

Trekking the Milford Track, New Zealand

Dairy Guest House, Queenstown
www.thedairy.co.nz

Real Journeys
www.realjourneys.co.nz

Ultimate Hikes
www.ultimatehikes.co.nz

Festival of the Sahara, Tunisia

Tunisia National Tourist Office
www.tourismtunisia.com

Souk shopping, Morocco

Dar Les Cigognes
www.lescigognes.com

Moroccan National Tourist Office
www.visitmorocco.com

'Lost World' river journey, Venezuela

Angel Falls in Venezuela
www.salto-angel.com

Embassy of the Bolivian Republic of Venezuela in the USA
www.embavenez-us.org

Walking the Wall, China

China National Tourist Office
www.cnto.org

Trekking Torres del Paine, Chile

Blue Green Adventures
www.bluegreenadventures.com

Chile Tourism Promotion Corporation
www.visit-chile.org

Pico Ruivo, Madeira

Madeira Tourism Board
www.madeiratourism.com

Reid's Palace Hotel
www.orient-express.com

Isle of Skye, Scotland

Skye The Island & Lochalsh
www.skye.co.uk

Bosville Hotel
www.bosvillehotel.co.uk

The Golden Temple, Amritsar, India

Amritsar Portal
www.amritsar.com

Yasawa Islands, Fiji

Fiji Visitors Bureau
www.bulafiji.com

Nanuya Island Resort
www.nanuyafiji.com

Newfoundland, Canada

Newfoundland and Labrador Tourism
www.newfoundlandlabrador.com

Sagar, India

Incredible India
www.incredibleindia.org

Atithi Voyages
www.atithivoyages.com

Jet Airways
www.jetairways.com

Hong Kong Island, China

Hong Kong Tourism Board
www.discoverhongkong.com

Mandarin Oriental Hotel
www.mandarinoriental.com

The Florida Keys, USA
The Florida Keys & Key West
www.fla-keys.com

Madagascar
Le Voyageur
www.madagascar-tour-operator.com
Air Madagascar
www.airmadagascar.mg

Stockholm, Sweden
VisitSweden
www.visitsweden.com
Stockholm Visitors Board
www.stockholmtown.com
Nordic Light Hotel
www.nordiclighthotel.se
The Archipelago Foundation
www.archepelagofoundation.se

Sri Lanka
Sri Lanka Tourist Board
www.srilankatourism.org
Jetwing Hotels & Travels
www.jetwingtravels.com

Big Island, Hawaii, USA
Hawaii Visitors and Convention Bureau
www.gohawaii.com
Mauna Lani Resort at Kalahuipua'a, Big Island
www.maunalani.com
Hilo Hawaiian Hotel, Hilo, Oahu
www.castleresorts.com
Ala Moana Hotel, Honolulu, Oahu
www.alamoanahotel.com

Sicily, Italy
Sicily Tourist
www.sicilytourist.net
Sicily Hotels
www.sicilyhotels.com

Socotra, Republic of Yemen
Universal Touring Company
www.utcyemen.com
Yemenia Yemen Airways
www.yemenia.com

Sark, Channel Islands, UK
Sark Tourism
www.sark.info

St. Lucia, Caribbean
St. Lucia Tourist Board
www.stlucia.org
Coco Palm Hotel
www.coco-resorts.com

Mont Saint-Michel, France
Mont Saint-Michel
www.ot-montsaintmichel.com/accueil_gb.htm.com
Aurigny
www.aurigny.com

Rapa Nui (Easter Island)
Casa Rapa Nui
www.explora.com

Angkor Wat, Cambodia
Embassy of Cambodia, USA
www.embassy.org/cambodia/tourism/
Ministry of Tourism
www.mot.gov.kh
Bangkok Airways
www.bangkokair.com

Grand Canyon, Arizona, USA
El Tovar Hotel, Xanterra Parks & Resorts
www.grandcanyonlodges.com
National Park Service
www.nps.gov/grca

Iguassu Falls, Brazil and Argentina
National Secretariat of Tourism, Argentina
www.turismo.gov.ar
Hotel das Cataratas
www.hoteldascataratas.com

Rio de Janeiro, Brazil
Riotur
www.riodejaneiro-turismo.com.br
Visit Brazil
www.braziltourism.org

Taj Mahal, Agra, India
Amarvilas Hotel, Agra
www.amarvilas.com

Petra, Jordan
Jordan Tourism Board
www.see-jordan.com
Movenpick Resort Petra
www.movenpick-hotels.com

Venice, Italy
Italian Government Tourist Board, North America
www.italiantourism.com
Tourist Board of Venice
www.turismovenezia.it/eng
Europa & Regina Hotel
www.starwood.com

The Alhambra, Granada, Spain
Alhambra
www.alhambra.org
Spanish Tourist Board
www.tourspain.es

Karnak Temple, Luxor, Egypt
Egyptian Tourist Authority
www.egypttourism.org

Galapagos Islands, Ecuador
Metropolitan Touring
www.metropolitan-touring.com
Ministry of Tourism
www.vivecuador.com

Lake Titicaca, Bolivia and Peru
Asociación Titicaca Al Mundo
www.titicacaalmundo.com/en
Peru Tourist Board
www.peru.info/perueng.asp

Santorini, Greece
Greek National Tourism Organization
www.gnto.gr

Lalibela, Ethiopia
Embassy of Ethiopia, Canada
www.ottawa.ethiopianembassy.com
Embassy of Ethiopia, USA
www.ethiopianembassy.org

Drakensberg, South Africa
Ezemvelo KZN Wildlife
www.kznwildlife.com
South Africa Tourism Board
www.southafrica.net

Machu Picchu, Peru
Machu Picchu Sanctuary Lodge
www.orient-express.com

Lhasa, Tibet
The Government of Tibet in Exile
www.tibet.com
China Tourism
www.cnta.com

Monet's Garden, Giverny, France
French Government Tourist Office
www.franceguide.com/us
GiVerNet
www.giverny.org

Uluru, Australia
Ayers Rock Resort
www.ayersrockresort.com.au
Northern Territory Tourist Commission
www.ntholidays.com

Samarkand, Uzbekistan
Tourism Uzbekistan
www.tourism.uz

Ngorongoro Crater, Tanzania
Abercrombie & Kent Travel
www.abercrombiekent.com
Sopa Lodge
www.sopalodges.com
Air Excel
www.airexcelonline.com

Makalu, Himalayas, Nepal
Nepal Tourism Board
www.welcomenepal.com

Yellowstone National Park, USA
National Park Service – US Department of the Interior
www.nps.gov/yell/

Temples of Kyoto, Japan
ANA
www.anaskyweb.com
Japan National Tourist Organization
www.jnto.go.jp
www.seejapan.co.uk

Amalfi Coast, Italy
Landscapes of Sorrento, Amalfi and Capri – Car Tours and Walks by Julian Tippett
www.sunflowerbooks.co.uk
Italian State Tourist Board
www.enit.it

Tour du Mont Blanc, Europe
Sherpa Expeditions
www.sherpa-walking-holidays.co.uk
French Tourist Office
www.francetourism.com
Italian State Tourist Board
www.enit.it
Swiss Tourist Office
www.myswitzerland.com

Tiger Leaping Gorge, China
In Depth China
www.indepthchina.com
China National Tourist Office
www.cnto.org

Morne Trois Pitons, Dominica
Dominica Tourism
www.tourismdominica.dm
British Airways
www.ba.com
Evergreen Hotel
www.avirtualdominica.com/evergreen.htm
Papillote Wilderness Retreat
www.papillote.dm
Rainforest Shangri-la Resort
www.rainforestshangrilaresort.com
Titiwi Inn
www.titiwi.com

Drovers' Roads, Andalucia, Spain
Andalucian Adventures
www.andalucian-adventures.co.uk
Andalucia Tourist Board
www.andalucia.org

King Ludwig's Way, Germany
Sherpa Expeditions
www.sherpa-walking-holidays.co.uk
German Tourist Board
www.germany-tourism.de

Fallingwater, USA
Fallingwater – Western Pennsylvania Conservancy
www.fallingwater.org
Pennsylvania Tourism
www.visitpa.com
Stepping Stone Farm B&B, Confluence
www.steppingstonefarmbnb.com

Canals of Amsterdam, The Netherlands
Netherlands Board of Tourism & Conventions
www.holland.com
Amsterdam Tourism & Convention Board
www.amsterdamtourist.nl
Mövenpick Hotel
www.moevenpick-hotels.com/hotels/Amsterdam/welcome.htm

Mount Kilimanjaro, Tanzania
Classic Tours & Safaris
www.theclassictours.com/kilimanjaro.htm
Tanzania Tourist Board
www.tanzaniatouristboard.com

Meteora, Greece
Greek National Tourism Organization
www.visitgreece.gr
Konstantina Papaefthimiou
(licensed English-speaking guide)
Email: konstantipap@yahoo.gr

Coast to Coast, England
England Tourist Board
www.enjoyengland.com
Coast 2 Coast
www.coast2coast.co.uk

Takesi Trail, Bolivia
Tim Best Travel
www.timbesttravel.com

Coyote Buttes, USA
Arizona Office of Tourism
www.arizonaguide.com
Page-Lake Powell Tourism Bureau
www.pagelakepowelltourism.com
Overland Canyon Tours
www.overlandcanyontours.com
Page Boy Motel
www.pageboymotel.us

Canal du Midi, France
French Tourist Office
www.franceguide.com
Toulouse Tourist Office
www.uk.toulouse-tourism.com

Yukon River journey, Canada
Kanoe People
www.kanoepeople.com
Tourism Yukon
www.travelyukon.com

Tracing the life of Gaudí, Spain
Spanish Tourist Board
www.spain.info
Turisme de Barcelona
www.barcelonaturisme.com

Horse-drawn caravan, Ireland
Clissmann Horse Caravans
www.clissmann.com/wicklow/
Tourism Ireland
www.discoverireland.com

By rail through Copper Canyon, Mexico
Hotel Divisadero Barrancas, Divisadero
www.hoteldivisadero.com
Hotel Posada del Hidalgo, El Fuerte
www.hotelposadadelhidalgo.com
Quality Inn Chihuahua San Francisco
www.qualityinn.com/hotel-chihuahua-mexico-MX043
Mexico Tourism Board
www.visitmexico.com

Into the ice bear kingdom, Canada
Hudson Bay Helicopters
www.hudsonbayheli.com
Travel Manitoba
www.travelmanitoba.com

Driving the Uyuni Salt Flat, Bolivia
Andean Summits, La Paz
www.andeansummits.com

Driving through fall colors, USA
The Foliage Network
www.foliagenetwork.com
New Hampshire Travel and Tourism
www.visitnh.gov
Vermont Department of Tourism
www.travel-vermont.com

On the *Road to Mandalay*, Myanmar
The Governor's Residence Hotel, Yangon
www.governorsresidence.com
Myanmar Tourism Promotion Board
www.myanmar-tourism.com
Orient Express
www.orient-express.com

Shackleton's voyage, Antarctica
Abercrombie & Kent
www.abercrombiekent.co.uk
International Association of Antarctic Tour Operators
www.iaato.org

Riding the Okavango Delta, Botswana
African Horseback Safaris
www.africanhorseback.com
Botswana Tourism
www.botswanatourism.co.bw

Driving along Route 66, USA
Arizona Office of Tourism
www.arizonaguide.com

Following the reindeer migration, Sweden
Kiruna Tourist Office
www.lappland.se
Swedish Travel & Tourism Council
www.visit-sweden.com
Vägvisaren – Pathfinder Lapland
www.pathfinderlapland.se

Tracking mountain gorillas, Rwanda
Discovery Initiatives
www.discoveryinitiatives.co.uk

Pyramid of Kukulcán, Mexico
Mayaland Hotel
www.mayaland.com
Mexico Tourism Board
www.visitmexico.com
Travel Yucatan
www.travelyucatan.com

Dead Vlei, Namibia
Namibia Ministry of Environment and Tourism
www.met.gov.na
Wilderness Safaris
www.wilderness-safaris.com

St Petersburg, Russia
Embassy of the Russian Federation, Canada
www.rusembcanada.mid.ru
Embassy of the Russian Federation, USA
www.russianembassy.org

Dubrovnik, Croatia
Croatian National Tourist Board
www.croatia.hr
Dubrovnik Tourism Board
www.tzdubrovnik.hr
Hotel Kompas
www.hotel-kompas.hr

The Bund, Shanghai, China
Embassy of the People's Republic of China, Canada
www.chinaembassycanada.org/eng
Embassy of the People's Republic of China, USA
www.china-embassy.org/eng
Peace Hotel
www.shanghaipeacehotel.com

Great Barrier Reef, Australia
Heron Island Resort
www.heronisland.com
Tourism Queensland
www.tq.com.au

Ephesus, Turkey
Hotel Kalehan
www.kalehan.com
Ministry of Culture and Tourism
www.turizm.gov.tr

Jaisalmer Fort, India
Jaisalmer Tourism
www.jaisalmertourism.com
Narayan Niwas Palace
www.narayanniwas.com

Great Ocean Walk, Australia
Auswalk
www.auswalk.com.au
Australia Travel & Tourism
www.australia.com

About the authors

Steve Davey is the author and principal photographer of *Unforgettable Places to See Before You Die* (the first book in the 'Unforgettable' series, which has been published in more than twenty languages worldwide) and *Unforgettable Islands to Escape to Before You Die*. Steve has turned his day job into a way of life, travelling compulsively to photograph amazing cultures, festivals and remote destinations. A constant thirst for adventure and change inspires his travel and the desire to show the world to as many people as possible directs his professional life. To pass on his knowledge, Steve has recently launched a series of travel photography tours. See www.stevedavey.com for details.

Marc Schlossman was born in Chicago and has been based in London since 1988. From a beginning in editorial photography and photojournalism, his work has evolved using documentary, landscape and photojournalism techniques to explore and make visual stories in locations around the world. Marc was the associate photographer for *Unforgettable Places to See Before You Die* and *Unforgettable Islands to Escape to Before You Die*. See Marc's website, www.marcschlossman.com, for further details of his work.

Steve Watkins has been a professional travel photographer and writer for 14 years. His work has featured worldwide in many magazines, newspapers and books, including *Wanderlust*, *Geographical*, the *Daily Telegraph*, the *Sunday Telegraph*, the *Daily Mail*, the *Sunday Express*, the *Times*, and various AA guidebook publications. He contributes to the *Wexas Traveller's Handbook*, writes a travel photography column for *Traveller* magazine and tutors on photography workshops for Traveller's Tales. His assignments have taken him to over 65 countries and every continent, including shooting voodoo ceremonies in Haiti with modern-day explorer Benedict Allen. His photographic exhibitions have included one on Australian Aboriginal art at London's Barbican Gallery. He is the Director of Photography for the Travellers' Tales Festival and markets his images through his website www.stevewatkins.com.

Clare Jones is a professional travel writer and photographer who covers destinations for a variety of books, magazines and newspapers. These include the *Sunday Telegraph*, *Mail on Sunday*, *Geographical*, *Health & Fitness*, *Traveller*, the *Scotsman*, and the *Herald*. She has co-authored several AA titles, including *Extreme Places* and *Key Guide to Spain*. Clare is also an assistant television producer, working on several BBC documentaries. On assignment in over 50 countries and five continents, she has explored on foot, by kayak, under sail, by bike and on skis. As a Winston Churchill Fellow, she sea-kayaked from Vancouver to Alaska, as part of the first British all-female team to undertake this epic 1000-mile journey; for which she won the Mike Jones Award. She is sponsored by Salomon and reached at www.clare-jones.com.

Acknowlegements

The authors would in particular like to thank Christopher Tinker and Nicky Ross at BBC Books, Bobby Birchall at Bobby&Co and Tessa Clark for their invaluable work and support in bringing this book together.

Steve Davey and Marc Schlossman would like to thank the following people and organizations for their support, advice and assistance: Athithi Voyages, Delhi; Naryan Niwas Palace; Air Rarotonga; Aitutaki Pacific Resort; Cook Islands Tourism; Mayaland Hotel; The Europa and Regina Hotel; Wilderness Safaris Namibia; Brazil Tourist Board; Las Cataratas Hotel; Macuco Safari; Helisul Helicopter Tours, Foz do Iguaçu; Royal Jordanian; Jordan Tourism Board; Metropolitan Touring; South American Experience, London; Orient Express; Sopa Lodge, Ngorongoro Crater; Abercrombie & Kent Travel; Air Excel; Hotel Arusha; Ezemvelo KZN Wildlife; Ethiopian Airlines; Qantas; Ayers Rock Resort; Heron Island Resort; Peace Hotel, Shanghai; Croatian National Tourist Office; Hotel Kompas, Dubrovnik; Madeira Tourism Board; Orient Express Hotels; Hong Kong Tourism Board; Mandarin Oriental Hotel, Hong Kong; Indiatourism, London; Atithi Voyages; Jet Airways; District Magistrate Roshni Sen; Golden Temple, Amritsar; Casa Rapa Nui, Explora Hotels; Fiji Visitors Bureau; Nanuya Island Lodge, Fiji; Le Voyageur, Madagascar; Air Madagascar; Aurigny Air; Sark Tourism; Sri Lanka Tourism Office; Jetwing Holidays; UTC Yemen; Yemenia Yemen Airways and the following PR companies who helped organize many of the trips: Lush PR; Indigo PR; Mango PR; Hills Balfour; Saltmarsh PR; Seal Communications; BGB Associates; PR Co; Oliver Relations; Southern Skies and Cut Communications; Coco Palm Hotel, St Lucia; St Lucia Tourist Board; Bosville Hotel, Skye; Nordic Light Hotel, Stockholm; Scandinavian Airlines; The Archipelago Foundation; Östanviksgard, Nämdö; Stockholm Visitors Board; Visit Sweden; Mauna Lani Resort, Big Island; Outrigger Keauhou Beach Resort, Big Island; Hawaii Visitors and Convention Bureau; plus all the guides who showed us their countries with such dedication and flair, but are too numerous to mention individually.

Steve Watkins and Clare Jones would also like to thank the following people for their support, advice and assistance with organizing trips and for sharing their laughter and friendship along the way:
John Brough, David Lanfear, Rhys Henderson at Salomon, Linda Lashford, Jo Carter, Roger Jones, David Holmes, Katia Vignes, Sian Pritchard-Jones, Bob Gibbons, Rianne Steenbergen, Sophie Palmer, Joke Herngreen, Maarten Coolen, Manos Hatzimalonas, Konstantina Papaefthimiou, George Vlachoyiannis, Helias Vlachoyiannis, Lindsey McNally, Philip Nelson, Elaine and Owen Jones, Katrina Milne Holme, Claire Hilton, Fernando Piaggio, Tim Best, Oliver Alvestegui, Sheila Nelson, Frank Nelson, Bryn Jones, Fflur Roberts, Sarah Watkins, Mel Watkins, Dilys Watkins, Kylie Clark, Mayu Okamoto, Matilda Granville; Susan and Andrew Collingbourne; Charly Moore, David Rankin, Dwayne Cassidy, Pearl Macek, Susie Tempest, Margel Durand, Marvlyn Alexander-

James, Keith and Janet Heath; Fred Phillips and Dr Janet Taylor; Jerry Fu and John; Monica Coleman; Alan Dow and Yvonne; Clinton Piper; Nigel Gifford; Graham, Farah, Aliyah and Suraya Bond; Pete, Kirsty, Oscar and Angus Dart; Guy, Ani, Will and Sam Alma; Keith Byrne at the North Face; Emily Grubb, Lalla Dutt and Martin Petts at BGB; Josie Heisig, Mick and Lucy Fleming, Charles Metcalfe, David Symes, Sarah Hopkins, Neil Rogers, Larry Hobbs, Jannie Cloete, Giovanni Biasutti, Charlie Wheatley, Jason Hicks, Phillip Hicks, Chris Simpson, Bob Burton, Martin Almqvist, David and Debbie Pain, Penny and Grace Porterfield and the Explorer II crew in Antarctica; Sara Rogers and Matilda Granville at Abercrombie & Kent; Sarah Barnett and Dee Byrne at BGB; Caroline Grayburn at Tim Best Travel; Sarah-Jane Gullick, Corne du Plessis, Pam McLean, Bongwe, Dany Hancock and Malise Scott-Barrett in Botswana; Lennart Pittja and family in Lapland; Emelie Klein at the Swedish Tourism Council; Lupita Ayala at the Mexico Tourism Board; Gillian Monahan at Tourism New Zealand; Javier and José at Andean Summits in La Paz; Dick Jones; Alexis Thornely at Discover the World; Chris Johnston and Julian Matthews at Discovery Initiatives; Mary Clissman and her team in Wicklow; Alun and Irene Newby; Suzie and Lydie; Anna Nash at Orient Express; the *Road to Mandalay* crew; Palm Equipment.

A FIREFLY BOOK

Published by Firefly Books Ltd. 2009

First printing

Publisher Cataloging-in-Publication Data (U.S.)
Davey, Steve.
Unforgettable places / Steve Davey, Marc Schlossman, Steve Watkins, Clare Jones.
[608] p. : col. photos. ; cm. Includes index.
Excerpts from: Unforgettable places to see before you die (2004); Unforgettable things to do before you die (2005); Unforgettable journeys to take before you die (2006); Unforgettable islands to escape to before you die (2007); Unforgettable walks to take before you die (2008).
Summary: A tour of 80 favorite destinations, including cultural and historical background, travel advice, and suggested activities for all sites.
ISBN-13: 978-1-55407-530-0 (pbk.)
ISBN-10: 1-55407-530-0 (pbk.)
1. Travel – Guidebooks. 2. Travel – Pictorial works.
3. Voyages – Guides. I. Schlossman, Marc.
II. Watkins, Steve. III. Jones, Clare. IV. Title.
910.2/02 dc22 G153.4D384 2009

Library and Archives Canada Cataloguing in Publication
Unforgettable places / Steve Davey ... [et al.].
Compilation of material previously published in Unforgettable places to see before you die, and 4 other publications.
ISBN-13: 978-1-55407-530-0
ISBN-10: 1-55407-530-0
1. Travel--Guidebooks. I. Davey, Steve
G153.4.U54 2009 910.2'02 C2009-901426-2

Published in the United States by Firefly Books (U.S.) Inc., P.O. Box 1338, Ellicott Station, Buffalo, New York 14205

Published in Canada by Firefly Books Ltd., 66 Leek Crescent, Richmond Hill, Ontario L4B 1H1

Commissioning editor: Christopher Tinker
Copy-editor: Tessa Clark
Design: Bobby Birchall, Bobby&Co, London
Production controller: Helen Everson

Printed in Great Britain by Butler Tanner and Dennis, Ltd.

The Random House Group Limited supports the Forest Stewardship Council (FSC), the leading international forest certification organisation. All our titles that are printed on Greenpeace approved FSC-certified paper carry the FSC logo. Our paper procurement policy can be found at www.rbooks.co.uk/environment